PORTRAITS OF THE NEW CENTURY

PORTRAITS
OF
THE NEW CENTURY
(The First Ten Years)

By

EDWARD RAYMOND THOMPSON

(E. T. RAYMOND, pseud.)

Essay Index Reprint Series

BOOKS FOR LIBRARIES PRESS

FREEPORT, NEW YORK

First Published 1928
Reprinted 1970

STANDARD BOOK NUMBER:
8369-1685-9

LIBRARY OF CONGRESS CATALOG CARD NUMBER:
74-117853

PRINTED IN THE UNITED STATES OF AMERICA

CONTENTS

	PAGE
KING EDWARD VII	9
SIR HENRY CAMPBELL-BANNERMAN	26
LITERARY SWASHBUCKLERS AND SENTIMENTALISTS	38
GEORGE WYNDHAM	63
THE "PRANCING PRO-CONSULS"	77
SOME DIVINES	98
PRESS MAGNATES	115
TREE AND ALEXANDER	139
ALFRED LYTTELTON	150
ROBERTS AND KITCHENER	164
WILLIAM HESKETH LEVER	180
TARIFF REFORMERS AND FREE TRADERS	190
LORD STRATHCONA	207
FIVE EDITORS	219
TWO ADMIRALS	243
HENRY JAMES AND MAX BEERBOHM	257
CERTAIN IRISHMEN	273
MINISTERS FOR WAR	288
MEN OF THE LAW	300
LABOUR LEADERS	313

SOME use has been made in the sketches here assembled of articles which appeared in *The Outlook*, *The World's Work* and the *Strand Magazine*. The author wishes to acknowledge with warm thanks the assistance he has had regarding certain subjects from Mr. D. Willoughby.

KING EDWARD VII

THE figure of King Edward VII, debonair and dignified, dominates the first ten years of the century. It stands out from the background much as a jolly Burgomaster does on a Hals canvas.

It was no slight man who could thus, emerging from the status of a superannuated Prince Hal, immediately achieve in his new part so marked an ascendancy. The "grace of station" has seldom worked so great a miracle. King Edward's reign, which nearly synchronised with the first decade, gave it the distinction of a period. "Edwardian" had become an accepted adjective before it became a convenient term of historical reference. King Edward's presence is felt everywhere and in all things during these years ; his character and outlook flavoured the epoch ; they influenced its politics ; they affected its philosophy ; they gave a distinct touch to its furnishings ; they bred a deportment which trimmed between the excessive straitness of Victorianism and the ultra-frankness of the Neo-Georgians. Had King Edward reigned thirty or forty years he would, it is certain, have stamped England, as Louis the Great did France, with his style and superscription. As things fell out, his short reign is seen as but the interlude between two considerable pieces. Edwardianism did not survive King Edward. But it is eloquent of his strong personality that, coming to the throne late and dying while still not old, he created an atmosphere equally distinct from that which went before and that which came after.

That personality might be thought, on first consideration, no great puzzle. Yet views so various have been taken by biographers pretending to large authority that the mere outside observer may well be cautious in dogmatising. The hearts of princes, even though they may be Constitutional princes, are inscrutable, and there may well have been sides to the character of this monarch, who lived all his days in strong light, which no one observer saw. Perhaps there were sides that no observer saw. It is a very common error, as Mr. Strachey hinted in his study of Queen Victoria, to forget that a monarch is, first of all, regal. A wise king is always something more (and perhaps also something less) than an ordinary man who is wise ; a crowned fool can never be quite like an ordinary foolish man. One might add that, just as a saint can only be understood by a saint, so only a king can fully understand the feelings and motives of another king. It needs no great imaginative effort for any intelligent person, who has sat on a Board of Guardians or watched the proceedings of a County Council, to enter the mind of a statesman oppressed by problems greater in degree but not very different in kind. Anybody who has debated whether to fine a wife-beater or send him to prison can imagine himself a judge trying a capital charge. Anybody who has made a few hundred pounds a year in Stock Exchange deals knows exactly what sort of qualities go to the making of that typical modern hero, the gambler swollen big. But to be an ordinary—possibly a very ordinary—human being, and yet to feel one's self in very truth the Lord's anointed ; to put on with a silk hat the personality of a man about town, and with tweeds that of a country squire, and yet in the robes of State to feel one's self one with Cœur-de-Lion and Edward of the Long Shanks : this is something not exceptional, but simply unique. The most ordinary

king cannot be an ordinarily ordinary man. He may
believe in nothing. He may believe in everything.
He may be a saint. He may be a cynic. He may be
a megalomaniac. He may, as Montaigne shows of
Maximilian, retain a realistic and even coarse sense of
his equality as an animal with him who does the lowest
menial offices. He may be tempted, as many besides
Alexander have been, to fancy himself of another
spirit from the rest of humanity, if not of another clay.
But, whatever he is, he is separated from all his fellow-
creatures, and not merely from the mass of them, by
something far more subtle than mere etiquette and
protocol and fiddle and faddle. He may seem to act and
think much like others of his general mental type. He
may be as penny plain as Farmer George or as tuppence
coloured as Kaiser Wilhelm. But Farmer George, we
may be sure, thought in many essential respects in
terms unknown to the proudest of his Whig peers,
and though Kaiser Wilhelm was in many ways a
popinjay and a cad there were things in him and for him
undreamed of in the philosophy of any of his subjects.

That graceful and adroit writer, Mr. A. G. Gardiner,
in a study of King Edward composed during his reign,
suggested that His late Majesty must have grown very
weary of the sound of " God Save the King." The
same idea was suggested by W. S. Gilbert in a now
forgotten opera :—

> The king who is bored by that song,
> Who hears it all day, all day long,
>   Who hears it loud shouted
>   By throats operatic
>   And loyally spouted.
>   By courtiers emphatic ;
> By soldier, by sailor, on drum and on fife,
> Small blame if he think it the plague of his life.

While his subjects shout loudly and long,
  Their king, who would willingly ban them,
With composure polite, endures day and night
  That implacable National Anthem.

Now a writer who is at once a loyal subject and a
fairly conventional Radical would feel obliged to say
something of the sort. The king had to be credited
with ideas concerning his own position which would
accord with those of the Liberal intelligentsia. He had
to be represented as psychologically attuned to his
status as head of a crowned republic. An " Odds-
Fish " sort of a king was repellent to one side of the
Liberal mind ; a king who took himself with full
divine-right seriousness offended another. He must be
serious, of course, to a point—carry out his functions
with due dignity and impressiveness ; but he must
stop short of viewing those functions as really worth
while, or at all comparable in importance to those of
Mr. Asquith. So we have the vision of a plain, homely
sort of man, longing to be natural, panting for the law-
less freedom of the bowler hat, hungry for the wild
irresponsibility of life at Muswell Hill, but content, for
the sake of his people, to play his part as legal fiction
with conscientious thoroughness, though the servitude
of it galled and wearied.

A touching picture, and, one would make bold to
say, a wholly false one. One imagines—it is impossible
to go further—that these islands never contained a
human being more completely satisfied with his position
than Edward VII as king. He might be a plain man
at bottom ; he might have occasional yearning for a
plain life. But nobody could see him for three seconds,
engaged in the business òf a king, without feeling how
thoroughly he enjoyed it. It was his trade, and he
relished the trade, even in its smallest details. Some

details may have bored him, as other men are bored, at one time if not at another, by a business they love but which they find it difficult to escape. But who shall say what bored him, and when ? Before we answer let us recall Johnson's story of the retired tallow-chandler who begged to be allowed to visit the factory—on melting days.

Very possibly there were times when, in the capacity of Royal Highness, he was irked by the monotony of " God Save the Prince of Wales." For that could only remind him of long years of frustration and self-suppression, of a weary apprenticeship which might outlast his life, of a man's work withheld and a man's liberty only half secretly enjoyed. " God Save the King " may well have sounded to him as an anthem of emancipation—a Marsellaise personal to himself. If when he ascended the throne at the age of sixty he was not free to do everything he liked he was quite ready to like everything he would have to do, from the coronation in Westminster Abbey onward. He was as far as possible from thinking of kingship, or any-thing connected with kingship, in the disrespectful terms imputed to him by Mr. Gardiner. On the con-trary he found the job equally serious and amusing. He enjoyed business, for which he had some head. He revelled in pomps and ceremonies, for which he had much heart. It may be safely said that, while he often saw others with humorous clearness, no man was ever less ironical with himself. There was no vestige of self-mockery in his view of the king or the Court etiquette. No Mason, or Buffalo, or Forester, or Druid ever wore his vestments of office with more complete and convinced reverence. He gloried in the sceptre. He was fascinated by the orb.

In Mr. Kipling's lines, written after his death, a good deal of the truth about him was told :—

" For to him above all was Life good, above all he commanded
    Her abundance full-handed.
The peculiar treasure of kings was his for the taking;
    All that men come to in dreams he inherited waking."

The assumption that all men have the same dreams is,
of course, incorrect, but if by some violent stretch of
the imagination King Edward could be pictured nobody and a dreamer he would probably have desired
those things which in actual fact were his. " Assemblies
upstanding " would have seemed to him to repay
performance of sundry dull duties of routine. As to
his " world-gathered armies," he adored them to, or
from, the last polished button, and resented jests about
them, such as are sometimes made on the stage or in
comic papers, almost as insults to himself. The navy,
it may be, interested him less, but, " when his war-
castles foamed in their places," the Fleet too was a very
satisfactory possession, and there were few pleasures in
the world comparable to that of showing it to the
nephew from Berlin who absurdly styled himself
" Admiral of the Atlantic." The political side of the
business of being king could sometimes be, no doubt,
tiresome. The time had gone when an English
monarch could exclude from the Cabinet on grounds
of taste a popular politician, and the King's taste was
undoubtedly offended by at least one of the then darlings
of the people. Still there was no need to have a personally objectionable statesman as Minister-in-Waiting,
and there were certain compensations for the unavoidable unpleasantness. All through the Prince of Wales
period he had wanted a part in the affairs of State. If
as king he found this part onerous, it was not for him
to grumble. These were the penalties of the position,
and to be taken philosophically.
Whether the King's actual influence in statecraft was

great or small is still a matter of some speculation. How much he had of statesmanlike abilities is yet disputed. During most of his mother's long reign it had been considered wise to minimise, or entirely to conceal, the queen's share in ruling the country. But towards the end of her long life there was a revival of royalism, and it was considered safe to let the truth be known. Gradually it came to be realised that Queen Victoria had been by no means a cipher, and the public, which had never cared much for Whig ideas about the Constitution, was on the whole gratified. On her son's accession it seemed, therefore, that loyalty to the throne, not to mention security for the existing order in general, could best be fortified by a certain parade of monarchy. In the beginning there was the muddle of the Boer War ; then the failure of the Balfour Government to deal with the problems of peace ; and then again, the disappointment of the Liberal administrations. But whatever causes of dissatisfaction there might be, England remained proud of her King—pleased with the urbane dignity of his activities within the island, flattered by the court and deference he commanded abroad. Europe, we were told, accounted him the first diplomatist of the age. At home, it was concluded, his influence must be no less strong and salutary. Only towards the end some qualms were felt. Class animosities had been roused by the question of the Budget and the House of Lords. Even the great achievement of the *Entente* with France was being criticised in some quarters as a dangerous entanglement. And a little while after the King died it was decided that there had been an error of tact in connecting him personally with policies which time might not approve. Let the praise or blame for everything be on ministers who came and went—not on the permanent institution of the throne.

In this mood of caution was written the account of King Edward's life, which is to be found in the *Dictionary of National Biography*. The truth seems to be that whilst his capabilities and activities had once been deliberately exaggerated, their subsequent belittlement was also overdone with intention. Most certainly the King was not fitted, nor did he aspire, to be his own Foreign Minister. On the other hand, he had all that sturdy common sense, that clear insight, which are so often lacking in the experts. If he was ignorant of everything they had at their fingers' tips, he had a knowledge of men, women and affairs beyond that of any English king since Charles II. The story of his sequestered education is common property. An effort had been made to mould him into a pedant of the German type, and it had failed completely. Afterwards there had been a strong reaction. Many fancied that the prince—"Prince Hal," as Disraeli called him— was nothing but a fribble, and even those who championed him were wont to deplore the company he kept. What they all forgot was that his way of living, if dangerous, might be extremely educative.

Like Charles II, the heir-apparent went on his travels, survived them, and derived from them the wisdom of experience. The experience was less wide than is sometimes assumed. King Edward passed with his subjects for a cosmopolitan, but there were vast patches on the map that did not exist for him. His France was Paris and its seaside resorts. His acquaintance with Central Europe, though not confined to Berlin, did not go far beyond Grosvenor Square (where lived Sir Ernest Cassel and Baron Eckhardstein) and its suburbs of Homburg and Karlsbad. Jewry he knew pretty well. America he probably imagined as populated by Goulds, Astors and Vanderbilts. But if a little learning is dangerous, all real knowledge is useful, and within rather narrow limits King Edward's knowledge of the world was deep. Also, narrow as it was, it was wider far than that of most royal personages.

It is said that Napoleon III was the first of the King's unofficial instructors, and whether this be true or no it is interesting to recall the Emperor's dictum that there is no better training-ground for rulers than the turf. The English people rejoiced that their King should be a sportsman, and had there been a Republican party in the country it would have been extinguished by Minoru's Derby. Yet few realised how greatly the King's judgment had been sharpened by racing. Whatever else may be thought of those who frequent stables, they are a shrewd race, and those who know the points of a horse seem usually to have some faculty of assessing with rough accuracy their fellow-men, at least to the extent of knowing whether they are trustworthy or the reverse, and exactly to what extent the best, and worst, of them may be trusted. The Prince had known men and women in wide variety. His foremost apologists raised their eyebrows over Tranby Croft, and marvelled at his friendship with Baron Hirsch, yet visits to country houses where baccarat scandals were possible, and companionship with a person who had been expelled from the French Jockey Club, went to the making of a worldly-wise man. He saw the underneath of various cards which are not Court cards. He knew from experience many things of which more conventional royalties had only hearsay or superficial information. That they did not make him a sadder man was but a proof that he had much natural sagacity and an excellent digestion.

"He like roulette and cards; dry champagne and sweet women." So wrote Max Harden, than whom he had no more discriminating, or cynical, admirer. In

B

Germany the tendency was to be shocked by his catholic taste in the matter of friendships. Harden, the spectator who saw most of the game, knew better. He understood how well it was for England that her King had not lived the life of a Dalai Lama. " He has lived," he wrote, " to know the cares of age after his dealing with Hirsch and Rhodes, the prince of diamonds, and Rothschild and Cassel, and as the friend of smart men of business has learned what life is. Such experience lifts him above a dozen other monarchs." In particular, it lifted him above his nephew, the German Emperor, and for a decade or more gave England a definite diplomatic advantage over Germany, as well as securing that, when the clash of arms came, England should enter the field as a partner in the stronger alliance.

That there was personal antagonism between uncle and nephew has never been denied, although Sir Sidney Lee, writing in 1912, reduced it to an affair of occasional tiffs. The King had had a surfeit of Germanism in early youth. He had heard too much of the genius and still more of the virtues of his father's people. In manhood he repeated John of Salisbury's question : " *Quis Teutonicos constituit judices nationum ?* " In his nephew was incarnate all that he resented in the Germanic idea, and, first of all, there was the ostentatious self-righteousness. Not all Wilhelm's friends were models of virtue or even of decency, but they were all high-born, and when they were caught tripping they were coldly flung to the wolves. For the crime of being found out, Wilhelm had no mercy. King Edward, on the other hand, chose his friends because they were useful or amusing, and stood by them through thick and thin. It had been thought he might drop some of them on coming to the throne, but his heart was warmer than Prince Hal's, and he did not turn his back,

when at Windsor, on the old acquaintances of East-
cheap. Considering the relationship, the German
Emperor's comments on this width were often un-
pardonably graceless. After the Tranby Croft trouble,
for instance, he had the audacity to complain that the
Prince of Wales had brought discredit on some
Prussian regiment wherein he had accepted an honorary
colonelcy.

Apart from affectation of pietism, there was the
ridiculous stiffness of the nephew, who did not realise
that Court etiquette, excellent at Court, is sometimes out
of place. There was his insufferable military swagger,
all the harder to bear because it did have behind it the
most perfect fighting machine in the world. There
was the pretence, again, to authority in intellectual and
artistic matters, very irritating to one who liked musical
comedy and could not read a book without yawning.
Also, there were family dissensions. The Kaiser had
been rude to his own mother, who was the King's
sister. In short, the Kaiser, while he could fairly be
called a magnificent prince, was in no sense a gentleman,
which King Edward, in every sense appropriate to that
sometimes misused word, emphatically was. If there
were good reasons for dislike on the King's part, the
Emperor's antipathy can be readily understood.
Wilhelm, with all his blinding pride, was clever enough
to have a notion that Uncle Edward, with his man-of-
the-world ways, could make him look a raw provincial.
Even where the younger man was undoubtedly the
superior, as in oratory and the art of phrase-making, the
older man was apt to score. For a few hours the
Kaiser's words were like blazing comets in the European
firmament. Peoples quaked when he spoke of the
mailed fist and Germany in shining armour. Then the
King, with an agreeable smile, made some banal
remark to somebody over an *aperitif*, raised his hat to

a crowd, and *tout le monde* suddenly discovered that the All-Highest was only a ranter with odd melodramatic talents.

In fact, uncle and nephew detested one another. For the rest, King Edward had a liking for the French, as far as he knew them, and rather disliked the Germans. Not that he wanted war. He would have hated to see his beautiful Guards begrimed by battle. Besides, he was a practical man, as well as kindly and humane. As Harden puts it, there was something of " the princely merchant " about him, and, indeed, in one who had associated so closely with the plutocrats that was inevitable. Again, as Harden said, " a nation of sixty-three millions, with great gifts for trade and industry, hard working, fecund, toiling for small pay, is not finally made harmless by blowing up some of its ships, and no great merchant with clear sight would invest money in so futile a speculation." But King Edward, while he harboured no insane notion of " destroying " Germany, did think Germany was dangerous, and that by diplomatic means she might be made less so. He did not, of course, invent any of the alliances or understandings into which England entered during his reign, yet he certainly approved them, and did much to make them not only possible, but popular. If for nothing else he should live in history as a man who dissolved prejudices. The French *Entente* was a triumph over Puritan and Protestant prejudices. The Japanese alliance was a triumph over colour prejudice. The Russian *Entente* was a triumph over Tory habits and Liberal principles. As official engagements they might have been made at any date. As engagements which ninety-nine out of a hundred people would have readily ratified, they bear the stamp of the Edwardian age. Because in social affairs the King had set the example of breaking loose from old conventions and restraints, the task of his Foreign Ministers was made easy.

The fact that he liked and was liked in Paris had its importance too, but as a clue to his character it has been misinterpreted. It meant a number of things, among them that he was an average European, who, without necessarily having any deep refinement of taste, appreciated civilisation. But it did not mean that he was a crowned Republican indulging a thwarted taste for liberty, equality and fraternity. Mr. Gardiner once quaintly advanced the King's affection for the French as a sign that His Majesty thought of himself merely as a sort of President. Of course it signified nothing of the kind. The French had, indeed, as Mr. Gardiner recalled, " swept the whole institution of kingship on to the dust heap," but, ever since, they, or, at all events, the Parisian crowds, have delighted in other people's crowned heads. If they had received King Edward as *Citoyen Edouard*, he would not have been in the least pleased. But because they showed so plainly that he interested them infinitely more than did the worthy individual for the time being *Monsieur le Président*, he found in their welcome something subtly more satisfying than could be found in the acclamations of a throng accustomed to a royal presence.

For, despite the catholicity of his friendships, King Edward never long forgot that he belonged to a special and exclusive guild. For that reason, if for no other, he would have worked to avoid a war. Wilhelm might be this or that, but Wilhelm was anyhow a member of the guild, and, in consequence, it would be deplorable to take extreme measures against him. King Edward may have had anti-German sentiments, but more than once he forgot them in his concern for monarchism. For example, he neglected Belgium, though Belgium was an ally to be courted, and the reason was a notion that Leopold II had been guilty of unprofessional, or unkingly, conduct. Again, though Serbia might be a useful piece to move in the supposed game of " encircling " Germany, he could not bring himself to recognise Serbia's existence after the crime of the Konak. When foreign diplomatists reasoned with him on the matter, he replied simply : " *J'ai mon métier de roi.*" How could he be on nodding terms with a people who had killed their King and Queen, even though the assassinated pair had been notorious undesirables ?

King Edward was, of course, fundamentally Conservative, though it is not to be concluded that he always saw eye to eye with the Tory party of his time. Although he found it hard to forgive Campbell-Bannerman for criticism of the Army in Boer War days, he had no antipathy to Liberals as a body. Often they were more respectful to the throne than were its boasted defenders, and Asquith, a straightforward Englishman, was in some ways preferable to Balfour, a philosophic Scot. Like Disraeli, the King seems to have glimpsed something wanting in the Conservatives' Irish policy, and he is known to have protested against certain items in the tariff reform programme. He thought taxing the people's food was madness. Imposts on the luxuries of the rich were what he wanted. In his simple fiscal faith he displayed his sympathy with the man in the street. Such taxes on luxury have in practice proved more plague than profit, yet in theory they are so attractive that ordinary people will always demand them and account the experts at fault when they fail to work.

But the King's influence on home politics was considerable in one direction only. It was he who gave, no doubt unconsciously, the last kick to the system of aristocratic government which had been established in

England on the fall of the Stuarts. During the last quarter of the nineteenth century, although the aristocratic and territorial families of Great Britain no longer led the way for wealth, there was no sensible diminution of their prestige. Politically they were still more important than the mere plutocrats. When Cabinets were formed, if some new rich man was included it was on his own merits, whereas places had invariably to be found for great noblemen and large-acred squires as representatives of a class. Socially, the established families yet retained a position that appeared to be one of unchallengeable supremacy. Their incomes might be small in comparison with those recently amassed in finance and commerce, and they might be positively growing smaller, but for the requirements of the age they usually sufficed. Extravagance could be eschewed and economies effected without fear of losing caste or dropping out of the social swim.

This state of affairs was, of course, due to the position of the Court. For the greater part of every year throughout the period in question the Court for all practical purposes ceased to exist. The Queen disappeared to the Scottish Highlands or to the Isle of Wight, and even when in London was seen only on infrequent and set occasions. Accounts of her occasional visits to favoured subjects suggest that her hosts and hostesses found them a tax upon their nerves rather than on their pockets. When Lord Beaconsfield entertained the royal lady at Hughenden he had a hundred apprehensions in advance, and heaved a sigh of relief at speeding the parting guest, but when all was said and done the whole thing had not amounted to much more than giving Her Majesty a cup of tea. If the Queen's distaste for shows and public pomp during the years of her widowhood had irritated the middle and lower

classes, it had undoubtedly been useful to those who
stood nearer to the throne, since it enabled them not
only to cut their coats according to their cloth, but even
to set about an idea that vulgarity lurked in coats which
were not a trifle scanty.

With the new century and new reign came an immediate change. The King whilst Prince had been an
expensive friend, but entry into his circle had been
optional, with no penalty for those who felt unable to
afford it. It might be said of them that they were not
of the smart set, but then the smart set was only a section,
and by no means the most exalted, of society. The situation was altered when the Prince became King, for if
the monarchy was politically limited it was still socially
absolute. Those who could not entertain the King
on the scale which the friends of his youth had taught
him was his due had to go into exile. Hence the
degeneration of a large tribe of peers to the status of
" backwoodsmen." Hence, too, the rapid impoverishment of that other section of the aristocracy which did
attempt to keep pace with the plutocrats. And not
only on pomps and vanities did the King expect lavish
expenditure from those about him. In a novel form he
revived the ancient custom of " benevolences," and in
his Coronation year the scale was set by the Cassel gift
of £200,000 which His Majesty dedicated to a sana-
torium for tuberculosis.

So the older nobility and gentry either ruined themselves or abdicated, and, either way, it came to the same
thing in the end as far as their influence in the nation
was concerned. The King had costly tastes, spacious
notions. It is not to be imagined that he worked
deliberately to alter the balance of power within the
State. Yet the thing was, in its way, a perfect revenge,
a piece of poetic justice. In the beginning of the
eighteenth century the aristocrats had destroyed the

power of the monarchy. Two hundred years later the
King destroyed them. It is said that King Edward had
a keen sense of humour. Had he possessed a feeling
for history as well, he would have appreciated the
piquancy of the thing.

SIR HENRY CAMPBELL-BANNERMAN

NEARLY twenty years after the death of Sir Henry Campbell-Bannerman it can be seen that the most important thing about him was his taste for French novels.

In the period immediately before and after the great Liberal victory of 1906 the chief problem for every serious statesman, as distinguished from the mere politician, was what should be England's relations with the Powers of the Continent. Splendid isolation had proved too dangerous. In the midst of the Boer War we had been threatened by a league of Europe. Thenceforward, the ideal course was to make friends everywhere, and the practical alternative to make friends somewhere. It was necessary either to return to the policy which for two centuries had linked our country with the German interest, or else to seek and to cement accord with France. Neither course seemed to possess an overwhelming advantage over the other when C.-B. was called to office. Balfour had, indeed, after some hesitation, come down on the French side of the fence, but it was open to any new Government either to strengthen or to weaken the new *Entente*. Joseph Chamberlain's plea for a German alliance was yet fresh in memory, and there was no quite obvious reason against further feelers in that direction, whilst Lord Rosebery, still the leading Liberal authority on foreign questions, had decided Germanic inclinations.

When a statesman finds something like a balance between the benefits and drawbacks of any given policy, his private and personal predilections are usually decisive. If C.-B., who himself had never gone very deeply into foreign affairs, had been a devotee of poetry, philosophy or science, with Goethe, Kant or Haeckel as his special idol, it is more than likely that we should to-day be writing the history of the world in different fashion. More friendly relations with the German Empire would then have been not his secondary but his primary object, and, inevitably, there would have been a cooling towards France. The European War might have been postponed for a few years, or it might have started rather earlier than it did, but England would have been arrayed, whether as belligerent or as benevolent neutral, upon the other side. As things were, C.-B.'s recreation was reading French novels. Balzac, Flaubert, Maupassant were the companions of his leisure. They laid the foundations of his affection for the country of their origin : an affection that was confirmed and given a serious tinge by sympathy with the political and social character of France, and was, no doubt, heightened by his pleasure in the good things of the table which France provides.

When Campbell-Bannerman had to choose which of the two countries should be England's first friend abroad, he seems to have surprised some of his colleagues by having the matter already settled in his mind. In the last days of 1905 Lady Oxford notes that her husband " was glad to find him (C.-B.) sound on Germany," and that the latter had admitted his dislike for the Kaiser, whom he thought " a dangerous, restless, mischief-making man." When the initial arrangement was being made for military co-operation with the French in case of eventualities, C.-B. was, of course, the presiding genius of the little inner Cabinet that knew all about them.

It is probable that his mere acquiescence in such

proceedings would at the time have startled a good many of his political friends and enemies. Throughout his career he had been misunderstood and misinterpreted, and, for his part, he had been content that it should be so. For one thing, it had always been assumed that he was a monument of what Disraeli called " the simplicity of the three per cents," but, in fact, his simplicity was sometimes near to Martial's " *prudens simplicitas,*" otherwise astute guilelessness. He was, no doubt, not a man of first-class intellect, but he was good second-class, and for most of his life he allowed it to be thought that he was third-class. Because in ordinary circumstances he was no match for Arthur Balfour, he allowed himself to be trampled on by the Brodricks and the Longs. In his own party it was the same. He was not apt to assert himself, and when, day after day, whilst leader of the Opposition, he was branded in the *Daily Mail* as " the incubus," quite a number of Liberals resented the epithet mainly because they believed that it expressed the truth. Gradually an idea arose that he was a stop-gap to be deposed or relegated to another place when Rosebery should emerge from his tent or when one of the younger men should reach age and fame to fit him for the leadership. During those years, C.-B.'s position, always uncomfortable, might have been made simply untenable by careful mining, but nobody thought elaborate preparation necessary. He had been elected leader because Harcourt and Morley would not serve. The Boer War had made him what he had never been before, actually unpopular. Surely, he was to be overturned by a single jostle. But when the moment came for giving him notice to quit, his younger lieutenants were amazed to find that, though listening with patient courtesy to their suggestions for his virtual supersession by one of themselves, he did not budge immediately. Instead, he promised to consult his wife. From the consultation he returned with " No surrender " as his unalterable reply, and the bevy of all the talents found nothing for it save to serve under him or to retire to obscurity and the back benches. " Easygoing to the point of laziness," says Lady Oxford of him. That was just where he had tricked his juniors. They had not grasped that to be easy-going is one way to conserve energy and purpose.

Similarly, belief in his simplicity had made many fancy that he had what some American journalist has called a single-track mind. To the Jingoes of Mafficking Night he had appeared a pro-Boer. His real attitude towards the South African problem had been expressed by himself when he remarked that he had " never been pro-Kruger, only anti-Joe," but his distrust of the Colonial Secretary and all that was then connoted by Imperialism was misunderstood. Liberals and Unionists alike thought it the equivalent of " Pacifism." They regarded him not merely as a normal man with a normal love of peace, but as one who would always advocate peace at any price, and, in consequence, could never be trusted to prepare against the possibility of war. It was a complete miscalculation. C.-B. was far too robust a being to be a disciple of Tolstoi. In his youth he had been an ardent officer of volunteers, and in the years he had spent at the War Office he had displayed considerable natural aptitude for the often hard business of getting on well with regular soldiers. The old Duke of Cambridge had called him " very nice, calm and pleasant," and such a tribute would scarcely have been given to anybody who regarded the Horse Guards as a mere Temple of Moloch.

When the Dogger Bank incident threatened armed conflict with Russia, C.-B.'s vigorous patriotism asserted itself, and he gave his promise of unqualified support to the Conservative Government of the day. South Africa had been another story. He resented what he styled the " insolence " of the Transvaal President, but he judged it the natural result of the methods of Chamberlain and Milner. " Sordid " was his adjective for the whole business, and though he agreed that hostilities were inevitable after Kruger's ultimatum he could not, as he wrote to Lord Buxton, see where there could be " any ground for cock-a-doodle-doo."

Later, when Majuba was being consummated by a series of Majubas, marked on the map as Spion Kop, Magersfontein, Stormberg and Colenso, he refused to join in the massed attack upon our generals. He would not even add to the chorus of abuse against the War Office. The Government had known, or ought to have known, the extent of the Boer armaments, and was culpable for having made war without the necessary preparations, but that, as he wrote, " was the fault of the C.O. and his Cabinet, and not of the W.O." and still less, of course, of the men in the field. If he felt that there was something mean about the whole war, he felt also that its greatest meanness was the effort to place blame for its disasters on the wrong shoulders.

Yet, before the end came C.-B. was accounted not merely his country's enemy, but as the man who had most shamefully traduced the British soldier. " When is a war not a war ? " he had asked, and his own reply had been, " When it is carried on by methods of barbarism in South Africa." It was the system, not the soldiers, he was denouncing, but the phrase was to rankle for years. C.-B. was not a Pacifist in the ordinary meaning of the term. He was rather a man of chivalrous nature, who in his single person combined a good deal of Harcourt's hatred of " damned nonsense " with some of the idealism of the younger Cecils. He would have faced war with Germany or

Russia less unhappily than war with the little Dutch republic, and when the campaign involved not only slaughter of fighting men, but starvation, disease and death for women and children, he turned sick and cursed. Such things, it may be, are inevitable in modern war, and he who protests against them may be a nuisance to his country while the war lasts. Afterwards, however, he may be an asset. Europe might be a happier family than it is to-day if Germany had had a C.-B. to protest against " methods of barbarism " in Belgium and elsewhere. On the morrow of the speech which exasperated seven-eighths of England C.-B. received a letter from a clergyman who called him " a cad, a coward and a murderer." But we have Botha's testimony that it was this speech which later made peace possible in South Africa.

None the less, the words were unquestionably a political indiscretion, and in the view of many Liberals an unpardonable indiscretion. It was bruited abroad that C.-B. always had been, and always would be, a bungler. It does many men no harm to say indiscreet things daily. They often, indeed, get thereby a reputation for genius as well as high spirit. But C.-B. was normally even ponderous, and one slip by such a man is serious. It is put down to stupidity. That, at least, is ever the judgment of the passing hour, yet time has a way of reversing the verdict. " Methods of barbarism " was immediately harmful to C.-B.'s party, but of eventual service to the whole country. " La Douma est morte : vive la Douma ! " shocked an ambassador, but it rang through the world with a sound that no professional challenger could have produced. "Enough of this foolery," coming from a man habitually courteous, awoke England to the fact that the verdict of the polls meant more than " strange faces in familiar places " : that it meant an actual change of masters.

Campbell-Bannerman had never striven to vie with men of more brilliant parts than his own. But, though modest, he was neither timid nor easily overawed. He had, indeed, a large quality of irreverence, and was always privately chuckling at the great luminaries of the political firmament in which he was so long a lesser light. What were Rosebery and Harcourt that the services of one or other should be counted a *sine qua non* for the very existence of Liberalism? Rosebery to him was just Barnbougle, and Harcourt was the Nymph, two queer creatures whom it were foolish to take quite seriously. And when all eyes were turned on the rising young men, C.-B. merely winked. " Master Asquith " and " Master Grey " and " Master Haldane " : what were they? Bright boys, perhaps, but their cocksureness were best treated with a little humour. When chosen leader of the party, he had described himself as " a person of pretty tolerant and easy-going disposition," and, on the whole, he was, in spite of feuds and plots, always on fairly good terms with his associates, that is to say his differences with them rarely involved personal rancour. Between him and Dilke there seems to have been a chronic hostility, for the latter's whirlwind energies and assumption of omniscience irked C.-B., whilst C.-B.'s tranquillity and show of ingenuousness enraged the other man. " Master Haldane " may have been another exception to the rule. C.-B. christened him " Schopenhauer," and one may guess that the reader of French novels had no spiritual home in common with the graduate of Gottingen. But as a rule the Liberal leader was content to let his rebels have their fling, and to handle them with jocularity rather than severity when it came to settling accounts. " Are you feeling cooler now? " he asked Mr. Lloyd George after the member for Carnarvon had been kicking over the traces at an awkward moment. As to the Liberal Leaguers, who gave him so much trouble, he admitted a desire " to damn their eyes," and did at least " dot their i's," during the celebrated war of knife and fork, yet before long he had forgiven all save one of them. Haldane, who had bored him as well as intrigued against him, he did not quite forgive. Haldane, in fact, did not find his grave at the War Office, but Pall Mall, when C.-B. sent him thither, was accounted the most unhealthy spot in England for reputations.

Of Campbell-Bannerman Lord Morley wrote, " Stout-hearted Sir Robert Walpole, though of heavier build, would have understood him, and so, although of lighter weight, would Lord Melbourne." The resemblance between C.-B. and Walpole is, indeed, marked. In both there was the same large core of fundamental honesty, the same sense of the ironical, the same ability and anxiety to put off their clothes and their cares together. If Morley was right in adding that C.-B. " did not think too well of human nature " a further link between the two Prime Ministers may be found. And, in a sense, Morley was right. C.-B. held to the true Liberal motto of " Trust the people," and was sincere when he spoke of " the good sense, the wisdom, the righteousness and the patriotism of our country," but that did not in the least bespeak a blind faith in masses, far less in individuals. C.-B. had ideals, but few illusions. Like Walpole, he could " smile without art and win without a bribe," but he too was quite aware that smiles are often artificial, and that bribery is one way to victory. If he had few enemies, he appears to have had fewer intimate friends. His wife was one. Another was Lord Ripon, a man of deep and sincere faith, without a single glittering ability.

And in C.-B. there was much of Melbourne also. They were akin in their ordinary easiness of temper. They resembled each other in their occasional bursts

c

of heat. They both lacked ambition of the pushful sort. They had in common a happy knack of managing their kings. Melbourne, explaining to William IV the vagaries of Brougham taking the Great Seal with him in a post-chaise when he went speechifying through the Highlands, can be neatly paralleled by Campbell-Bannerman expounding to Edward VII the significance of Mr. George's Biblical jokes or the insignificance of Mr. Burns's attacks on hereditary privilege. A twentieth-century young Disraeli would surely have jibed at the Liberal chief for " lounging away the glories of an empire," and " sipping the last novel of Paul de Kock "—for de Kock, of course, read Gyp or Abel Hermant.

Here it may be noted as a fact not entirely unimportant that C.-B.'s sipping in French fiction was by no means confined to novels of the classic type. The frivolous Gyp, the amusing Hermant, and the wittily improper About were among the authors whom he fancied. Liberals, taking them in the mass, are over-solemn people. The colossal figure of Gladstone towers between them and the sun ; the tolling of chapel bells is in their ears ; the images of certain secular saints are in their hearts. Temporarily, at least, C.-B. did something to correct this fault. Everybody said he had a " pawky " humour, derived from Scotland, where his forebears had tilled the soil and traded, but he had also a lighter touch, probably of Gallic origin and acquired in the course of light reading. By its exercise he could round sharp corners at times. It helped, for instance, in his relations with King Edward. Had they, from lack of other subjects, been forced to devote all their interviews to politics, the strain might have been unbearable. As it was, C.-B. could discuss intelligently with his sovereign the respective merits of halibut boiled and halibut baked. Also, C.-B.'s light side won the confidence of a public which, even when it thinks Liberalism a sound creed, is distrustful of its exponents as including a band of sour-visaged cranks. His way of whispering "*pas trop de zêle*" to earnest members of the party clamouring for reforms that were dreaded by the majority, was frequently denounced as levity, but it was really shrewd sense. "Old Lawson, battle-axe in hand," ready to smash bar, butt and bottle, was one of those he kept resolutely in check. As to the "efficiency" preached by Rosebery's Liberal-Socialist followers, he knew that it meant upsetting everybody and everything, was contrary to English tradition, and spelled an end of personal liberty. With delightful aptness and lightness he dismissed it from his programme as "a mere *rechauffé* of Mr. Sidney Webb." C.-B. was, perhaps, the last English statesman who not only believed in freedom for individuals and nations, but was willing to battle for his faith. Though he could flame to indignation over "the underfed twelve millions," much that is now called "social reform" left him cold. Melbourne's "Why not leave it alone?" must have often been in his mind when discussing with his colleagues their legislative projects.

C.-B. was a Radical, but he was not a Progressive. In his personal habits he was an enemy to change. He hated motor cars and liked to drive in a carriage behind a pair of horses. "In the whole trend of his mind," said Dilke, "he is one of the most conservative members occupying a seat on the Liberal benches," and, though the verdict was given in anger, its basis was truth. What Dilke did not see was that it was just his essential conservatism which kept him always true to the Liberal and Radical faith whilst others went whoring after strange gods. Some ran along the all-red route towards Imperialism, others towards the redder dawn of Socialism, but C.-B. remained upon his plain buff-coloured rock. It might almost be said that the practice of Liberalism as a definite creed, not as a halting between two opinions, died with him. He never went with the tide, and would never have minded being left by the tide. He knew that every tide has its ebb and flow.

C.-B. may be called simple, but of that simplicity which implies merely a healthy synthesis of component singularities. He was decidedly not simple in the sense of being deficient in subtlety. He had his full share of complexities. There was a suspicion of artifice in his homely shrewdness : there was irony mingled with his honesty. If he were in effect a plain-dealer, he could see as much in a horse's mouth as the most tricky of copers. There was something majestic in the way in which, at the appropriate time, he put in their places all kinds of clever people who, as the phrase goes, had once thought it " a shame to take his money." It was inspiring also to see how, as a Prime Minister, he rose immediately to the dignity of his position. Six months before people had laughed at the mere idea of his directing an administration. Before his first session was over he was accepted as irreplaceable, and in fact he was never replaced. He was a Liberal because he really did believe in liberty. His most applauded and his boldest peace of work was, of course, the grant of self-government to the conquered people of South Africa, and he never wavered in his personal conviction that the Irish problem could only be solved by Home Rule. He was a Radical chiefly from his dislike of privilege. He was not a self-made man, but his family had risen in a generation from nothing to something, and if he had a quite measurable reverence for mere talent, he had none whatever for wealth or birth. In his first speech made in Gladstone's presence, he had dared to speak disrespectfully of university education. That a man was a man for a' that was the first article in his creed, and it decided his place in politics from the beginning to the end of his career. Had he lived a while longer he might have enjoyed a struggle with the Lords, though we are also free to fancy that in his lifetime the incidents which led to the actual conflict could not have happened. Tolerant and easy he may have been, even inclined to laziness, but he possessed that fundamental wisdom which objects equally to sluttish neglect and fussy interference, and refrains instinctively from driving men or institutions into a corner. One figures him dealing with " Master " Lloyd George in 1909 much as he had done with the other " Masters " in 1905. Had C.-B. remained another half-dozen years on earth, in short, the Liberal party might still be in vigorous being. As it was, he remained just long enough to settle England's place in the European scheme of things, and that, after all, was no small man's work.

LITERARY SWASHBUCKLERS AND SENTIMENTALISTS

IT is not easy to give a satisfactory explanation of the combativeness of so many of the literary men—some of them happily still with us—who were at the summit of their vigour in the first ten years of the century.

They had their being in a standing quarrel—with things in general, with various things in particular, with their enemies, and above all with their friends. No doubt some of this pugnacity was due to reaction from the " art for art's sake " of the 'nineties. The Green Carnation, it has been observed, made these people see red. The Decadents held that art must have no object. The Anti-Decadents held, on the other hand, that art is nothing without an object : it must hit something, and what more pleasing than to hit somebody else's head ? Violence is the note of the time : hot with Mr. Belloc, cold with Mr. Shaw, bland with Mr. Galsworthy. There is a logical extremism even in those who are reasonably moderate in language.

It was, I suppose, Mr. Kipling who started the thing. The " genius without aspirates " killed the author of that sneer. For in Kipling there was unquestionably art, and high art in patches, and as surely it was not art for art's sake. The art was exercised for a dozen reasons : to make money, to amuse the author, to advertise the Empire, to oblige a friend, to down a pet aversion, to help a charity, to boom a soldier, to blast a politician. It was never employed for itself alone.

Mr. Kipling was directly, as well as indirectly, a

great destroyer. But he was also indirectly, as well as directly, a considerable creator. He founded no permanent school. The melancholy brood of pseudo-Kiplings that swarmed for a time—the people who thought the secret of his success lay in the use of " ye " and " far-flung "—belonged to a special kind of journalism, not to any kind of literature. But Kipling's hostile followers, those who came after him, but with a snickersnee, were as much of his creation as were his servile imitators. For example, Mr. Kipling was the spiritual parent of Mr. Chesterton—parent, that is to say, as the insect is parent to the oak-apple. The insect bites the oak, and raises a lump which grows and grows until it has developed an organisation and character of its own. Mr. Chesterton was the very considerable lump raised by Mr. Kipling, and the growth of Mr. Chesterton both widened and intensified the polemics of the period. The more fervently Mr. Kipling sang and preached of Empire, the more decisively did Mr. Chesterton embrace the parish pump, honouring it as a symbol if not as a source. The higher rose Rudyardian rhapsodies over Medicine Hat and the Notched Kaikuras, the more valorously did Mr. Chesterton shout the glories of Notting Hill and of the chalk downs. Mr. Kipling idolised the gloomy strong man ; it was but natural that Mr. Chesterton should exaggerate the qualities of the cheerful village idiot. If not himself specially the friend of millionaires, Mr. Kipling was certainly a friend of their friends ; it needed no better reason, though there were others, to enrage Mr. Chesterton, only less than Mr. Belloc, first against Beits and Albus, and then against all money-lords. Mr. Kipling was fascinated by the mere machinery of the modern world, though rather contemptuous of much that is characteristic in its spirit. Mr. Chesterton, therefore, must needs retreat into the Middle Ages somewhat further than was strictly necessary. With Mr. Chesterton, as the lawyers say, Mr. Belloc, and the two together managed to get on barking or biting terms with almost everybody else. There were, of course, personages and things to fight about in those happy days, or, at least, names. Some Tories, if they did not sincerely deify Mr. Balfour, did most sincerely diabolise Mr. Lloyd George. Some Radicals thought Sir Edward Carson almost as lost a soul as Sir Edward Grey. A prominent statesman could then only be God or devil; nobody conceived him as but an embarrassed wretch. Also there were causes : Tariff Reform or Free Trade for the herd ; Socialism or Personal Liberty for the intellectual few. One feels pity for the survivors of those jolly quarrels. By force of habit they go on fighting, but the foe, following the fashion of modern war, has gone to ground, whilst, in most human affairs, causes have become unfashionable. The old contests are maintained by the elderly writers without regard for the fact that compromises, coalitions, making the best of bad jobs, and shoulder-shrugging are the order of the day for the majority of mankind that has outlived the European War.

As everyone knows, there is only one comfort greater than that of a trusty friend. It is an entirely constant and reliable enemy. So, perhaps, it is lack of dependable heroes and bugbears to-day, combined with a blurring of most moral problems, that has led many bonny fighters of the first decade to theological or semi-theological speculations. On theology one can always get up a good fight. Mr. Chesterton and Mr. Belloc derive, perhaps, more fun from attacking Pithecanthropus and the Neanderthal man than from their tilts at millionaires and politicians. Mr. Wells has found more joy in brief fealty to the Invisible (and Incomprehensible) King and in his fierce repudiation of " Mr. G." than he can have taken from his feud with fellow Fabians. Mr. Shaw's dissatisfaction with concrete victims who once contented him may be the secret of his later mysticism.

I would leave others to decide who among these swashbucklers was the best armed. Was it Mr. Kipling, alternately using a cunning Eastern scimitar and a Lee-Metford of the latest mark, complete with " bay'nit " ? Or Mr. Chesterton, capable of infinite finesse with Excalibur ? Or Mr. Belloc, of the straight Roman blade ; or Mr. Wells, with acids and gasses and embryonic tanks and aeroplanes ; or Mr. Shaw, with his assorted bombs ? But if it is hard to decide who was the best armed, or the best fighter, I should unhesitatingly give Mr. Wells the distinction of being the best hater. Mr. Wells, as far as too limited chances have allowed me to judge, is personally the most charming of men, and, should he be in the right mood, contrives to make an entire stranger feel that he has at least found a thoroughly understanding and sympathetic soul. Nothing becomes him more than his kindliness to humbler followers of his craft. But intellectually he is about the most satisfactory hater I know. It is really an achievement to hate St. Athanasius as if he were a " little, red-haired, busy, wire-pulling " curate actually living, and in unavoidable proximity to one to-day ; to detest Constantine as if he were the Kaiser ; and Demosthenes as if he were somebody like " Pertinax " or Count Westarp. But Mr. Wells manages even this.

Largely, no doubt, it is with him a matter of early training. England has never made any systematic effort to secure that young persons of genius who happen to be born poor shall have their full chance. " A child of excellent abilities, and with strong powers of observation, quick, eager, delicate, and soon hurt bodily or mentally," says Dickens in his character of Copperfield, " it seems wonderful to me that nobody should have made a sign on my behalf." Those youthful years in the blacking factory were mightily revenged on the Victorian age. All the preaching of Ruskin and Arnold against complacent Gradgrindism had less effect than phantom accusers such as Copperfield, Tiny Tim and Jo. What the blacking factory was to the son of John Dickens, a broken clerk, the Folkestone drapery establishment was to the son of Joseph Wells, a poor professional cricketer who had failed as keeper of a general shop. It was bad luck for many ancient institutions that H. G. Wells was Kipps, Hoopdriver and Mr. Polly before he became Remington, M.P., Porphyry Benham or William Clissold. Whether it was bad luck for Mr. Wells himself is a very different matter. His mind is naturally of the scientific cast, his instincts are pedagogic. But for evil years of youth, but for contemplation of suicide as a boy of fifteen, Mr. Wells might have been only a mediocre hater, and, perhaps, a dullish dog not very unlike some of those academic teachers whom he loves to scarify.

Although the depth and number of his hatreds was but imperfectly known when the first decade of the century ended, a fair idea of them could have been gleaned by any intelligent reader of his novels and romances. From *The Time Machine* one might have extracted his impartiality in contempt for the leisured classes and dislike for the proletariat, and from *The Island of Dr. Moreau* his notion that beasts were beasts and men in general only a degree better. The same poor regard for humanity at large was repeated with variations in *The War of the Worlds* and *The Food of the Gods*, in both of which books are visions of superior beings who will anon give us our deserts if we do not mend our ways. Private property had been condemned in *In the Days of the Comet*; nationalism in *The War in the Air*. In *When the Sleeper Wakes* Mr. Wells had gone further. He had passed from cursing things as they were to cursing things as he imagined they would soon be. *When the Sleeper Wakes* is a very curious book. If you found a copy that did not bear the author's name you would guess, by its predictions of the Servile State, and a mechanical hell in full-going order upon earth, that it must be the joint work of Mr. Belloc and Mr. Chesterton. And by its testimony we may know that Mr. Wells is even capable of hating those few things on which as a rule he seems to dote, such as moving roads and gramophones.

The novels of the period tell the same tale as the romances, though rather less plainly. For in those days Mr. Wells was a real novelist and reluctant to interrupt a story for a tirade or sermon. But in *Love and Mr. Lewisham* could be glimpsed his impatience with educational gentility, with marriage and the family as obstacles to a man's career, not to mention spiritualism, in which, it may be, he discerned a dangerous counter-attraction to materialistic science.

In *Kipps* and *The History of Mr. Polly* there is plenty of good humour, but the cross-grain is only partly hidden. It is with Mr. Wells as with Voltaire: although the total of his thoughts may be chaotic, he thinks clearly upon almost every subject that he touches. But in *Kipps*, apart from the excellent narrative, the one subject he tackles is that of etiquette, and, despite a mocking air, he has gone for it in a blind fury. His japing at Chester Coote and " the gentlemanly little people " and " the gentlefolk who have to manage " can be justified. Such as they have simply put themselves in bonds. They have invented a number of vague rules about social inferiorities and superiorities,

and obviously would have a better time if they scrapped
the lot.   In practice, they must be constantly stretching
their rules, and, in consequence, they and the rules are
alike made a butt for everybody, high or low, with a
sense of logic or of humour.   But Mr. Wells is wide of
the mark when he connects the Coote tribe with the
perfectly ordered scheme of monarchical society, or, as
he puts it, with " everybody walking backward " at
Court.   " Everything that is realised is right," Wilde
wrote once, and at Court everything is realised.
Nothing is vague : nothing is stretched.   Nothing is
improvised ludicrously for the occasion because everything is cut and dried.   There are no trumpery disputes
about who shall stand next to the King or bow first
before the Queen (and somebody, after all, has to be
next or first), because the whole system was arranged
exactly centuries ago.   There are no futile nuances
about which people can quarrel.   Consequently, there
is no snobbery.   A marquess does not hate a duke or
despise an earl as Coote hated or despised the man who
in his sphere was for no plain cause rated one step
above or below him.   We have never had a war for
which we were prepared, but let the monarch die, or
even his second cousin, and the Lord Chamberlain and
the Earl Marshal (or whoever it is) are ready in every
conceivable detail.   The greatest triumph of British
organisation, its most signal example of clear thinking,
is, no doubt, a coronation.   All this, however, was
hidden from Mr. Wells because etiquette as practised
at a Coote tea-party had made him cross ; crosser than
any man of parts should be at a display of human
infirmities.

And what of *Mr. Polly?*   Mr. Wells has never written
a jollier book, but it is also a violent book.   As a preliminary to rising from the lowly estate of a small
draper to the lonely grandeur of general factotum and

chucker-out at a village pub, Mr. Polly has burnt down half a town. " What a crime ! " exclaims the moralist. " What a waste ! " bemoans the economist. " Not at all," answers Mr. Wells with perfect calm. " Arson is the appropriate fate of most things in a civilisation like ours."

Finally, there came *Ann Veronica* and *Tono-Bungay*. The former is not a book about which anybody would trouble nowadays, but it had its success of scandal, and was an assault on current notions of propriety. In *Tono-Bungay* the author indicted the British public for allowing itself to be fleeced by a charlatan who knew how to get rich quick in our disorderly society. There was the suggestion that under Socialism things would be different. But here is a curious thing to note. Mr. Wells was angry only with the public. For Uncle Ponderevo, who exploited it without remorse or shame, he had something like affection. There is one class of men that Mr. Wells adores : the scientists. There is another for whom he has a sneaking tenderness : the big, bold money-makers. Many classes he detests, notably squires, Anglican parsons, classical scholars, professional soldiers and Whig politicians. But he detests peasants far more bitterly than any of the rest. They, he says, are the enemy. In *Tono-Bungay* he actually took off his hat to the abominated county families, because there was this one mark to their credit : they had exterminated the English peasantry, and so made England in that one respect at least a better land than could be found anywhere on the continent of Europe.

As Mr. Kipling helped in the making of Mr. Chesterton, so did Messrs. Chesterton and Belloc help in the making of Mr. Wells. It is highly improbable that Mr. Wells has ever been in intimate contact with a peasant. It has been enough for him to hear the peasant praised by those two writers who dare affirm, among other things, that the last word about evolution was not said by Huxley, what time Herbert George Wells was sitting at the master's feet.

Mr. Galsworthy, though he, too, was in the thick of the fray, would doubtless wish to be judged a man incapable of hate. From the first, he was always trying to be charitable : he succeeded in being as cold as charity. When I was (to my exceeding benefit and enjoyment) refreshing my memory of Mr. Galsworthy's works a while ago, there entered my head something that had no right there just then, something as far removed as possible from *The Silver Box* or *The Country House*. It was a scrap from the duet in *Ruddigore*, wherein the ex-bad baronet and his ex-mad wife deliver themselves of something like the following :—

> " In fact we rule a national school :
> It's rather dull, but we're not complaining ;
> *(Business)*
> This sort of thing takes a deal of training."

Mr. Galsworthy does not exactly rule a national school. His wares suggest Ibsen, Tolstoy, Brieux, and, perhaps, a German or two. But he is a schoolmaster, and shows pathetic patience, as though it were " rather dull " (though he would never think of complaining) to be always addressing a class of imbeciles. Were he to tell us that his " sort of thing "—every sentence chiselled, every syllable effective—took " a deal of training," we should all agree. It must. Mr. Galsworthy is trained to the last ounce. There is no " native wood note wild " about him—one would say no hint of genius. But talent has been cultivated assiduously, and there is odd contrast between the passionate enthusiasms of the man and the rigid discipline of the artist. That very competent critic, M. Chevalley, is surely right in saying that had Mr. Galsworthy been born French he would, after one or two assaults, have gained admission to the Academy. Of few English writers could as much be said in praise or blame.

In his style and method Mr. Galsworthy betrays not only the Harrow boy and Oxford man, but also the solicitor's son and the barrister. His temperament tends naturally to the loosest sentimentality. His pity for " all who are afflicted and distressed," whether a woman who cannot get on with her husband, or a son with his father, or a workman with his employer, or a cab-horse with its four-wheeler, is so exquisitely developed as occasionally to mislead. Were it not for the legal backbone in him, it would make Mr. Galsworthy quite molluscoid and incredible.

Mr. Galsworthy is, in fact, a lawyer out of sympathy with the law, and with a special objection to the law of property. His plays are brilliantly drawn indictments ; his novels eloquent pleadings. Especially is he master of one very difficult branch of the forensic art. Whilst acting as counsel he can nearly always induce the ladies and gentlemen of the jury, simple persons for the most part, to imagine that he is the judge, and that his speech, whether delivered for the defence or the prosecution, is a judicial summing-up. He is always careful to show that the people against whom he seeks a verdict have charming manners or good intentions, and are the men and women whom we should not only like to meet at dinner, but would most readily admit to our intimacy. Those for whom he pleads are, on the contrary, often presented as disagreeable, or else as vagabonds none too trustworthy in the neighbourhood of pretty women or silver spoons. Only after all this does our barrister make his irresistible appeal to our sense of justice. Our prejudices, he admits, must be against his clients, and our prejudices do us credit, but as a jury we must shed them. We must give our decision on the facts of the case, and the facts, as he has stated them for our benefit, are always and overwhelmingly on the side of the scurvy-looking rogue or the woman who has bolted from a respectable home or the mad dog who has bitten the man. In France, M. Bourget, for the other side, uses the same artifice with like cunning. His rebels are always delightful creatures : his " right-thinking " characters dull and frequently unpleasant. But his right-thinkers are none the less right, or, at least, they get a verdict from the unprejudiced jury.

The one trouble is that Mr. Galsworthy's people are seldom alive. They ought to be, for there is an immense amount of mere fact in Mr. Galsworthy's work : the police-court scene in *The Silver Box*, for example, is a mass of facts, accurately observed. But the characters are not men and women who, one feels, might do anything if Providence allowed, but lay figures who must do only one strictly relevant set of things, because the author wills it. They are the John Does and Richard Roes of fiction and the drama. In one respect they are the unreal creatures of a lawsuit brought only to test a great principle : in another, perhaps, the personified platitudes of an allegory. There is much art in their effective opposition : much skill in the presentation of the case for and against. But there is no human conflict : only a conflict of personified causes and ideas. In a Hamburg theatre the audience was once so affected by the prison scene in *Justice* that the play could hardly be brought to its conclusion. In England, where people care about people a good deal, and about causes and ideas very little, Mr. Galsworthy has always been heard and read with respectful calm.

On the whole, one is sorry for Mr. Galsworthy.

Despite his triumphs in the literary law courts, he seems to be a man painfully conscious of his limitations. There is no thinking of him without recalling the man in *Fraternity* whose pity for a girl was prevented from growing into love because she had dirty nails. Mr. Galsworthy has evaded or overcome the brutality that is occasionally bred by Harrow and Oxford, but in life as well as in letters he is in thrall to the fastidiousness that is sometimes the complement of their brutality. Up to a point, Mr. Kipling can make friends with common soldiers in a canteen, Mr. Chesterton can make merry with mixed company at an inn, but Mr. Galsworthy has never been anything like at home save in the most refined society. And at home he must have been always unhappy with his conscience telling him he should be with the least kempt and fortunate of his clients in the streets. These things, it may be, explain in part his extraordinary affection for dogs.

To dwell here on Mr. Kipling would be out of place. For the best part of the decade his Imperialism was out of favour. His South African verses only provoked derision at a time when men were nodding approval at Mr. Belloc's satires.

> " The little empty homes forlorn,
>   The ruined synagogues that mourn
>   In Frankfort and Berlin ;
>   We knew them when the peace was torn—
>   We of a nobler lineage born—
>   And now by all the gods of scorn
>   We mean to rub them in."

Not yet had Mr. Kipling become a classic, and in the interval he was reduced to writing stories for the

D

young, which, delightful as they may be in their own
way, are not fit matter for the criticism of adults. But
to say that the first ten years of the century were
Mr. Shaw's greatest period might, though bold, be not
quite wrong. From a literary point of view he had
written nothing to approach *St. Joan* or the first part
of *Back to Methuselah*, and his philosophy was, perhaps,
still comparatively crude. He had still to win success
in the biggest way at the box-office. Few owned as
yet to taking him seriously, most imitating Max in the
assertion that Mr. Shaw was a man standing on his
head. But, secretly, he was taken rather more seriously
than he is to-day. The plaudits he receives at this
hour are the proof that he has been found essentially
innocuous.

When good King Edward ruled the land one of
Mr. Shaw's plays was still under the censor's ban, and
the Lord Chamberlain is almost always wise in his
generation. Mr. Shaw just then seemed dangerous.
Several other plays of his early and middle period were
of a kind that would be described as "subversive."
Arms and the Man made war ridiculous ; *John Bull's
other Island* threw contempt on the Radical reformer ;
The Doctor's Dilemma was highly disrespectful to an
intensely serious profession. But in all these matters
Mr. Shaw was but a day before his time. War, in its
biggest and most hateful manifestation, has since also
shown itself at its most ridiculous. English ineptitude
over Ireland has ended, earlier than anybody expected,
in something that nobody expected. Doctors command
higher fees and do more wonderful cures than ever,
but are no longer revered, as in Victorian days, as a
mixture of magician and saint. We have here one of
the main facts concerning Mr. Shaw. He has always
been, so to speak, topically anticipatory. He has an
assured eye for the very next thing coming, and he has

got all out of it before others make it tiresome. He has always been enough in advance of his age to extort respect as a tipster, never enough to be accounted, except by hysterical admirers, as among the major prophets. Mr. Wells has a sense of the future which is at least impressive. One hopes, on the whole, that he may be wrong, but feels that he may quite possibly be right ; at any rate he deals in possibilities, and makes his world to come a three-dimension affair, fantastic perhaps, but more or less rational. Mr. Shaw, when he looks forward as far as thought can reach, finds himself forsaken by the one quality which makes his view of contemporary things valuable and interesting. He loses his magnificent clarity and cocksureness. He becomes woolly and ambiguous.

It is curious to note how quickly the public has caught up with Shavianism. The extravagances of Mr. Shaw's middle life have become banalities in his age. One remembers how he wrote that the hall of the Ptolemies would, because of its lack of upholstery, seem ridiculously bare to a rich Englishman. Fashion in furniture now decrees that there shall be bareness in the rich Englishman's halls to correspond with the nudity of the rich Englishman's womankind. The *Life Force* has been domesticated, and is familiar in every provincial debating society. The growth of Christian Science in the residential suburbs is due as much to Mr. Shaw's exposure of sundry medical practices and malpractices as to the gospel preached from Boston, Mass. With the idea of the Superman we grew only too familiar when the Geddes clan was in its heyday. Eliza Doolittle's naughty word is heard in every smart night club. That is why Shaw plays " date " rather badly. Even *Man and Superman*, the most finished of the early works, and the one in which the author most consciously strove to compress his

whole philosophy, is not exempt.   We find a chauffeur
with an eager interest in cars, natural enough in
experimental days, but strangely contrasting with the
bored efficiency of Straker's successors.   Meanwhile
Mr. Shaw, who took eighteenth-century models for his
style, has contrived to prolong his heterodoxy by
slipping backwards, in thought no less than in expression.   He is now piquantly old-world in many
respects.   He, who at one time protested against
discipline even for children, emerges in the introduction to *Saint Joan* as something very like an authori-
tarian, and has given perhaps the best apology for
religious intolerance penned by a modern.   Only in
one thing he is still the young Shaw—in his very noble
hatred of cruelty, whether to men or to animals.
Otherwise, while far higher in literary stature, he has
lost significance;   rather commanding respect than
inspiring hopes or fears.

Indeed, it is now seen that Mr. Shaw, to outward
seeming the least conventional of men, has always in
essence shown a pretty close affinity with the conventional.   He has long been quite conventionally rich ;
he has always been quite conventionally business-like ;
his political ideals, wild as they may appear in incidentals, are at bottom tame;   he has none of that
itch for kicking over the traces which possesses Mr.
Wells, and led him to glorify the " free man of the
steppes " over the humdrum (I think Mr. Wells's
own adjective is " frowsy ") Roman.   Mr. Shaw's
philosophy in his subversive days was, it is true, very
much opposed to that of the conventional man, but it
could not have existed in the conventional man's
absence.   For early and middle period Shavianism
reveals itself on analysis simply as conventionalism
twisted or reversed.   The three important points to be
noted are an excellent style, an almost unhealthily keen

eyesight, and an impish desire to smack respectability
in the face on all occasions. The style needs no
comment; it is the perfect vehicle for everything but
emotion; Mr. Shaw is only feeble when he rants
love, philanthropy or mysticism. Of the eyesight
something more may be said. It is just too good for
the purpose of seeing. It has put Mr. Shaw in the
uncomfortable position of Gulliver in Brobdingnag,
who was shocked by the coarseness of the Court ladies'
skins, when, in fact, by all standards of common sense,
these young women were marvels of delicacy. Vision
of this kind sees a multitude of facts, but plays the very
mischief with the truth. There was thus in Mr.
Shaw's early work much of that pitiless illumination
that belongs to a kind of day in the English spring—it
may arrive any time between March and June—when
the east wind saws and grits, when a Bokhara rug loses
all its colour and a Turner seems to be done in greasy
monochrome, when everything you touch is scratchy,
when the cold glare decomposes all beauties and
makes all ugliness malignantly alive, one of those days
when ugliness chokes you like a sandstorm and beats
you like a cudgel. It is significant that as time has
weakened Mr. Shaw's sight it has mellowed his judgment, and made him more human and tolerant. The
third singularity is that, himself eminently respectable,
and even in his essential tastes bourgeois, he created his
personality, as a man and a writer, on a passionate
detestation of respectability. Probably the hatred was
more ethical than æsthetic, based on a sense of the
selfishness, the egotistic self-satisfaction, the unfeeling
complacence concerning social injustices which distinguished the respectable classes. But there was also,
unquestionably, a large element of "devilment,"
which, it is significant, he has himself denoted as the
fount and origin of all good work. It gave Mr. Shaw

pleasure to see people writhe and hear them revile. He may have taken up heretical music because he admired it, but the annoyance of the orthodox was an added relish. Of Ibsen he had, no doubt, a high and even exaggerated opinion, but he did like rubbing in Ibsen the faces of people who thought Ibsen mere dirt. He was the surer of his Socialism when respectability spluttered that it was of all heresies most damnable. With a natural preference for water as a drink he appreciated it also as something to throw in the face of a rosy port-loving bishop or don. It added zest to his dish of herbs that he could jeer the better over the annual dinner (if there be one) of the Society for the Prevention of Cruelty to Animals. His whole joy, in fine, was to shock Mr. John Bull, Mrs. John Bull and Miss Joan Bull (the latter-day imperviousness of the last must have pained him), and to ridicule all they held sacred—Sir Henry Irving, Harley Street, the Archbishop of Canterbury, Shakespeare and the musical asses, the marriage service, fox-hunting, the capitalist system, major-generals, and county cricket. But an anti-John Bull must, of necessity, be as insular as John Bull himself, and as limited. There is, accordingly, a kind of narrowness in Mr. Shaw's breadth, a kind of sectarianism in his superiority to all denominations. His wit, when it can be dissociated from his thought, is imperishable, but his thought is not; it would be charming if we could have all leading articles as sparkling as his plays, but most of them are, in fact, leading articles (written not for the day but for the day after next) and, like other leading articles, they do not improve by indefinite keeping. Mr. Shaw takes his place, and a dignified one, among men who, like Carlyle and Ruskin, Arnold and Morris, exercised a considerable and on the whole salutary influence on the minds of their contemporaries. But the time had passed, even before the end of the first decade, when it could be thought that, like Rousseau, he might be included in the little band of writers who have changed the course of history.

From the literary propagandists we may turn to the artists. In the year 1908 appeared a book entitled *The Old Wives' Tale*. To say that the author, Mr. Arnold Bennett, has ever pursued art wholly for art's sake would, to put it mildly, be an exaggeration, but this one novel can be cited as a pure artist's work, just as all his other novels can be invoked as the work of a skilled, and often of a very highly skilled, artisan. Born in the heart of the Potteries, where the god of getting-on reveals himself as a pillar of smoke by day and a pillar of fire by night, Enoch Arnold Bennett yielded early worship to the gracious divinity. " Fame and a thousand a year "—mainly, perhaps, the thousand a year—stimulated a mind chiefly fascinated by the concrete. Had other means of getting there conveniently lain handy, the Five Towns might still be voiceless. In a handsome brick house, replete with every appurtenance of middle-class comfort, Mr. Bennett, manager and junior partner in some pottery concern, might now be entertaining the prosperous people he has put into his books. Circumstances, however, drove him farther afield, that is, to a high stool and a low salary in a solicitor's office, and so to London and two hundred pounds a year, which appeared to be the end of it. A certain restricted fame was his, through " cunning in the preparation of costs and a hundred and thirty words a minute in shorthand," but the gulf between two hundred and a thousand was clearly unbridgeable. Then, with manful decision, if with some qualm, the still young Bennett threw away the small certainty, and embarked on the great gamble of journalism after having a story accepted by *The Yellow Book* and gaining a prize in *Tit Bits.*

Seven years later, at the beginning of the century, he resigned his editorship of *Woman,* and retired to a cottage in the heart of that Fontainebleau Forest where Corot saw his vaporous nymphs dancing under the shade of fairy trees. On the last day of the previous year he had recorded in his diary the fact that in twelve months he had written 335,340 words.

So began one of the greatest recorded triumphs of industrialised literature. It is not belittling Mr. Bennett to describe him as the supreme living example of the tradesman in letters. On the whole, the trades-man—the genuine tradesman, not the false pretence of one—is the truest and most satisfactory thing we have left. It is wholly blessed to turn from amateurish reachings after the right word and perfect sentence to the work of the deft artisan who knows he is near enough. Such an artisan is, and was, Mr. Bennett. That neatly written " copy " of his, delivered (like Shakespeare's) " with scarce a blot," tells its own story of the professional competence that is not afraid of being a little less than faultless.

Men have often gone into the wilderness to make their souls ; it is rare to repair thither to make great fortunes. Yet the Bennett hegira was calculated common sense. Mr. Bennett has himself said that he left London to avoid its distractions. In the next ten crowded and prolific years, he travelled from the Grand Babylon Hotel, where Mr. Oppenheim might nod to him in the lounge, and Mr. Le Queux acknowledge their common status in the bar, to his own stately mansion, in which he could without ridicule hang among the portraits of his intellectual ancestors a full-length of Balzac. The flight to Fontainebleau was as good for the quality as for the quantity of what American publishers call his "literary output." Carlyle insisted that all great men retain the capacity of wonder; to lose it is to cease to be great. Mr. Bennett had not the holy wonder of the mystic, but he started with all the hungry receptiveness of the provincial up for a royal procession. We often talk of keeping an open mind; Mr. Bennett has, so to speak, had the supreme luck and wisdom to keep his open mouth. Others rejoice to have their angles rubbed away; Mr. Bennett wisely escaped from London for the very purpose of preserving his. Other writers who had much his experience in his provincial youth have yielded to the superstition of the capital. They regard late dinner as a law of nature; treat the latest philosophic craze as a final answer to the riddle of things; forget that most of England is still provincial, that the social writ of Mayfair runs not an inch beyond Baker Street, and that Spurgeon and Herbert Spencer sway more minds than Inge and Einstein.

It is, in short, Mr. Bennett's strength that he has retained what may be described as virginity without innocence; a sort of vestal knowingness. He has kept alive in himself the perception of his own England. Old unhappy far-off chiffoniers and glass-cased humming-birds of long ago are at once a vivid and a blessed memory; they work up into more magic than the choicest Chippendale. As he puts on an evening-coat he remembers the carnivorous five o'clock meal of the pottery magnates, who sometimes sat down to it in their shirt-sleeves. As he speaks fluent French in a Parisian literary circle a sense of miracle overwhelms him; his fellow-townsmen are still talking Five Towns dialect—at least to the servants. He has kept the appetite as well as the memory of the avid provincial. The fun of the fair is still fun to him. He rejoices in

the fatness of the Fat Lady, and in the telling of the
tale of her fatness we lose no ounce of her.   The best
of Mr. Bennett is that he takes nothing for granted,
least of all himself and the place to which he has climbed.
The Five Towns are always in the background of his
mind, and during the Fontainebleau decade, when
The Old Wives' Tale was published and the *Clayhanger*
series was beginning, they were all the background.
At the end of it, from the fame and fortune point of
view, his career had but just begun, but the most
masterly of his novels had been written, or, if not written, planned.   Why the later books have to be placed
on a slightly lower level, and are left on a higher and
less accessible shelf, is not quite easy to explain.   The
Pretty Lady, with all her carefully described frailties,
with or without her no less carefully described flounces,
is entertaining.   *Mr. Prohack*, passing from one night
club to another by way of the Turkish bath, provides
diversion.   But there are, perhaps, regrets that the
master shoemaker has left his last.

If I say nothing here of Stephen Phillips, although
one responsible critic ranked him with Sophocles and
Dante, whilst another proclaimed him to be the younger
Dumas speaking with the voice of Milton, it is because
few readers of this book are likely even to remember
the name of that meteoric poet.   And if I say no more
of Joseph Conrad, it is because appreciation of that
great writer was confined to a very small circle of
connoisseurs until more than ten years of the century
had gone.   Maurice Hewlett has more claim to notice
in this chapter; yet I hesitate.   It is a matter of
personal taste, and the chapter would grow too long
were I to dispute about it, but I hold that in *The Forest
Lovers* only did Hewlett produce anything of special

worth. And, as it happens, *The Forest Lovers* belongs, chronologically, to the 'nineties.

For failure to touch upon the problem of Sir James Barrie, however, I could find no good excuse. The years with which we are dealing here were, as far as he was concerned, a time of transition, and, like most times of transition, extremely interesting. He had already accomplished much, yet it was fairly plain that he had still a long way to go before reaching the limit of his powers. Moreover, there was no telling in what direction he would go. The *Kailyard* belonged to the past; there could be no return to *Thrums*. One George Douglas had broken up the school of the Scottish sentimentalists with a single well-aimed and horribly poisoned dart. But the Barrie of those days was free to move in any direction he pleased, save that he might not return on his tracks. He might, it seemed, accomplish anything.

In the end, as all know, he accomplished *Peter Pan*, and, from his banker's standpoint, no doubt, he has thus exceeded the highest hopes of him. But in the transition time there was more than a possibility of success of a rather different order. The penniless Scot who had advanced from a base at Kirriemuir, by way of journalism in Nottingham, to the conquest of London, was to be judged, among other things, essentially a man. As an undergraduate at Edinburgh he had thrown a " divot," that is, a bit of turf, at Lord Rosebery. " He was a peer; those were my politics." Pelting a Liberal lord in these days would show nothing but bad manners, but in Queen Victoria's reign it meant Radicalism of the really sturdy sort. You might hate the politics, but you had to admit that the youngster who practised them was made of tough stuff. And when he came to full manhood there was reason to hope that whatever he did would be done robustly.

Some, indeed, were hopeful enough to look to Barrie for the great comedy of manners which would owe nothing to topicality, which would give to England something of the everlasting glory Molière gave to France. Only a few years ago, when I was in the midst of writing an article on Sir James Barrie, O.M., I went to a revival of his *Admirable Crichton*, and the first act was not over before I determined to tear up the whole thing. For there was a specimen of pre-*Pan* Barrie at its best—wit, humour and philosophy blended in a delicious whole. What impertinence, I reflected, with something like a blush, to take up any attitude towards so delightful a wizard in words save that of closing the mouth and opening the eyes and ears to take whatever he might care to give. Yet, when it was all over, I could not help thinking that I had been right after all, and that *the* thing remained to do. *Crichton* was very near it. When first played it could only have seemed a guarantee that the thing was going to be done very soon. At the revival, alas, after the last curtain I could only reflect that the thing would probably be left undone for ever and ever.

In the interval the author had produced *Peter Pan*. Of that work, I, as a confirmed adult, am incompetent to speak, and am ready to accept (this side of idolatry) the view of those who profess competence. But it may be suggested that the triumph was not altogether a good thing for the man who achieved it. Thenceforward the lines of his development were determined for him. After *Peter Pan* the genius of the author was canalised, and the greater the apparent variety of his work the more actually monotonous it became. A Barrie play began to be as much a trade-term as a Sheraton cabinet or a Derby dinner service. It had to be " whimsical," with " elfin mischief," " inimitable humour," " delicate irony," " fresh and playful fancy," and so forth. As long as each new production satisfied in its intention, the critics took the line of least resistance, and were silent as to the rest. Had *Peter Pan* been followed by a gloomy drama they would have been pained. Things would have been made difficult for them. They would have had to scrap all the adjectives which had been buzzing in their heads on entering the theatre, and, particularly, the blessed word " inimitable " which, by the way, can never be used until an author has learned to copy himself (or some other) with unfailing accuracy. Mr. Barrie also went on the line of least resistance. He took his cue from the success of *Peter Pan*. Thereafter, every editor could go to bed in peace without bothering about the proof of the criticism on a Barrie first night. Nothing could be wrong with a full column of " delicate," " dainty," " winsome," " playful " flattery headed " More Real Barrie—Puckish Humour at the Banality Theatre."

Whether Sir James Barrie goes to bed in peace is another question. Barrie anecdotes have this in common, that they all represent him as a person of solitary disposition with an affection for monosyllables and a humour that is saturnine rather than strictly Puckish. His eyes, big and sorrowful as a seal's, hint at chronic weariness ; he wears the moustache one associates with lost hopes ; the dome-like forehead is lined with the wrinkles of incurable care. In one of his playlets there is a pantaloon whose business in life had, it seems, been to make people laugh by falling into a barrel, and this funny fellow is haunted by an idea that he is less funny than he used to be, that the trick is losing some of its attraction. Sir James Barrie is not, of course, to be confounded for one moment with a mere tumbler, but since *Peter Pan* he has depended on the repetition of a trick, albeit a most refined and complicated and extremely clever trick.

Possibly he has lived in groundless fear that it is wearing thin. More probably he has grown a trifle tired of it himself, and has found it difficult to credit the sincerity of the encores he has received. And almost certainly he must have often sighed for that man of promise who flourished about a quarter of a century ago, over whose all too mortal remains the monument of the boy who would never grow up stands in Kensington Gardens.

The moral of it all is that Fairyland is an excellent place for a day trip, but that one should never lose the return half of one's ticket. Like any captured human child in the old stories, Sir James Barrie has been kept there, a prisoner in perpetuity.

GEORGE WYNDHAM

In one of Mr. Galsworthy's plays the heroine goes to the bad through being " too fine and not fine enough." That, I always thought, was the *vraie vérité* concerning George Wyndham. There was much in him that was really superior, but it did not give him the freedom in which it could best develop, but rather contributed to his dependence. He was too fine for the ordinary party game with its shams, its self-deceptions, its catchwords, its log-rollings. He was not fine enough to be indifferent to its petty prizes, or to escape infection from its vulgarities. He could not hopefully compete with the Rigbys or even the Tadpoles and Tapers. But he was not quite big enough to play the kind of game which is the despair of those estimable people. Which, after all, is only to say that he failed where such a man as Disraeli did not wholly succeed.

At the beginning of the century he was eminently the man of promise. He was strikingly handsome. He was well-born. He had all the grace of manner which seems to be as much the heritage of the Wyndhams as the pleasing family face. But, though of high lineage, he was neither menaced by a title nor handicapped by immodest wealth. With all the opportunities, he had most of the inducements for a career ; and there was that in him which fascinates men of the most various types. He was the kind of officer who is an idol for his men and good copy for the war correspondents. The literary were flattered by the friendship of one who paid them the compliment of plying their trade in an amateur sort of way and yet was not industrious enough to compete with them. But he also won the goodwill of those who cared for none of these things. " I thought he was a spring poet," said Cecil Rhodes, " and, instead, he is all chapter and verse." When he entered politics, he " took up " the right questions. In the late 'nineties he was recognised at Westminster as one of the senior members for South Africa, and, on the South African Commission, his knowledge and adroitness gained him not only the gratitude of Rhodes, whom he championed, but the admiration of Labouchere, the most redoubtable of his adversaries. Now and then, of course, one heard a sneer about " the Adonis of the Treasury Bench," but a man is, indeed, happily circumstanced when nothing but his good looks can be flung against him. Someone said of Wyndham that he was so handsome as " to take one's breath away." But there was nothing insolent in his perfection of feature ; he was not in the least the kind of handsome man who makes other people feel their drabness. His good looks were at once a joy to others and an asset to himself.

Under-Secretary for War and spokesman for the War Office in the House of Commons when hostilities began in South Africa, he had early an ample opportunity to prove his mettle. By the pro-Boer faction he was, indeed, held to have been one of the chief authors of the conflict. He had been, it was said, in the " conspiracy " to dislodge Salisbury, Hicks - Beach, and those older and steadier Conservative leaders who had favoured looking before leaping. However that might be, there could be no denying that Wyndham was an uncommonly brilliant Under-Secretary. The mood of the country was to accept almost any excuse advanced for the war, or to dispense with excuses altogether, but with regard to the conduct of the war it was sometimes angry and always critical. Wyndham, called on constantly to defend the indefensible, neither faltered nor failed. "Wyndham, Mr., Brilliant Defence of the War Office," is an entry to be found in the index to Hansard, under date 1st February 1900, and the compliment, so rare and so striking in the Parliamentary Reports, was well deserved. If, eventually, he did not persuade the country that all was well with our military arrangements both at Whitehall and at the Front, he did, during the most critical months of the campaign, keep the home public from plunging through doubt into despair, and, in so doing, he established his own reputation. It was remarked by opponents that, while a good party man, he remained nice upon certain points of honour. The "khaki election," with its slogan of "every vote given to the Liberals is a vote given to the Boers," was repugnant to him. He regarded it as a sharper's move, and seems to have felt instinctively that time would bring its revenge.

Delight in an adventure for its own sake never wholly left George Wyndham. An almost boyish love for pirates, highwaymen and the more picturesque types of rogues survived into his manhood. To those who risked much he was ready to forgive much. In his essay on "Elizabethan Adventure" one is struck by his light and easy glossing of the "blacker thing than blood's own dye" which "weighed down great Hawkins on the sea." As a young man, at all events, he appeared to be a little indiscriminate in his sympathy with "Empire builders." It was natural enough that Rhodes should occupy a high place among his collection of gods, but at one time he was a little too kindly in his judgment of less complex characters among the South African magnates. Years were to pass before he was disillusioned, but disillusion did come. He was troubled concerning the effects upon the national

E

character of the Boer War. Wilfrid Scawen Blunt has left on record his prediction that its results must be a lessening respect for law and personal liberty. He lived long enough to see his opinion justified in mournful enough fashion.

The George Wyndham who went to Ireland as Chief Secretary was in some respects a different man from the Wyndham of South Africa. He had matured, and he had emancipated himself. It had been the correct thing for young Tories to take a particular line about the Transvaal, and Wyndham had taken it at a joyous gallop as befitted an officer of the Coldstream Guards. It was no less correct to take a particular line about Ireland, yet he refused absolutely and from the first to take it. Scawen Blunt has written that, whilst the " Castle " party disgusted him by its sycophancy, he took an instant dislike to the Orangemen on account of their " sour bigotry." To either he preferred the Nationalists, and, making little or no attempt to hide his sentiments from his colleagues, he realised from the beginning that he might at any moment be hunted from office as a heretic. His sympathy with Irish Ireland has been ascribed by some to his descent from Lord Edward Fitzgerald, the evergreen hero, or " this ill-fated gentleman " as he is styled in *Burke's Peerage*, but, without underrating the possible influences of blood, it may be urged that the sympathy was due rather to the genuine conservatism of his temperament. Like Disraeli, he felt the absurdity of the successors of the Cavaliers governing Ireland after the manner of the Roundheads, and, unlike most contemporary Unionists, he was very much a Cavalier.

Fortune for a while favoured his schemes for a new Irish policy. Mr. Balfour, looking back on his own experiences, decided that coercion was not a panacea, and was ready to let his brilliant lieutenant try experiments. Mr. Ritchie, who has been described as the most " obliging " politician that ever lived, was, as Chancellor of the Exchequer, quite willing to provide the necessary financial aid. But, despite this backing, he might never have been able to go far had it not been for the political complication of Free Trade and Protection. His Irish Land Bill, it is said, commanded in the Cabinet a bare majority of one, and Chamberlain was among its opponents. In the circumstances, however, his adversaries were not inclined to go far in opposing him. There was, obviously, one rift coming in the party, and everybody was anxious to avoid another. Moreover, as the final controversy grew in volume, disputes on other questions were automatically shelved, and the Tariff Reformers, at all events, began to think it might be advantageous if the Chief Secretary could contrive an Irish alliance. Finally, both factions were anxious to secure Wyndham's own support. At this time he seems to have been more or less neutral, or rather balanced in his dislike to both parties. Later, he threw in his lot with the whole-hoggers, but in truth the nakedly commercial imperialism of the new school appealed little more to his imagination than did the equally commercial internationalism of the Cobdenites.

Thus favoured by the differences between his colleagues, he went straight forward to the greatest Parliamentary triumph ever won by a minister responsible for Irish affairs. The general scheme of land purchase had, of course, been agreed in Ireland between the representatives of the tenants and a considerable group of landlords, but it was uncertain how either Ulster or England would receive it, and the actual measure had to be so framed as to gain at all events English approval whilst retaining that of the Nationalists. On points of detail, opposition from all sides had to be expected, and explanations, too, were bound to be difficult. "I must," Wyndham said, "*imprimis* be understood by Irish patriots and city brokers," and, in the event, he contrived to make both understand without scaring either.

The triumph was, or seemed, complete. Perhaps, from the point of view of the statesman, it was too complete. The success of his land purchase scheme was too great to be forgiven him. The Ulster Unionists, scandalised by seeing a Conservative Chief Secretary on terms of cordiality with Papists, sullenly set about a policy of pinpricks while waiting their opportunity to strike home. And while friends were estranged, enemies were not placated. Gratitude, unhappily, has neither the vigour nor the longevity of malice. A section of the Nationalists, while accepting the benefits of the Act, detected in it an effort to kill Home Rule by kindness, and, as their alarm increased, they too started to whet their knives. Wyndham himself was not content with his victory. To him the settlement of the agrarian problem was but a preliminary to a larger synthesis. He wanted to tackle education. He wanted to carry Irish self-government to a point undistinguishable, by whatever name it might be called, from Home Rule. On his side were Lord Dunraven and other southern landlords; he had the wholehearted support of William O'Brien, and, to all appearances, Redmond was as eager to stand by him. In Dublin he had installed Sir Anthony Macdonnell, a retired Indian officer and an avowed Home Ruler, as his Under-Secretary, whilst for Viceroy he had Lord Dudley, a nobleman who, whatever were his own convictions, was unlikely to prove a serious obstacle to the plans afoot. There was, however, only one chance of success for this scheme. If it were to be done at all, it had to be done quickly. It could only be carried by a rush,

before the hostile forces had time to organise. Time
was given them.

When the land-purchase measure became law George
Wyndham went abroad for a complete rest. He had
worked hard. The financial provisions of the Act,
which were generally believed to be the work of some
competent man of business, had in fact been of his own
devising. At least by fits and starts Wyndham had
the capacity for toil, though most people thought of
him as a man of happy-go-lucky, touch-and-go brilliance,
a *sabreur* with a streak of genius. To correct this view
it is only necessary to look at his literary essays. Their
volume, it is true, is small, but they are finely wrought,
and much reading, thinking, and writing must have
gone to every page of them. Gifted with a natural
trick of agreeable expression, he could, with a tithe of
the trouble, have produced—and that without the
reproach of vapidity—ten times as much. But that
was not his way. In his prime, at any rate, whatever
he did was done with all his might. Yet even in his
prime he appreciated the sweetness of doing nothing.
When he went abroad he took a holiday from politics,
and he took it so thoroughly that, it is credibly said,
weeks passed without his opening a newspaper. Holidays of this kind must always have their danger for the
politician. The lawyer can spend his long vacation in
the desert if it pleases him ; nothing can happen to the
prejudice of the cause for which he is briefed so long
as he comes back with the judges. The fashionable
physician can leave his patients when tired of the
pleasant routine of fee-taking ; if they choose to die
that is their affair ; if, more happily, they find themselves the better for his desertion, it still matters
nothing ; the supply of rich people, ill or fancying
themselves ill, is, for practical purposes, illimitable.
But in politics things still go on happening, and those

who take too many chances will not indefinitely escape a mischief. Wyndham's holiday was more than a mischief. It was a disaster. While he was away the new style Home Rulers—Devolutionists as they called themselves—upset the apple-cart by an excess of zeal. A sort of manifesto was launched. It was all quite loyal, quite respectable, and quite Conservative. But there was no doubt that it meant self-government for Ireland. Immediately the Orange drum began to beat. Colonel Saunderson, the hero of Protestant Ulster, squared his fists and announced that the policy had been framed " under the direct orders of Mr. Wyndham " by Sir Anthony MacDonnell. To this there was no rejoinder. No word came from Wyndham. And Wyndham had no notion that a word was necessary. Wyndham, probably, was reading Plutarch and Ronsard, or studying the modern French Romantics, or, it may be, merely enjoying the sunshine. At all events, he was not reading *The Times*.

Wyndham, certainly, was not conscious that his lassitude was imperilling the design he held dear. There is no doubt whatever of his sincere interest in Ireland. He had refused the War Office for Ireland. He could have had the Colonies for the asking. The Exchequer itself had been within his reach. Yet he remained Chief Secretary, in the belief that he, and he alone, could do what was needed in John Bull's other island. The opportunity, however, had been missed. When he returned in the early autumn of 1904 the storm which broke in full force took him by surprise, and he went down before it. With clear conscience and without damage to his reputation he could have announced that the Devolution scheme had been published without his consent, and that, in its details, it did not meet with his approval. But the disavowal which he issued went much farther than that. It read, and was clearly meant to read, like a complete disavowal of the whole Devolution policy to which, as all his intimates knew, he had long been converted. On the face of it the declaration was a betrayal of all the men in Ireland who had stood by him, but it is a curious tribute to his personality that these were the very men who sought to find excuses for him. They admitted disappointment, but, said they, if Wyndham had become renegade, who could wonder ? Redmond had been now hot, now cold, for the plans of conciliation with which the Chief Secretary had been associated. Other Nationalists had been all along jealously suspicious. With Ulster now rampant, what else could be expected ?

These charitable excuses, we now know, had little relation to the facts. Wyndham was not the man to take his hand from the plough because his furrow was to be a more or less lonely one. He was not the man to be, for any light argument, disloyal to those who had trusted him. Least of all was he likely to give up, without a strong compelling reason, his ambition to settle a great question. To-day there is no doubt as to the explanation of his conduct. After a talk with him, Blunt wrote : " He has sacrificed himself to party necessities and his devotion to Arthur Balfour." The personal affection for Balfour, the desire to spare that harassed leader more worries than the fiscal controversy had already put on him, is comprehensible. The Prime Minister was, perhaps, the only member of the Government for whom Wyndham cared much, or whom Wyndham found congenial after the disillusionment of the Boer War. But the personal explanation alone is insufficient. " Party necessities " were foremost in his mind, and for a good reason. Wyndham believed that war with Germany was coming. With Mr. Balfour and Lord Lansdowne he was one of the three ministers chiefly responsible for the *Entente* with France, and his share in the authorship may well have been considerable. Mr. Balfour and Lord Lansdowne approached the business without prepossession ; they might almost as easily have taken part in founding a cordial under-standing with Germany.   Wyndham, on the contrary, loved France.   Like many Conservatives of his kind, he was apt to be scornful of the Third Republic and all its works, but behind and above that not very attractive political façade he saw not only a peasant people, appealing strongly to the countryman in him, but also the Nation which he, as a man of letters, specially reverenced for its part in maintaining and in spreading that type of civilisation which distinguishes Western Europe from the rest of the world.   To him the *Entente* appealed not only as a measure of national security ; it was also a labour of love.   And until the *Entente* had been consolidated he must have felt that a change of government would be a catastrophe for England, and indeed for the world.   Any further split in the Conservative ranks had, therefore, to be avoided at all costs : even at the cost of sacrificing Ireland ; even at the cost of sacrificing his own reputation.

The rest of Wyndham's record is a story of slow decline.   His remaining months in office were wretched. The Ulster Unionists persecuted him without remorse, and, with the idea of Devolution abandoned as an item in practical politics, there was no special reason for him to remain at a post where he was abominably uncomfortable.   Anon, he who had made a sacrifice for " party necessities " was sacrificed for party.   The Orangemen continued like wolves upon his track, and when the chase grew hot his chief flung them their victim.   George Wyndham resigned from the Cabinet. He talked even of leaving Parliament.   " I have," he wrote, " a wife, a son, a home, six good hunters, and a library of Romance literature. I mean to enjoy them. If I am wanted I can be found." But when the General Election came in 1906 he stood again for Dover, and was among the few Conservatives of standing to be successful at the polls. Yet, though when the House met he was by far the most distinguished Conservative it contained, he was not conceded even the honour of the temporary leadership. Until a seat was found for Mr. Balfour the place was taken by Mr. Aretas Akers-Douglas.

" A soldier," Wyndham wrote in his essay on North's *Plutarch*, " may as well complain of bullets in a battle as of stupidity in his colleagues." He murmured at none of the slights put on him. Outwardly he endured everything in stoic style, and even talked to his friends of a new and strange ambition—to remain in the Commons until he should be Father of the House. Certainly he had too many interests in life to be positively unhappy. One of his friends (Mr. Charles Boyd) has written : " He loved books, the open air, music, the sentiment of wine and fellowship, games, gardens, the far-away illimitable spaces at the ends of the Empire, the misted valleys and water meadows, encompassed by vast downs, of his own countryside." Perhaps it would have been better had he actually left politics. There was work for him to do in letters : work of another sort as a landowner. At Westminster on the other hand, he could only wait for the day which never came, for the day when he should be wanted. In his *Poetry of the Prison* he had written of Charles d'Orleans as " an idler growing old in idleness," and there were some who feared that such a fate would be his own.

That he remained in Parliament from a high sense of duty must, however, be allowed. " The gentlemen of England must not abdicate " was a saying often on his lips, and he does not seem to have realised that they had, in fact, been deposed. He himself was intelligent enough not to see the end of all things in the Lloyd George Budget. If he had been in authority he would, no doubt, have favoured a very different policy from that into which the Conservative party was seduced, to its disaster. But when the Lords had thrown the Budget out he threw himself into the thick of the fray on the Diehard side, and once again was full of notions for an alliance of Tories and Irish against the Radicals. In 1911 he deluded himself with a fancy that the party leadership could be his for the asking, and plainly did not understand that he had come to count for less than Mr. Austen Chamberlain or Mr. F. E. Smith, and for no more than Lord Willoughby de Broke. Some said he was too literary and romantic ; others that he cared over-much for the " sentiment of wine." Scawen Blunt, his friend and cousin, wrote that he had become " self-indulgent."

" It is clear to me," Mr. Boyd reports him as saying in his later days, " that the British race has one foe— Cosmopolitan Finance with an Oriental complexion." Had he satisfied his ambition and become the Conservative leader, it is interesting to speculate what crusades he might have attempted. His political ideas, as privately expressed, were rarely orthodox. He was in favour of Home Rule. " The State," he wrote, " ought to launch the young, and provide a haven for the old. Between youth and age the State should say that a good man deserves a living." He was emphatically of the " Country Party." The English fields and the plains of Ireland must, he said, be held against " the weasels of pure finance," whom he saw sucking them like eggs. But, accepting this point of view, it is still evident that there were some things he never came to understand. He thought too much of his own class, and too much of his intellectual peers. For the people, at all events for the people of England, he took thought, but only as patron and protector. In his political theory, as in his literary criticism, he often went wrong through his too slight respect for the commonplace. " Romance," he wrote, " results from welcoming the strange," whereas, of course, it results from welcoming the everyday thing, from taking it to our hearts and into our minds until the wonder of it is revealed by love. Again, writing of the French Romantic movement, he could be so blind as to give the credit for it to Saint Beuve, whilst never hinting that the way for it had been cleared by the uprising of the people that was the Revolution. According to Mr. Whibley, " his only outpost in the modern world was Sir Walter Scott." One could wish that he had strengthened himself by extending his outposts at least as far as Charles Dickens.

His devotion to a Conservative party with which, at least towards the end, he had but slight sympathy, and to which, certainly, he owed no gratitude, may seem curious, but it was a part of his philosophy. Throughout his life Plutarch's statesmen served him frequently as models, and of them he had observed how they bent to " the use and manners of their times," how they endured all things whilst they lived, and at last died quietly, " not for an abstract idea or a sublime emotion, but for the compromise of their day," and though they knew it for a compromise and foresaw its inevitable destruction. So it was with Wyndham himself. His ideals were not those of his party or his time, yet for the party of his time and for its compromises he gave most of a life that might have been spent in a score of other ways, all more satisfactory to a man of his temperament. And in the end he died quietly. So quietly that only his intimate friends were more than dimly aware of his passing. When he died England had forgotten him, though Ireland, indeed, rendered his corpse some tardy honours. In his passage through life he had undoubtedly lost much. Rural England and his library, he told Wilfrid Ward, were his last remaining interests. But despite disappointments, despite fatuous Diehard forays, despite many bowings to compromise and party, like Cyrano he retained his *panache*. After all, it is that which distinguishes him from every other politician of the twentieth century in this country. In good or ill repute, he alone among them wore the *panache*.

What was wrong with him ? Perhaps he was self-indulgent. Perhaps, despite his infinite capacity for labour, he was really only a dilettante. Perhaps the worship of his literary friends, who naturally believed that in politics, which was his business, he must be even more brilliant than in literature, which was his recreation, conspired, with the respect paid to him by politicians as a man of letters, to make him believe himself exempt from the ordinary laws relating serious effort and high reward. Perhaps he was too much of an aristocrat. But, it may be, his chief misfortune was that the only discipline he ever knew as a mature man was the discipline of the party system. For one of his character something else, probably religious belief, was needed. " I am not much of a believer," he told Scawen Blunt. The creed he lacked would have been useful at least as ballast.

THE "PRANCING PRO-CONSULS"

"Prancing pro-consuls" was a phrase often heard in the years following the Boer War.

Its import was plain. The country, which then as always meant rather more than half the country, was deadly sick of everything that smacked of adventurous imperialism, and looked with suspicion on those personages whose task it was to govern the remoter parts of the Empire. The pro-consuls who did such work inconspicuously, whose names were unknown to the man in the street, who were from his point of view nonentities, escaped censure. The others, who were writing or had written their names in history, who furnished copy for the press, were in varying degrees suspect. They were said to prance.

In fact they did not prance. The word suggests a gay expansion which was not included in their characteristics. Milner may not have been a model of the sagacious man of affairs. He certainly did not fill the ideal of a "statesman old, in bearded majesty." But he did not prance. One could not imagine him doing anything so light-hearted. Nor did Curzon prance. Whatever else he forgot, and he forgot (or never knew) nine-tenths of what is a commonplace to the average Englishman with a tenth of his intelligence, he never forgot his dignity. One sees him most fittingly placed (where Mr. Dulac put him in a memorable cartoon) on the back of an elephant, and the elephant is not a prancing beast. As to Lord Cromer, the third of the famous pro-consuls of the period, even the most perfervid little Englanders only thought of him as prancing when their tempers were very bad indeed. If Milner was a man of the study, Cromer was no less surely a man of the office. " Cautious, measured, unimpeachably correct," Mr. Lytton Strachey has written of him, and the verdict is final. Such men may infuriate, but by coldness, and not by ostentatious challenge.

Milner, when he was made High Commissioner of South Africa and Governor of Cape Colony, was very well known to a small circle at home and very little known to the world at large. There was German blood in him, and he had been partly educated in Germany, but probably the most important thing about his early years was his connection with Balliol. When he became a journalist and was working under Stead at the *Pall Mall Gazette*, it was said of him by a colleague, whose mixed feelings of admiration, annoyance and impatience are easy to divine, that he had " the University tip." If the " Oxford manner " be, as some claim, a phantasm, " the University tip " is a definite reality, and it is the mark of those who have been at Balliol. Milner in a peculiar degree kept it throughout his life. One of its effects was to make nearly all Balliol men his allies. Another was to make almost everybody else at least a potential enemy.

In the interval between the *Pall Mall* and South Africa, Milner had been employed mainly in Egypt. It was none too good a training ground for the work before him. On this point there is truth in two observations made subsequently by Kruger. Milner, the old Dutchman wrote, had learnt " to look upon the fellahs as creatures of an inferior species," and " he forgot that the Afrikander is a different creature from the Egyptian fellah."

Long residence among coloured people undoubtedly incapacitates a man from dealing with whites. And this not necessarily because he becomes obsessed with the colour line : the worst examples are often men who have yielded to the fascination of old Asiatic cultures, and, in many respects, are more Indian than the Hindoo, or more Chinese than the Chinaman. It is simply because such a man gets used to thinking of all who are not colleagues as inferiors. Never needing to consider the criticism which is not expert, he simply cannot understand that, while the expert may sometimes err, the common man may occasionally be right, and that even when the common man is conspicuously wrong, it will not suffice merely to tell him so, and have an end on't. Milner, dogmatic by nature, was confirmed in his dogmatism by his early official experience, and was perhaps the last man for the task committed to him in South Africa.

He went to Cape Town with firm intention to keep the peace. But from the first he was confused and mystified. On the one side of him were the Afrikander Dutch, a stubborn peasant people, quite uncultured in the mass, but with no more sense of inferiority to the English than a peasant of the Auvergne feels for a Parisian, and having among their leaders a certain number of men who, in education and capacity, were the equals of the statesmen he would have met in most of the smaller European capitals. On the other side were Cecil Rhodes, a crude but competent adventurer, at once vulgarian and visionary ; the loyalist English, obsessed by hatred of the Dutch ; and the powerful body of the Rand and Kimberley millionaires, with their following, opportunist in the racial struggle, fishing eagerly wherever the waters were troubled.

From the very beginning Milner inevitably made enemies all round him. He committed the mistake of despising the Dutch, thinking they needed nothing but the strong hand to control them. True, he did not always approve of Chamberlain's methods with them, but the distinction he himself drew between his Balliol behaviour (described by one Afrikander as "autocratic superiority") and the cruder style of Birmingham was not appreciated on the back veldt. Also, he could not help coming into conflict with Rhodes and antagonising the one man who, had he so desired, might have used his knowledge and influence to reconcile the races. Between the Oxonian who saw the world from a Balliol window and the Oxonian who saw it from the Matoppo Hills there could be no friendship, but the clash was no less unfortunate. As to the Uitlanders and their kind, he sensed quickly something not quite right, but was puzzled how to deal with them. He knew the serpentine character of Orientals, but these Orientals who had houses in Park Lane, and were called, as they called themselves, Englishmen, were beyond his scope and experience. Then, in his search for honest allies, he lighted on the loyalists, the people who really did want "to wipe out Majuba"—probably the least intelligent section of the whole community, not excepting Kruger's own individual partisans.

Lady Oxford has written of Milner's "mild, slightly downish eyes, narrow, rather bureaucratic views, fine character and distinguished address," and has expressed her wonder as to "what it was that had produced the violence of his mind." On the same point Stead felt astonishment. At the Pall Mall, Stead, prophet turned journalist, had written furious diatribes, and, under the Morley rule, Milner had been given the task of turning them into leading articles meet for a Liberal newspaper. Stead says, altogether credibly, that he had usually emasculated them in the process. Under Stead's editorship, Milner was, of course, given other work, but Stead was afterwards to say that his writing was "clear and colourless," whilst his notes were "not remarkable for snap or point." We must believe this evidence. Milner's eyes did not belie him. Mild and downish he was, even to excess, and not by nature violent at all.

There was, in fact, something unnatural in his indiscretions in South Africa. His outbursts on "breaking the power of Afrikanderdom," on the readiness of British South Africa "for extreme measures," on "helots . . . calling vainly to Her Majesty's Government for redress," came, not from a fierce, a masterful and an unscrupulous mind, but only from a mind befogged and bewildered. His neglect of, and impatience with, Butler's warnings as to the criminal absurdity of running the risk of war with no adequate force to wage it are traceable to the same puzzlement. This mild man raged and stormed because he could disguise his impotence in no other way, because he was in a corner and could see no way out of it save the passage which the bravos about him were panting to cut. Sometimes he roared in hope of bluffing the Boers into belief that they heard the authentic voice of the British lion; sometimes to drown the clamour of the loyalists; and sometimes because he really wanted England to intervene with arms and end a situation with which he could not cope by finer methods. Mild men are often like that. In certain situations they are afraid of everything but most of their own mildness, which they subdue mercilessly. It has been said that there is no wilder animal than a mad sheep. In Milner there was always a strain, if not of the sheep, then of the German professor, a being deficient in fire but peculiarly liable to be hypnotised by fire-eaters. At last he seemed as unreservedly on the side of war as any schoolboy.

Olive Schreiner wrote of Milner when he first came to her country: "He must have the large and rare

F

qualities springing more from the heart than from the head, which enable him to realise that sympathy and comprehension are more potent than coercion in government of men." Milner was exactly the reverse of the man she pictured as the possible peacemaker. What qualities he had were essentially cerebral. His defects, or many of them, came less from the heart than from the stomach. In early life he had suffered much from indigestion, and under hard work or strain he always wilted and deteriorated. It is doubtful whether he ever recovered from the strain of his South African experiences. At the end of the Boer War, he was the least reasonable and conciliatory of the Vereeniging negotiators. When he returned to England to play a part in home politics, he failed lamentably. " Damn the consequences " is, perhaps, the political dictum by which he is most remembered ; and by the consequences he was damned.

There was no place for him in the English scheme of things, and he could not make one. He was, more or less, a Liberal-Unionist. At least, he had once been a Liberal and he had left the party. He was certainly an Imperialist, and had taken up Tariff Reform largely because he liked the resemblance of Chamberlain's scheme to the German customs union, but there was a spiritual gulf between Birmingham and Balliol which meant that the alliance could never be an understanding. For a while attempts were made to bend the Conservative Party into such a shape that he could be useful in it, and anon lead it. He was, of course, as are most men who have been through a Germanic training, a sort of Socialist, the particular sort that Germans call a Socialist of the chair. The *Morning Post*, under Fabian Ware, was the organ in which his opinions were proclaimed and echoed. But it was all in vain. England may one day yield to Socialism of the tub, but to

Socialism of the chair it will always be averse. It is suited neither to the excitable side of English character, which finds it far too cold, nor to the phlegmatic side, which wants to be left alone. Much of it may be, and has been, introduced by underhand legislation, but the politician who openly announces his faith in it is doomed. Milner's belief in good government, strong government and lots of government attracted a good many young men who felt themselves embryonic autocrats, but it was no use as a party programme. Tories may and do preach a jovial paternalism. Milner only managed to seem a well-meaning and severe stepfather. In 1909, when Tory Cabinets were being constructed on paper, he was commonly awarded the India Office. This meant that late in the day, yet quite clearly, his South African record was being scanned by the party which it had most damaged. His blindness to the fact that men who have once been free sigh always for liberty, and must be given at least its semblance, had been illustrated by his dealings with the Boers before the war, by his advocacy of Chinese labour for the Rand mines, by his opposition to self-government for the conquered republics. By 1909 it was realised that he must be kept as much as possible out of English affairs. But possibly he might be the right man for India.

"An unrivalled union of fascination and intellect," Lord Rosebery said of Milner. The fascination is not easy for a non-intimate to discover, but it must have been there, for many intelligent people who were in close personal contact with him swore to it. The most obviously agreeable trait in him was his continuous interest in youth. "Milner's young men" were once supposed to be a galaxy of all the talents. They have since been represented in affairs by Mr. L. S. Amery and in journalism by the authors of deep and rather scornful articles in the lesser read monthly reviews. Neither outcome can be called altogether majestic.

George Nathaniel Curzon, K.G., G.C.S.I., G.C.I.E., M.A., P.C., F.R.S., D.C.L., LL.D., J.P., D.L., Marquess Curzon, Baron Scarsdale, Baron Ravensdale, Viscount Scarsdale, Earl Curzon of Kedleston (I am indebted for these particulars to Frederick Edwin Smith, P.C., D.L., D.C.L., LL.D., Earl of Birkenhead, Viscount Furneaux of Charlton, Viscount and Baron Birkenhead), may not have originally had much in common with Lord Milner, and to the end they were sharply differentiated types, but they had the common link of Balliol.   If we want to realise the two side by side we cannot, perhaps, do better than note that whilst Milner stood for Balliol plus German *kultur*, Curzon was Balliol superimposed on Eton and Kedleston Hall. At Eton, of course, Curzon had been accounted in various ways unusual, but his unusualness had been of a kind which, even at public schools, where most are compelled to follow the middle way, commanded admiration.   I remember receiving from the late Oscar Browning a wonderful letter recalling his youthful beauty and genius.   Others have written of him that he was " shapely " and inclined to " too sumptuous teas."   But it was also observed that he was very clever and worked very hard.   Apart from collegers, who were paid to study, it was said that there were only two Etonians who really did work at that time.   One was Brodrick, the other Curzon, but the former only plodded.

The Curzon who was Viceroy of India seems to have been much the same Curzon who, not so very many years earlier, had doubly astounded fellow Etonians by his capacity for hard labour and by his magnificence.

In a passage worth quoting in full, Mr. Shane Leslie
has written of him as—

" . . . the philosopher king who reformed India, until its
calm was broken by bombs—a cold, scintillating ruler, not
unworthy to succeed Warren Hastings, on whose virtue or
iniquity historians cannot agree. He explained the use of
commas to his officials, and introduced the Dalai Lama to
armed civilisation. It was no anomaly on his part to give a
gorgeous durbar in time of famine. Roman Emperors sated
the crowd with ' games and bread,' *panem et circenses.*"

Curzon went to India with a sincere and laudable
desire to make his reign memorable by the great
benefits he would confer upon the people, materially
by his boons, spiritually by his presence, but without
the faintest notion of consulting the people of India as
to their own desires. Even so does some alien man
of wealth occasionally descend on an English village
he has lately acquired. Curzon, who had travelled in
the East and made the Orient his special study, was
well aware that the government of India was in many
ways terrible defective. The compromise between
British ideas and native prejudices had left a number
of loose and untidy ends. The native population
could be divided into two sections : one that thought
and was more or less dissatisfied, and another that
seemed not dissatisfied, because it did not think at all.
The British migrants were always dissatisfied when they
arrived ; in the end, most of them were satisfied to the
extent of holding that things, humanly speaking, could
not be bettered. Curzon set no such vulgar limitation
to thoughts of what he might accomplish. Other
viceroys had left India only a trifle better or worse
than they found it, but then they had not the advantage
of being George Nathaniel Curzon. Being George
Nathaniel Curzon made, in his view, all the difference.

His début was all that could be desired. Asia is a weary continent, and anything or anybody promising relief to its chronic state of boredom is assured at least of a temporary welcome. Native opinion—that is to to say the opinion of natives who cared at all for such things—was mildly interested in this young man who had risen by his almost unaided abilities to a pinnacle higher than the throne of the Moghuls. British residents who had yawned at the humdrum Scottish ways of Lord Elgin were exhilarated by the advent of his brilliant successor with the beautiful and fabulously wealthy wife.

Curzon was met on his arrival with the inevitable petitions for reforms here and reforms there. Some years later he expressed wonderment because these same persons who had come to him with their prayers and grievances were begging him to let reform alone. Yet for every change he made or proposed grave arguments could be advanced. For instance, there was his handling of the municipal administration of Calcutta, where he reduced the elected members from a majority to a minority. It could be urged that the old body had been ineffective and corrupt, that everyone had grumbled at it. Why should there have been such uproar at his intervention ? Again, there was the far more momentous division of Bengal, about which the two certain things are that it was fully justified on grounds of convenience and that it provoked a tempest of passionate grief comparable to that which broke after the hanging of Nuncomar. So, too, Lord Curzon's educational policy had much to recommend it. He found in India a number of universities of which many were giving a third-rate education to students who did not benefit from it all. He observed that these places were flooding the country with " failed B.A.'s," who thenceforward had no way of making a living conformable to their ambitions save by political agitation. To bring these seats of learning nearer to the Eton and Balliol standard he conceived that something might be done by raising fees. Thus, he reflected, they would be able to give better teaching, and at the same time the dangerous class of needy knifegrinders would be kept away from them. What could be more plausible ? Yet, what more blind, and what more calculated to create opposition ? Curzon could not carry his educational reforms. The cry that he was going to starve the poor of knowledge was too loud to be neglected.

In his dealings with the native princes he was no more fortunate. With their ways, no doubt, much fault was to be found, but the reformer had to be tactful, and tactful Curzon was not. His edicts against visits to Europe without viceregal permission had to be quietly withdrawn. Rather obviously, if a maharajah was to exercise even a show of authority and exact even a show of respect in the eyes of his subjects, he could not be asked to apply for an *exeat*, schoolbon fashion, whenever he wanted to consult a physician iy London or to take a cure at Contrexéville. In a despatch to one feudatory, whose position had been disputed, Curzon wrote : " You are permitted as heretofore to generally administer the territory of the Seraikella State . . . the right to catch elephants in your state is granted to you as a personal concession and as a matter of favour." It was very much as though an English squire of the old school, in letting a parcel of land to a small farmer, had graciously given him leave to shoot rabbits.

Lord Curzon's views on his Indian subjects, whether the latter were "untouchables" or chiefs to be saluted with many salvos of artillery, may not have differed greatly from those held by ordinary Englishmen in the East.

Said Dr. Arnold of Rugby: "There is an essential inferiority in a boy, as compared with a man." It is not unnatural that an Englishman in India should become no less convinced that there is an essential inferiority in a native, as compared with himself. But if there are times when the wisest man may thoughtlessly parade his conviction, there are equally times when people, not specially wise, will conceal it. A fairly tactful person will take up the pose of being rather different than superior. Also, if he stands punctiliously on his own dignity he will be anxiously careful in observance of the complicated business of native etiquette. Curzon showed a frankness which, to put it bluntly, was proper only to a divinity. Having come to the conclusion (which others had reached before him) that Bengal was mainly inhabited by cheats and liars, he said so publicly. His own pride of birth and place never seemed to take cognisance of pride of birth and place in the very home of caste.

His famous Durbar has often been attacked on the ground that its splendour and extravagance were specially out of place in the midst of famine. "A viceroy," according to Sir Henry Maine, "has to regulate his watch to keep true time in two longitudes." In other words he must consider England and India both. But Curzon's policy was ever that of a single longitude, and his sole meridian was that of Kedleston Hall. The curious thing is that the Kedleston mind offended chiefly those which might be supposed to be nearest to it. The conjuncture of the Durbar and the Indian hunger, no doubt, hurt the more sensitive western susceptibilities. It is less likely that it appeared particularly shocking to the Eastern mind. Native potentates, it may be, felt no qualms about their people dying of starvation whilst they themselves were flaunting gems worth kings' ransoms, and the starving people had the experience of centuries to teach them that such indifference was to be expected. Moreover, the famine was not being neglected. There is no proof at all that its relief was impeded by the costly spectacle staged at Delhi. Lord Curzon may therefore be acquitted of any sin against humanity. His offence was really against taste, and Western taste at that.

But other features of the Durbar did certainly cause consternation in the East. On the plea that they would fatigue the viceroy, the usual visits of courtesy were not paid to the native princes, and for some reason their salutes of artillery were not fired. If the elaborate show had been prepared for Lord Curzon's sole glorification, if the rajahs and maharajahs had been bidden there to serve no purpose but the advertisement of his importance in the scheme of things, the arrangements would not have needed much revision. All this *orgueil*, which made the representative of an absent monarch assume more than majesty present in the flesh would have done, was natural to Curzon ; it sprang from his overpowering belief in himself and his total lack of humour. In comparatively small matters his self-confidence was advantageous. For example, when a native cook in a crack cavalry regiment had been murdered, he met the attempts of the regimental authorities to shield the criminal with prompt degradation of the regiment. His action was furiously resented by the British community, and caused a sort of demonstration against him at the Durbar, but it may be doubted whether he observed it, and it is certain that he would not have cared if he had done so. He had the impartiality of his lonely pride. His bitterest adversaries were compelled to own that he ruled without fear and favour, and was to be trusted to dispense impartial justice.

In larger affairs his inability to see with the eyes of

others was inconvenient. When he described the area from Arabia to Siam as "the glacis of the Indian fortress," he gave a jar to friendly relations with at least half-a-dozen European and Asiatic nations. His diplomacy, suitable enough for bringing to reason the smaller tribes of the frontier, threw Afghans, Persians and Tibetans, one after the other, to look towards Russia for protection. In his dispute with Kitchener, when he appeared as the champion of the civil power against the military, all Liberal opinion at least should have been rallied to his side, but, in fact, he won small support anywhere. The almost universal view was that the one constitutional principle for which Curzon was striving was the entirely novel one of his own personal authority.

When he returned to English politics he was from the first astray. He could no longer play the autocrat, and for any other part India, added to his natural temperament, had unfitted him. Tariff Reform was one of the first questions he had to face. Economics, it may be surmised, did not interest him much, but he may well have disliked Birmingham ascendancy in the Tory party. At first he was a Free Trader. Later, he was some sort of a Protectionist, because, he is reputed to have said, all the young men were going that way. But he was too stiffened and aged with premature dignity to lead these young men.

Again, in the struggle over the 1909 Budget, and in the subsequent constitutional crisis, Lord Curzon vacillated painfully. If, like the Duke of Plaza Toro, he had a "pose imperious" and a "demeanour nobly bland," he had also the habit of leading his regiment from behind. The Lansdowne leadership in the Lords was, in those days, rather a nominal affair. It was to the brilliant Curzon that the peers looked for guidance, and his advice was given for rejection of the Budget.

Afterwards, when the whirlwind was being reaped, none stood firmer than he for the death-rather-than-dishonour policy of the Halsbury Club until the hour for decisive action had all but struck. When Balfour was prepared to temporise, to agree to a limited creation of peers for carrying the Parliament Bill, Curzon's " This will never do " gave new hope to the Diehards. But in the end Curzon ranged himself against them, and with what proved to be the predominant faction. " He is a fool," said Wyndham, " for he might have been the next Prime Minister." Decidedly he was not a fool, but it is probably true that he then lost his chance of the Premiership. Years later, when the choice lay between him and Mr. Stanley Baldwin, the high Tory elements in the party showed a distinct preference for the midland manufacturer. They preferred a blank sheet to one on which so much glory, and so much laborious application, chequered with so much indiscretion, had been charactered. The high sense of public duty, which, after all, redeemed a character disfigured by an exorbitant arrogance, did not suffice to commend him as the master of the party. Lord Curzon once playfully complained that he had suffered all his life from a " wicked undergraduate gibe." But he was, in fact, unfortunate, being so " superior," to be thrown into an age in which those who will rule must have, or affect, some sort of feeling with the ruled.

It was just after the rejection of the Budget by the Upper House that Mr. Lloyd George took occasion to draw a lively comparison between the records of Lords Curzon and Milner on one side and of Lord Cromer, who had spoken against rejection, on the other.

" Lord Cromer," he said, " is the man who, finding a province devastated by its government, desolated by war, left it a land of abounding and smiling prosperity." Cromer, certainly, was one of those men of whom nearly all England conspired to speak well, and there is no doubt that, within certain limits, the general eulogy was justified. What he did for Egypt is a plain matter of history. One grants immediately that he gave the land abounding prosperity. But the smile appears only in Mr. George's rhetorical flourish. A balance-sheet may provoke a groan or a chuckle or even a wink : it has no power to produce that sign of *gaieté de cœur* which is a smile.

Lord Cromer belonged to a family which has won considerable distinction since it was first established in England, at the close of the seventeenth century, by the son of a Lutheran pastor from Bremen, who settled in Devonshire as a merchant and manufacturer of cloth. Francis Baring, the pastor's grandson, moved to London, by practical experience became an authority on finance and currency, and received the inevitable baronetcy from Pitt. In later generations other Barings acquired the peerages of Ashburton, North-brook, Revelstoke, and, finally, Cromer. Evelyn Baring, the pro-consul and first holder of the last title, was born in 1841, served in the artillery as a young man, and whilst still in military employment produced a volume entitled *Staff College Essays*. In 1877 he was appointed a Commissioner of the Egyptian debt, and so began his long association with the country of the Sphinx and the Pyramids. It was a curious post for a soldier, even for a soldier who had done more with pen than sword, but his hereditary aptitude for the work was, no doubt, taken into consideration.

And, it should be added, heredity counted for much in this member of the great Baring family. His

management of Egyptian finance was, according to all
financiers, masterly in the extreme, and at this time of
day it would, indeed, be superfluous to add any emphasis
to the testimonials he received upon this point from all
the best authorities. What has drawn less notice is
that he seems to have derived almost as much from the
Lutheran pastor as from his better-known banking
ancestors. In a biography of him by Mr. H. D.
Traill, several of his personal characteristics have been
set forth by one who is described as an appreciative
observer. "Loosely kept accounts," one reads, " vague
statements as to the extent of a debit balance, his soul
abhors." Bad book-keeping does, of course, annoy
any mortal man with a head on his shoulders, but,
probably, the soul is only stirred by it when banking
is in the blood. From the same source one learns that
when Lord Cromer chanced to pick up a novel that
offended his moral taste in other directions, his habit
was, not simply to close it, but actually to put it on the
fire. Ordinary bankers do not behave in that way.
But it is legitimate to fancy that the minister from
Bremen would have found satisfaction in such symbolic
gestures. The ordinary banker, even when dealing
with a worthless cheque, only returns the offending
piece of paper to the drawer. The need for purging
flames is not apparent to the merely financial conscience.

Somewhere in Cromer, the man who devoted the
chief part of his life to making Egypt a paying concern,
there lurked a good deal of the stern Puritan. Mr.
Lytton Strachey says he was " cautious, measured, unimpeachably correct," and that " his temperament, all
in monochromes, touched in with cold blues and
indecisive greys, was eminently unromantic." The
sketch of him, as far as it goes, is excellent. It explains
the fatal antagonism that existed between him and the
hotly Romanesque Gordon, but it explains in part only

either his success with Egypt or his failure with the Egyptians. Probably a more complete portrait could be constructed from his own book, *Modern Egypt*. Therein one reads of a man who has pursued one task with unfaltering determination, but with hopes severely limited. Foreign critics often wrote of him as an administrator who cared solely for material ends, to whom sound finance and improved irrigation were the Alpha and Omega of his duties. His own testimony is abundant proof that his mind was frequently occupied by very different questions. He was perpetually distressed by the moral condition of the people round him. He regarded it as almost unspeakably low, and, whilst he held it incumbent on himself and every European from the West to set a high example of moral rectitude, he had no idea that there could or would be perceptible improvement.

The English in Egypt had not the status of the English in India. In the business of government they could not simply ignore the Egyptians, and do what seemed to themselves best. Also, they had frequently to consider the susceptibilities of other Europeans, particularly the large French colony. Cromer was often praised by Liberals in England for having made use of native talent, but he had no choice in the matter, and there is no doubt that the obligation irked him. The Orientals had not his standards. They were prone to cheat and steeped in sensuality. For these things he could not forgive them, still less those Europeans who were more tolerant, perhaps laxer, than himself. It has been said that he knew by heart the prophecies of Isaiah and the book of Job, and he certainly had kinship with those old Hebrews who so often found themselves lonely and righteous in a society of evildoers.

For all the boons he gave to Egypt, Cromer was

detested. Had he been less a Puritan in his outlook, rather more willing to allow for relativity in morals, he probably would have done more to establish the position of England in that country. The influence of the French, always a little more perceptive than the English of an alien point of view, he resented strongly, but, with his character, he could not counter it. His paternal rule, so little tinged with affection or imagination, could only be harsh and unpopular ; and it reached what was, perhaps, its only logical conclusion in the executions at Denshawi.

"With a patience as indomitable as his energy," Sir Valentine Chirol writes of Cromer, " he transformed a bankrupt country into a land of plenty and contentment unprecedented in its own annals." The plenty must be granted, but, in fact, the contentment did not follow. It may be that a touch of romantic sensibility in his nature would have been an asset. The building of the Assuan Dam was, of course, a great feat that created wealth and relieved distress, but there was a loss to be put against the gain, for the dam entailed the submersion of Philæ : of Philæ the sacred and the beautiful. To Cromer it may have seemed that the island mattered to none save Pierre Loti and a few crack-brained writers and painters, but it is likely enough that he was wrong. The belief that man cannot live by bread alone is shared by more persons than financiers will ever know. Love of beauty and the historic sense are stronger things than the Puritan can ever guess.

In English politics Lord Cromer did not win even such success as was obtained by Milner and Curzon. He was considered for the Foreign Office, as an alternative to Grey, when the Liberal Government was being formed in 1905. Four or five years later, when there was talk of coalitions or of a Unionist administration with a Free Trade policy, his name was invariably

mentioned for important posts.   It was, of course, only
the haphazard of circumstances that prevented realisation of these ideas, but it cannot be said there was ever
a moment when the public looked to Cromer for
leadership or demanded that his talents should be put
to use.   He was thought sagacious, but he was thought
dull.   Himself utterly without imagination, there was
never a moment when he appealed to the imagination
of the people.   He was with the Liberals on Free
Trade : but when Mr. Asquith introduced Old Age
Pensions, Cromer gave up any notion he may have had
of definitely throwing in his lot with them.   He had his
own pension, but five shillings a week for old men and
women who might have done nothing to earn them,
save avoiding the poor law and the undertaker, seemed
to him fantastic.

Needless to say, he was shocked by the chimerical
finance of the " People's Budget," but quite as much
so by the wildness of the Tories in thinking it could
be successfully combated by invocation of the House of
Lords.   Inevitably, he was opposed to all the plots
and projects of the Diehards.   Subsequent history, it
may be, has proved that Lord Cromer was more often
right than any other statesman of his day, but then he
was always right in the wrong way.   Mr. George,
speaking of Curzon and Milner, said that the one
sense they lacked was common sense.   Common sense
was precisely what Cromer had, but common sense is
not enough in English politics, and too much of it
may be a burden.   There was something very depress-
ing in the consistency with which Cromer discovered a
flaw in every cause that here or there aroused enthusiasm.   In office and power he might have been as good
for England as he had been for Egypt.   But it is likely
that he would have exasperated the English no less
than he had exasperated the Egyptians, and brought

nearer the day of revolution which politicians without a tithe of his sapience have postponed. " His mind," it is written in the Traill biography, " is like a large bureau with many pigeon-holes, and labelled with a docket specifying its contents." The mind which an admirer can liken to a piece of office furniture is, no doubt, a valuable mind in many respects. But a piece of office furniture, when it is not meant simply to be sat on, will not serve in the more human kind of purpose. One does not ask a disgruntled set of workmen to interview the safe or the roll-top desk.

SOME DIVINES

" THE leading Anglicans," says a Roman Catholic writer, " are generally laymen." There is truth in this observation, and the fact is not so strange as it might at first appear. The dignified clergy do not as a rule lead, because leadership implies motion, and their main business is to move as little as possible. Rightly or wrongly they regard themselves as responsible for the defence of a citadel which may be endangered by temerity or provocation. They discourage alarums and excursions : they deprecate defiances and trailed coat-tails. With few exceptions they are what in the slang of oversea politics are called " standpatters."

As it is now, so it was at the start of the century. During the Victorian time the Anglican Church had been torn by intestine feuds. It had been attacked fiercely from without. During the Edwardian decade the civil war died down, and external assault ceased. There was a little lawlessness here and there in the matter of incense or an ikon, and from time to time Mr. Kensit and his preachers managed to produce a brawl, but these things were mere ripples on the surface of a truly pacific ocean. Between " Highs " and " Lows " a sort of working compromise had been reached, and toleration for an artistic ritual, as long as it was art for art's sake and had no hidden meaning, became general. Outside enemies ceased seriously to vex the Church. Save in the wilds of Wales the cry for disestablishment was no longer heard. For a year or two, indeed, there was bitter controversy about rates and church schools, but, when three Liberal Ministers of Education had failed to settle it, the whole business was discovered to be rather unimportant after all. When the decade ended, the Church of England as by law established was in a position of almost unexampled tranquillity.

Merely to state the facts is to pay the most fitting tribute to the statesmanship of Randall Davidson, Archbishop of Canterbury and Primate of All England. A Scot by birth, and of Presbyterian origin, he had, before entering the Anglican establishment, surveyed it in a manner impossible for those who are, so to speak, born under its roof, and to whom it is a hereditary home. No man ever realised more fully than he the truth in John Inglesant's saying that " the Church of England is a compromise." He saw it rent by factions, but, instead of intervening on one side or the other, instead of harshly bidding the contestants hold their peace, he succeeded somehow in embracing both, and, if he could not quite bring them to mutual cordiality, he did persuade them into an attitude of mutual and respectful forbearance.

" Mr. Crisparkle," said the Dean of Cloisterham, " keeping our hearts warm and our heads cool, we clergy need do nothing emphatically." These words might have been the text on which the Archbishop has founded any number of charges and encyclicals. One always knew in advance what his answer would be on any proposed innovation. If his reply were negative, it would surely be accompanied by words to the effect that, whilst he himself saw no great harm in the practice, it was wiser to refrain lest the reasons for it should be misunderstood. " Misunderstood " is what he would say or write, though " understood " would more probably be what he meant. And if his reply were affirmative, it would be no less guarded. The fervent priest who received it would find attached to it one of those saving clauses which make men realise that there may be more joy in defeat than in victory.

When a former archbishop bade farewell to Heber, on the latter's departure for the missionary field, he instructed him to preach the gospel and to put down enthusiasm. Dr. Davidson, of course, would never use words so tart. He knows that enthusiasm is a splendid thing and to be encouraged. He has seen its value exemplified a thousand times in the person of Dr. Ingram, Bishop of London, to say nothing of innumerable obscure curates who popularise religion by training themselves into boxers or by learning to bowl googlies. But no man is better aware that enthusiasm, unless properly directed, runs to waste, and may be even dangerous. Are not the canals of Holland of greater service to humanity than the rushing torrents of lands where nature has been less completely subdued by man ?

During Dr. Davidson's primacy the relations of the Established Church with other religious bodies have sensibly improved. There have been Lambeth Conferences in which union with the Dissenting Protestant bodies has been discussed, and, if nothing tangible has come of them, they have at least created an atmosphere of amiability. There have been Malines Conferences, on which the Archbishop has at least smiled with benignant vagueness, to consider reunion with Rome. In treating, directly or indirectly, with Nonconformists or Papists, the Archbishop has followed the course pursued in dealing with those of his own communion. He has always kept a single eye on what the broadminded agree are the essentials of Christianity. He may have hinted to Baptists that their concern with baptism is excessive, to Congregationalists that the congregational form of Church government has its possible disadvantages, and to Papists that a thought less fuss might be made about the Pope. Were he to have dealings with the Holy Rollers, he would surely try to persuade them that the rolling attitude, while indicative of abounding spiritual vigour, is not necessarily holier than some others. If only all these people would forget their peculiar foibles, then would Christendom be reunited and conterminous with the Church of England, as His Grace envisages it. What exactly would be its theology none can say, but it would certainly be a useful auxiliary to the Charity Organisation Society and the police. At all events, hostility to a Church presided over by one so ready to agree with everybody who agrees with him has become impossible. There may be some who say that the price of such peace as Dr. Davidson has given the Church of England is high, and that anodyne, indefinitely continued, would make the sleep of anæsthesia merge into that of death. But that he has given peace is undeniable.

But during the first decade of the century the Archbishop did not, perhaps, seem quite so representative of the Anglican body as he does to-day, for in sharp contrast to him stood the figure of Dr. Gore, in succession Bishop of Worcester, Birmingham and Oxford, and for a while it was doubtful which of these two would prevail. The Archbishop was a courtier, an ecclesiastical politician, and withal a good man. The Bishop was a zealot, an ascetic, conceivably a saint. The Bishop was, in addition, the one of his order who might be fairly called a leader, for to him the High Churchmen of the day looked for leadership. That most of them eventually outstripped him is nothing to the point. The common fate of leaders is to be passed in due course.

Strangely enough, Dr. Gore first attained wide fame as editor of a book entitled *Lux Mundi*, of which the tendencies were, at the time, considered modernist. As Father Ronald Knox put it in some witty verses, the work gave " a maximum and minimum of creed." Its aim was to be at once " high " and " broad." In a few quiet, decisive, yet not unkindly phrases Dr. Gore disposed of the claims of Evangelical Protestantism to be a religion for intelligent people. " It is, we may perhaps say, becoming more and more difficult to believe in the Bible without believing in the Church." The significance of the words is clear. Science and scholarship are assumed to have overthrown one form of Christianity and are hailed as having opened a way for the restoration of another. Literal acceptance of, say, the books of Moses may be no longer possible, but that does not matter, in fact is all to the good, since the Church has now the task of interpreting dark passages. But if Dr. Gore's words be examined carefully, a certain weakness in his position becomes evident. Whilst he claims authority for the Church, he, a Churchman, is hesitant. The " we may perhaps say " is in the conventional manner of the curate who is not quite sure either of his own ground or of the approbation of his congregation.

However, in the days of *Lux Mundi* Dr. Gore was envisaging the possibilities of a modernised Catholicism. He was scornful of the " Romanist system," and denounced it as obscurantist. " It is," he wrote, " the test of the Church's legitimate tenure that she can encourage free inquiry into her title deeds." Yet when he moved from Pusey House to the Bishopric of Worcester, and then to Birmingham, there were signs of change in him. It would be unfair to say he no

longer encouraged free inquiry, but it would be entirely
true to say that he showed a certain sternness with
those whose inquiries did not lead to the same con-
clusions as his own. The broad priest was accounted
a narrow bishop. Narrowness may result from firm
conviction : but it is also sometimes a consequence of
perturbing doubts. Dr. Gore often seems like the
man in *The Ancient Mariner* who " turns no more his
head," because of the fearful fiend behind him. His
complacency when he can twist the admission of an
opponent into support for himself is occasionally a little
pathetic. He is altogether too delighted, for example,
when he notes that Harnack ascribes the Acts of the
Apostles to the authorship of St. Luke. " To be
conservative in criticism, then," he cries, " is not always
to be wrong." So much reassurance at finding a
German exegetist on his side displays at once an
unrobust confidence and some lack of humour.

On the whole, there can be little wonder that even
Dr. Gore, after a while, lost his influence. Whatever
else the Anglo-Catholic party may be, it does not lack
self-assurance. The author of *Painted Windows* has
proclaimed that without Dr. Gore the party must
perish. He has apparently formed this opinion because
(as he holds) not many of its younger members are
scholars or gentlemen. Scholarship and gentility are
good things in their way. But are they of supreme
importance in those who believe themselves to be
priests ? In the composition of Dr. Gore they may
even have been defects. For Dr. Gore has always been
a scholar, if not a deep scholar, and for seemingly deep
scholarship he has always entertained a somewhat
idolatrous reverence. When it has taken him an inch
or two out of his intellectual depth, he has always shown
signs of alarm. Equally, he has been handicapped by
being too consciously a gentleman. A Christian

Socialist, an "advanced" politician, he has signally failed to reach the people. He has appealed to the emotions on their behalf ; he has never appealed to their emotions. He had never known the way, and, had he known the way, it is doubtful whether he would have used it. Harrow and Balliol would have forbidden.

Outside the Establishment, the two most remarkable religious movements during the Edwardian period came through the short though vigorous campaign of " Passive Resistance " and the promulgation of the " New Theology." In the days of Passive Resistance, Nonconformity had its Indian summer. The grievance which produced this brief stir was perfectly genuine, though there is good reason to doubt whether many would have felt it had not a strong light been turned on it by one of the political parties. In the heyday of Nonconformity, indeed, there would have been no need to stimulate revolt against paying rates for the upkeep of Church of England schools. When Baptists, Methodists and Congregationalists all had perfectly definite creeds, their violent objection to subsidising the teaching of another faith could have been taken for granted. But by the beginning of the century, the theology of the dissenting bodies, save in certain country parts, was, to say the least of it, amorphous.

In the person of Dr. John Clifford the strength and weakness of the religious rebellion were alike exemplified. In appearance he filled the part of rebel leader to perfection. He had the dangerous eyes of Hew-Agag-in-Pieces, and he was as hirsute as any Hebrew prophet in a pictorial Bible. Moreover, he had the right antecedents. At the age of ten he had spent his days, and a good part of his nights, working in a lace-mill. Still earlier in life he had been a bright boy at school, and there had actually been talk of educating him for Oxford, but between him and a university had stood the barrier of the Church catechism. So it was that iron entered into his soul. To the end of his days, John Clifford, though Doctor of Divinity by grace of an American university, remained an uncultured man, and, in consequence, immensely vigorous. As a preacher he had the vehemence of style which at once made and broke pulpits. At a mere glance one would have marked him as of those Covenanters, "baited into savageness and stubbornness," whom Macaulay glorifies in print, but seems, in the recesses of his mind, to dislike. But careful note of the matter of his sermons showed that it was often less forceful than the manner. Dr. Clifford, if he never acquired culture, had nevertheless given himself the maximum of education that can be obtained from popular encyclopædias and had gained his B.Sc. and M.A. at London as a result. In the process he had become sceptical of certain dogmas which had been the rudiments of religion to his forebears. On the problem of predestination as an article of the Baptist faith he had fought and worsted Spurgeon. Clifford was, indeed, a negative rather than a positive force. It was easy to understand why his father, a Derbyshire warp-machiner, with a long and definite creed of his own, should have objected to John repeating the "lies" of the Anglican catechism. It was somewhat less easy to understand why the son should so strenuously object to the public paying for other children to receive Anglican teaching. His own creed was comparatively short, personal to himself, and it may be doubtful whether he would have held any part of it essential to salvation. He had no touchstone by which to show that there was less truth in Anglican doctrine than in any other.

Dr. Clifford has been called the last of the old order of Nonconformists, but he was also the first of the new order, for he heralded the advent of what Mr. Chesterton has called " the creedless chapel." With a foot in each camp, he seemed to be the ideal and obvious leader for the solid opposition of the dissenting bodies to the Balfour Education Act. " Our best friends," wrote Joseph Chamberlain, " are leaving us by scores and hundreds." Dr. Clifford, holding a fiery cross aloft and denouncing clericalism, rallied to Radicalism the great band which Gladstone had scattered with his Home Rule policy. But soon it became doubtful whether the cross had really been a cross and not a mere flail wherewith to beat Tory backs. When the Liberals in office failed to remove the grievance of rates for denominational teaching, the habit of refusing payment fell gradually into desuetude. After all, the Education Act was, from the educational point of view, a progressive step, and the younger generation of Nonconformists, after the first turmoil had subsided, was rather readier to take the teacher's opinion of the measure than the pastor's. Moreover, it may be doubted whether the anti-clerical agitation could have been prolonged in existing circumstances. Punching the Archbishop of Canterbury was as disheartening as belabouring a feather bolster. Dr. Clifford and he provided a striking contrast in ecclesiastical temperament, and their views on, say, Chinese Labour were no less sharply opposed. Dr. Clifford was nothing if not a man of great rages. Replying on one occasion to the taunt that Dissenters were jealous of the Establishment, he cried : " What ! Jealous of a Church whose proudest alliance is with the beer-barrel ! " During the educational wrangle Mr. Balfour flatly refused to meet so vituperative a person. But Dr. Clifford and the Archbishop, if politics could have been forgotten, would surely have found common ground for an amicable meeting. When all is said, Dr. Clifford's

theology was too small a store to contain much of the
odium theologicum, whilst Dr. Davidson's was spread
so wide that at some corner or other of it he could have
found a point in common with every professor of religion.

As the education controversy gradually petered out,
it became evident that Nonconformity was by no means
the solid phalanx it had appeared when the hosts were
mustered to resist the rates and to down the Tories
and the prelates. At the City Temple, London's
Cathedral of Dissent, a youngish man named Campbell
had been preaching for some few years. By birth an
Ulster Presbyterian, he had been educated at Oxford,
where, whilst occasionally taking part in Methodist
ministration, he threw himself heart and soul into the
Anglo-Catholic movement, and had the intention of
taking Holy Orders. But shortly before the end of his
undergraduate career, he came to feel, as he himself
has put it, that " if the Anglo-Catholic theory of the
Church were the true one, I should not feel safe outside
Rome." In consequence, he changed his orientation,
and, after taking a second-class in history, accepted
charge of a Congregational chapel at Brighton.

If Mr. Campbell's opinions had shown something
less than adamantine firmness, it had been suggested
that they were at least consistent in running to extremes.
At the City Temple he was to prove as much. He who
might have been an Anglican priest and ritualist of the
ritualist but for a logical urge along the Roman road
was soon to startle England by rejecting even that
minimum of orthodoxy expected of him as a Free
Church minister. His Biblical criticism was unusually
severe. He was emotional and feverish. His appearance was remarkable. Frail in body, his face had a
beauty at once feminine and spiritual. What precisely
was the " New Theology " that he began to preach not

many knew, yet he preached it and wrote about it in a way that could not escape the attention of the newspapers. Whatever else he was, Mr. Campbell was terribly quotable. " Everyone believes in God if he believes in his own existence " is a perfectly shocking example of the *non sequitur*. But it was eminently the sort of thing to be repeated under the rubric of " Sayings of the Week." And so Mr. Campbell became famous.

He declared that the New Theology was " the religious articulation of the social movement." As he had become a member of the Independent Labour Party, his assertion was, of course, taken to mean that his theology was the religious articulation of the Socialist movement. Again, he asserted that the New Theology was " the religion of science " and " the denial of any possibility of dissonance between science and religion." Here were fine words that might mean almost anything, but inevitably they were read as meaning that Mr. Campbell had jettisoned all the miraculous elements in Christianity to which Huxley and other materialistic scientists had objected. To make matters worse, Mr. Campbell wrote of his religious system that " the word ' theology ' is almost a misnomer." What could that mean if not that he was preaching an ethical code in which God was " almost " superfluous ?

The Clifford-Spurgeon controversy had proved that modern Nonconformity preferred a minimum to a maximum of creed, but its minimum was, temporarily at least, an irreducible minimum. Mr. Campbell overstepped the limits of its tolerance, and although the spell of his personality kept the City Temple faithful to him, he was, so to speak, excommunicated and anathematised by the general body of Protestant dissenters. Dr. Gore's refutation of his teaching was felt to be a particularly black, not to say scarlet, blot

on the Congregational scutcheon. Mr. Campbell's
own explanation only made matters worse. The most
latitudinarian of his fellow-Nonconformists, who were
ready to agree with him more or less on points of
faith, were alarmed at his teaching upon morals. Sin,
he seemed to say, was the legacy of the ape and tiger
to humanity, and there was the logical inference that
we could not help it, and that as it would disappear
in man's upward and onward march, guaranteed by
the evolutionary hypothesis, we need not distress ourselves unduly about it. In the pulpit he would call
sinners to mend their ways, but his written words
might be interpreted as raising dark questions as to
how they could, or why they should.

The lay press had not in those days found religion,
but for months on end it gave prominence to Mr.
Campbell. And during those months Mr. Campbell,
combative as any other man from Ulster, laid about
him with gusto. When the storm subsided, he subsided with it. Calmer thought told him that the New
Theology was in various ways unsatisfactory. He
decided that he had turned the doctrine of immanence
into something very like pantheism, and concluded
that the fault was due to his own unconscious exaggeration of sacramental ideas. Once more, his thoughts
may have turned towards seeking safety in Rome.
Then the war came as a confusing issue. The attitude
of the Vatican disappointed patriotic Britons, though
surely it compared not unfavourably with that of the
I.L.P. However, Mr. Campbell, at the cross-roads
again, turned his eyes once more towards the Anglican
Church—" the historic Church of my own dear land "
as he wrote a little later. In March 1915 he withdrew
his volume of heretical theology from circulation, in
October preached for the last time at the City Temple,
and, in the following year, was ordained deacon and

priest by his old antagonist, the then Bishop of Birmingham, Dr. Gore.

Of the Roman Catholic divines of the Edwardian period Mgr. Benson was the most influential, and Fr. Bernard Vaughan the greatest pet of the newspapers. From the point of view of the Church he joined in early manhood, Hugh Benson started life with an exceptional advantage. The son of an Archbishop of Canterbury, he was a convert at whom all the world must stare, and whom not a few would surely follow. A story of him as a boy goes some way towards explaining the man he was to be. On a certain occasion no fewer than a dozen bishops were assembled, and Hugh, looking down upon their heads from a cedar in which he was secreted, invented a nickname for each. Which, being interpreted, means that he had in him by nature quite as much of mischievous humour as of reverence. In fact, in his gradual passage to Rome, as well as in his novels, a spirit of mischief was often at his elbow. Mere desire to flutter the timorously conventional is discernible in his early hankerings as an Anglican curate to use goodness knows what in the way of vestments and ritual. That he worked at fiction mainly as at a sport is beyond question. The priest writing novels with a religious theme must, as he well knew, be suspected by the crowd of propagandist intentions. Very well : he would give the public exactly what it did not expect.

Both as man and priest he was of an unusual gentleness. To that the many converts whom he made all bear witness. His religion seemed to be all sweetness and light. What Protestants would have called his Mariolatry was, of course, a sign of his special attachment to the side of Catholicism which is tenderness, which is

feminine rather than masculine. But in his novels none
of this is apparent. As a novelist he was harsh and
grim, wearing the weed of Dominic rather than that of
St. Francis. In one of his most widely read books, *The
Dawn of All*, picturing a Roman supremacy upheld by
the civil sword, ground sharp and wielded hard, he
contrived to alarm co-religionists, who saw that it
would be interpreted as a plea for the revival of Smithfield fires. Another novel, *Loneliness*, appeared to
have been written in yet fiercer mood. There is a
moment in it when, as his biographer, Fr. Martindale,
has said, " God begins to strike." First, the author
took pains to win sympathy for a pair of lovers, and
then he displayed his poor puppets being pounded to
the dust by divine hammer blows. In *Imitation* he was
less inhuman, but still terribly austere. All things
considered, one can scarcely imagine his novels directly
winning converts, whilst one may fairly surmise that
not a few who took them too seriously were scared
away from a Church which seemed to contain such
dark and uncomfortable corners.

Hostile critics called him brutal and heartless, and he
had a Puck-like joy in arousing their resentment. He
realised that in Protestant countries there is a common
idea of Catholicism as an asylum for the weak-kneed,
and it pleased his sense of humour to show the other
side of the picture. But now and then he had to throw
off his mask of seriousness. When everything else
in his tales is forgotten, there will probably linger
a memory of the pious old lady in one of them
who kept a parrot and chastised it for its profanity
with a rolled-up religious newspaper. A member
of his family has written that in playing games,
Hugh Benson was always a derisive and provocative
adversary. His way was to win by annoying the
other fellow into anger. When he took pen in hand,

he pursued the same tactics, but, probably, with less success.

None the less, Mgr. Benson did reach a vast audience with his stories, and, by virtue of their circulation and his own name, did much to keep Roman Catholicism in the public eye in England. Essentially he was a mystic, but that in him which was most real was least known. From his boyhood he had been solitary. Religion in his father's household, according to his elder brother, had been treated rather as an affair of " solemn and dignified occupation than as a matter of feeling and conduct," and in such an atmosphere Hugh could only be a stranger. " He went to his grave without even one really intimate friend," says Fr. Martindale. Before he had thoughts of taking orders, he had a strong distaste for the idea of marriage, and in no communion could he have made a successful parish priest. But the Church he entered found work for him to do, and, doubling every task given him with another self-imposed, he killed himself with work. When Manning died, there was a danger that the Catholic revival in England would be checked for lack of any commanding leader. The vacant place could not, indeed, be filled, but Mgr. Benson, thrusting and laughing in the breach, was a very gallant figure, and the admiration he won meant a steady flow of recruits for the white and yellow Papal flag.

That anybody who has come to maturity since the Edwardian period will grasp the importance of Fr. Bernard Vaughan is unlikely. Decidedly, he was among the ephemeral figures of ecclesiastical history, yet there were two things he did accomplish. Gaining notoriety for himself, he made people talk and think of the Church to which he belonged—the Church which

in England is always in danger of being forgotten—
and in this matter he simply supplemented Benson.
But he also compelled the public to a fresh estimate of
the Jesuit order. Fr. Vaughan, in Mr. Shane Leslie's
words, "decrying the sins of society to audiences
which were neither sinners nor society," may be passed
in retrospect as an almost comic character. The
"sins," when judged by standards of our looser age,
were venial sins, if sins at all. The "society" was,
outwardly at least, very decorous. Of that fringe
of it which was called "the smart set," Lady
Dorothy Nevill wrote truly enough : "These people
do little harm, for their amusements are generally
more silly than vicious." Why Fr. Vaughan should
have so thundered at their doings is difficult to
understand. Was he, one asks, just a simple, saintly
being to whom a little frivolous naughtiness stunk as
a crime ?

I might suggest a more plausible explanation.
Vaughan had made a careful study of the times in which
he lived, and he knew that they were vulgar. Another
ecclesiastic might have turned away in disgust, but he
was not fastidious. Vulgarity is, after all, not wicked-
ness. It is allowable as a weapon as any other. Vaughan
knew the churches were being deserted. He knew
that Anglican and Nonconformist congregations were
dwindling. He realised that the same peril beset his
own Church, and in a peculiar degree, since for nearly
three and a half centuries it had been treated in England
either as a dangerous growth or else as a negligible
body. In consequence, he resolved to advertise it.
It should provide copy for the press.

And advertise he did most effectively. For every
one who followed Mr. Campbell on the New Theology,
five followed Fr. Vaughan on the Sins of Society.
Among those who read of him, some went to hear him.

H

At least a few who heard him stayed. At all events, whilst he volleyed and thundered at what was, after all, no more than a stage army, there was no forgetting Rome in England.

Jesuitry ? But nobody had ever imagined a Jesuit like Fr. Vaughan. Jesuits were scholars who went pad-footed about the world, and conspired in secret places. Fr. Vaughan was, or appeared to be, a plain, bluff man on the stump, rather forgetful that a pulpit was not a synonym for a tub. If he were a Jesuit in the accepted Protestant meaning of the word, he was the profoundest Jesuit that ever lived. Anyhow, he was a magnificent advertising manager ; and his policy was to make a noise, just as surely as Dr. Davidson's policy was to keep very quiet.

PRESS MAGNATES

OF the two newspaper magnates who bestrode like colossi the first decade of the century, Cyril Arthur Pearson looked, for some part of the period, like outstripping, in all but money and money-power, his model and rival, Alfred Charles Harmsworth.

Pearson, it is true, never gave, as Harmsworth did even to the most careless observer, the impression of genius. Harmsworth's genius was very narrow and specialised, but there it was, without any doubt. Nobody could exchange half-a-dozen words with him, nobody could even cast a second glance at him, without being aware of something unusual. There was a whole world of significant contrast between the mere physique of the two men. Pearson was well-looking enough, though disfigured by the thick glasses which were always a necessity to him ; but men of his type are seen in every company. But Alfred Harmsworth, with his clear-cut features, his large and beautiful eyes, and his naturally dominating manner, was bound to command attention wherever he went. He was the sort of person who may attract one man and repel another, but is felt by all men. He was well aware of his power, and used it consciously ; he was prone to little theatricalities and Alexandrian gestures ; but the power resided not in these, but in something more fundamental. Pearson had none of this gift of personality, any more than he had Harmsworth's uncanny way of arriving at the results of thought without thought itself. But he possessed other qualities which might have more than

compensated for such deficiency so far as concerned
the attainment of real influence in his time and generation. If not himself a very serious person, Pearson
had the knack of getting on terms with the serious,
and winning (at least in a limited way) their confidence.
Harmsworth, in those days, was not only very little
trusted—he was very little known. His wife had gone
into society, and had had success there ; but of the many
distinguished people who dined in Berkeley Square, or
even week-ended at Sutton Place, very few had established much more than a nodding acquaintance with
the future baronet, baron and viscount. He took
some pains, in fact, to seclude himself. Anonymity
was both his taste and his policy at this time. Always
shy, he had, in the first flush of success, so far com-
pounded with his disposition as to display his name
for strictly business purposes. There were Harmsworth encyclopædias, Harmsworth magazines, Harmsworth classics. But this was a phase that passed.
The great business of the Amalgamated Press, so long
the most important and lucrative of the late Lord
Northcliffe's activities, rapidly became as impersonal
as the Bank of England. While *Pearson's Weekly* and
Pearson's Magazine were destined to keep their founder's
name before a public which had almost forgotten his
personality, there was little to remind the man in the
street of his most successful student and exploiter.
Mr. Balfour gave Mr. Harmsworth first his baronetcy
and next his peerage, and naturally these transactions
raised a ripple of discussion—there was nothing
extraordinary about them, but distinctions were still
conferred with relative parsimony, and the nature of
the consideration occasioned some curiosity. Above
all, the politicians were interested to know whether the
stormy independence of the *Daily Mail* was to disappear,
and whether the erratic free-lance of yesterday was to

be henceforth a well-drilled party servitor. But the
larger public was much less interested than it had been
when Sir Thomas Lipton was given his knighthood.
The Harmsworth coronet had little significance for the
ordinary man ; indeed, it was for a time rather an
extinguisher than a *panache*. But Pearson, remaining
for many years longer a plain " Mr.", did manage to.
make himself a figure. He got the public to talk about
him. He got the politicians to take note of him. He
got Joseph Chamberlain to believe in him. He won
over a most cautious and canny Scot in the person of
Alexander Henderson, later to be known as Lord
Faringdon. Chamberlain gave him political credit.
From Henderson's vast wealth he drew financial
support. Thus it was that he acquired control of the
old *Standard*, with its considerable tradition. He
seemed at one time likely to acquire control of *The
Times*. He was a power in " serious journalism "
during years that saw Harmsworth only as the con-
troller of a volatile popular press ; and for a while it
seemed quite possible that he might win a position
compared with which—cash, of course, apart—that of
Harmsworth would be insignificant.

Pearson was interested in politics, in the sense, at
any rate, of liking to know politicians and to be on
the fringe of intrigue. Harmsworth, who never
developed the political mind, had at that time not even
this kind of fancy for the game. He was interested
in his papers and the power they gave him, but I fancy
the power he most enjoyed was that which he exercised
over the individuals about him. It was more fun
being the divinity of a sort of domestic Olympus than
being a distant object of fears and hopes on the part
of people he never saw. He was vividly interested in
the circulation of his newspapers. He was vividly
interested in their advertisements. But Parliament did

not sell his newspapers ; Parliament did not advertise
in his newspapers. Football, flying, motoring, mur-
ders were all better sellers than debates and " crises."
A cigarette manufacturer or a big draper was vastly
more important from the other point of view than the
stateliest Right Honourable. For the rest he had all
the contempt a man of great but narrow capacity will
feel for what he cannot do or can but imperfectly understand. In some directions Lord Northcliffe's capacity
amounted, as I have said, to nothing short of genius.
He was an inspired showman, who could have given
Barnum points and a beating at Barnum's own game,
and who was engaged in a game which Barnum could
not have begun even to understand. Let me give one
story, which I believe to be true, in illustration of his
sure instinct in everything connected with an appeal
to the mass mind.

One of his concerns had published a cheap book on
the German peril. It was not a success, and apparently
no ingenuity of salesmanship could make it one.
Harmsworth happened to inquire how it was going
and elicited the facts. Then he sent for a secretary
and dictated at lightning speed the heads of an article
to appear in one of his dailies next morning. It was
of something like this tenor : " THE BOOK THAT WILL
NOT SELL. WHY? Here is a book, judged a sure
winner by a firm that prides itself on knowing what the
public wants.—An excellent book, the masterpiece of a
distinguished writer who has made its subject a life-
study.—Vivacious in style, engrossing in matter.—Yet
it will not sell.—Subject of great practical interest to
every Briton, and to every Briton's wife and little ones,
being nothing less than whether his country is to go,
within a year or two, the way of Carthage and Rome.—
Yet it will not sell.—As a matter of strictly human
interest as fascinating as any novel.—Yet it will not

sell.—Everybody that is anybody is reading and talking about it, from Miss Marie Corelli to the Prime Minister.—Yet the general public will have none of it. Why ? Again why ?—Perhaps somebody will offer a suggestion in a matter that baffles experts.—A hundred pounds for the best explanation—enclosing coupon—editor's decision to be final—reaching this office by 1.30 on Monday next."

The next day everybody was asking for the book, and I have no doubt that it went off by the hundred thousand.

That was the sort of genius Harmsworth had in greater measure, probably, than any newspaper man since newspapers were. I have given but a trifling example, but I think a significant one, of his swift perception and his audacious originality, and also of something which his biographers, partial though they are for the most part, have not sufficiently stressed. I mean the peculiar honesty which was one of his characteristics. He hated a falsehood almost as much as he hated an indecency—and that is saying much. An adroit specimen of something else—what shall I call it ? perhaps manipulative virtuosity may meet the case—he might not only tolerate but admire. One could say that he appreciated tricks that were merely adroit and that he detested tricks that were merely dishonest. There was room in his concerns for much doubtful ingenuity. There was none for undoubtful want of integrity. I have remarked somewhere on the paradox that, while the editorial opinions of his newspapers were always in a state of violent fluctuation, their finances had vastly more than the stolidity of Government securities. In this they were an accurate reflection of his own mind and character. He was intellectually flighty. But to such standards as he had he clove.

The qualities I have indicated in this trivial context were, of course, shown equally in great affairs. I should say that he never set himself to reflect methodically on any project or problem ; he just let it simmer in his mind for a time and then guessed. Thus it was natural that he should tend to underrate men compelled, by character or circumstance, to less rapid processes. Like a woman (and he was in many ways very feminine), he despised and was bored by logical exposition. His idea, for example, of the perfect " leader " was a succession of short, snappy sentences, each conveying a dogmatic affirmation. To reason appeared to him to savour of pusillanimity. " I'm not arguing with you : I'm telling you " was his constant attitude. And from his own point of view he was right. For while no man was better at telling, few were worse at arguing. He was probably incapable of producing a statement of any length at once complete and logically water-tight. Therefore he indulged a deep dislike for all sophisters and logicians, and a scorn for those arts which enable public men to make the best of a strong case or conceal the unsoundness of a weak one. Politicians were only one of the many classes he held in sovereign contempt, a contempt, no doubt, tinged with envy. He despised what they did, but he would have rather liked to be able to do it. To the end of his life this mixture of feelings prevailed. Even when, as Lord Northcliffe, the indubitable master of some public men and the possible rival of others, he coveted a statesman's share in the peacemaking, there was a disdain for the mentality mixed with a desire for the authority of the politician.

Pearson had nothing of this. He was a much more typical Englishman. He lacked, by that fact, Harmsworth's gift of seeing the human fool naked behind all his decorations and uniforms and fiddle-faddle. But he had, in other ways, a juster appreciation of the facts of the world it most behoved him to know. In some aspects he may be considered as merely a reduced copy of Harmsworth, and perhaps something of a caricature. On certain sides he was more frivolous than his model. I once heard it acutely said, by the best possible judge of such matters, that the difference between the then *Daily Express* and the then *Daily Mail* —the difference that explained all other differences— might be expressed by saying that if anything in high politics had happened to please the Ottoman nation, the headline in the *Daily Mail* would be " Satisfaction in Constantinople," and the headline in the *Daily Express* would be " Turkish Delight." This jocose disposition may have been inherited from Pearson's father, a Church clergyman with an odd passion in his spare moments for puzzles, rebuses, riddles and such trifles. But Pearson inherited other qualities— including a certain respect for the established things in English life. He had been at Winchester. He possessed a social disposition and some social talent. He had something of the vague kindliness and geniality of the English ; something, too, of their snobbishness. Harmsworth, Irish by extraction, was neither snob nor philanthropist. Pearson took a warm interest, not wholly without ulterior motive, no doubt, but also not insincere, in slum children, long before he became, under the inspiration of his own great affliction, a sort of patron saint of the blind. Harmsworth had small concern with inefficients of any kind ; his protéges were highly sophisticated and pushing people, motorists, aviators and such, who could make a splash for him as well as for themselves. In a word, Pearson was the more human figure, the more respectful of mediocrities, the more tolerant of fools, the more capable of ordinary loyalties and enthusiasms. He got on better with people generally, and with politicians in particular. They could understand him, and he them. He " knew

his place " also, as the phrase goes. He was content
to be one of a team, and did not aspire to direct his
leaders. When he accepted a point of view he could
stick to it ; he had no inconvenient spasms of originality. When he swore loyalty to a chief he could feel
something of the thrill of self-dedication—the Buddhis-
tic rapture of absorption into the infinite. He was not
afraid of a little unpopularity. Shouting vehemently
for his own side, he was not terror-stricken by the
clamour of the opposite party, or of the populace.
Harmsworth, on the other hand, showed immense
courage in public affairs of, so to speak, a semi-private
character. He could be bold enough when he was
fighting some person or coterie for whom or for which
he shrewdly guessed there was no great or inalienable
public support, when his personal interest was enlisted,
and when he was supported by evidence which fully
convinced him he could face a temporary outcry. But
he had a wholesome dread of being permanently out of
sympathy with great masses of public opinion on the
many large questions regarding which his own mind
was uncertain. Thus he chopped and changed, veered
and wobbled over the Chamberlain policy. It rather
appealed to him as new and spirited, but on the other
hand it rather deterred him as probably unpopular.
He could not bear to be quite out of the fashion, and
was afraid to be quite in it. He was scornful of the
academic Free Traders, if only because they were
academic, and most unjustly contemptuous of Campbell-
Bannerman, because Liberalism seemed for the moment
to be *vieux-jeu*. But some instinct told him that what
he called " stomach taxes " would not go. In all this,
of course, he was in spiritual harmony with perhaps
a majority of the nation, which wanted neither Free
Trade nor Protection, but all the advantages of Free
Trade combined with all the advantages of Protection

—if haply that could be managed. Pearson, once a Chamberlainite, simply wanted victory for Chamberlain, and recked nothing he should do to advance it.

Pearson failed, but the time was when victory seemed well within his grasp. With the *Standard*, the *Daily Express*, and a retinue of provincial papers, he had at least the potentiality of great influence on the one hand over the classes who compose, and on the other over the masses who make Governments. Yet nothing came of it all, and when he relinquished management of his papers they were, relatively and perhaps absolutely, weaker than when he assumed it.

His failure may be variously explained. He let personal likings influence his judgment, but, in truth, without such weakness his judgment would have been faulty. Perhaps he made fewer mistakes on the great scale than Harmsworth — who made some quite enormous mistakes, the original penny *Daily Mirror* for women being one of them—but he went on making mistakes all the time. He was, in one respect, more like Napoleon than the man he copied ; that is to say, he never consolidated his victories, making each enterprise pay the cost of its successor, but passed from one incomplete achievement to another, ever putting more and more to the hazard. It was exactly the opposite with his rival. *Answers* and its like were a gold-mine before any attempt was made to invade the field—even then expensive and chancy—of daily journalism. The *Evening News*, again, was an extremely solid success before the *Daily Mail* was launched. The strength of the Harmsworth press was all in the foundations ; Pearson reared a showy superstructure on an inadequate and shifting bottom.

Pearson, I fancy, was undone largely by his amiable qualities. He had a certain expansiveness of disposition which resembled, and may have been, generosity.

He liked people whom he liked to like him.   It may
have given him no particular pain to do an unjust
thing, but I think he always squirmed a little in doing
an unkind thing.   Macaulay somewhere lays to the
charge of Charles II that he was that worst of all
monarchs—the monarch who regards the feelings of
the few individuals he meets, and recks nothing
concerning the millions he will never see, who, to please
a favourite courtier or mistress, will plunge a distant
province into distress.   There was just a touch of this
kind of affability in Pearson ; he did not always detect
talent where it existed, unless he happened to relish the
other qualities of the possessor, and his partiality often
saw talent where it was invisible to a neutral eyesight.
Harmsworth was not so handicapped. He had his pets,
like Elizabeth, but, unlike the Stuarts, he never permitted them to be his counsellors.   If he wanted
flattery, he went to one set ; if advice, to another. And
he recognised in the most practical way the relative
value of these commodities ; on the whole the courtiers
did much less well than the statesmen.   A sort of
mystical worship of " efficiency " was his master
passion.   I should say that there were very few men
he really cared for as human beings, and the kind of
man who might really have cared for him, who could
have loved the much that was genuinely lovable, as
well as delight in the vitality and charm which were
so richly his in his splendid youth, was not the kind
of man who would readily serve him.   It was, in truth,
not easy to remain friends with him on perfectly equal
terms.   Few men, I think, emphasised less the millionaire grandee side ; his attitude towards his staff,
imperious though it was, was rather that of one who,
to the full, claimed superiority of talent and experience
in his craft, but cared for no other precedence. But
he was intolerant of the least opposition, and sooner or

later people who had no axe to grind found his absolu-
tism a bar to the closer kind of communion. True
friendship is a republic which cannot recognise even
a citizen king, and he always wanted to be Commander
of the Faithful. His companions were, therefore, to a
large extent his dependents, and his dependents were
mostly of one kind. Merciless to many kinds of inferiority, he was not more friendly to most kinds of
superiority. He could not but despise the man who
would never stand up to him, but he was so constituted
as to feel a growing irritation against the man who did
stand up to him on any considerable scale or for any
considerable time. Thus, amid all the great crowd of
people who hitched their small waggons to his enormous
star, there were not many for whom he retained, or in
whom he inspired, the sort of affection that wipes out
the distinction between master and man.

Pearson, on the contrary, had some colleagues who
almost loved him, and many who found him pleasant
and amusing. But this talent for friendship, while it
might have been made a business asset, was in fact
rather a handicap. Choosing his lieutenants partly
because they were humanly interesting, he was at a
disadvantage as against Northcliffe with his genius
for discovering the right kind of Robot for his every
purpose. No doubt Lord Northcliffe, as one who had
been a journalist, had some fellow-feeling for his
journalistic aides-de-camp. He paid most of them
pretty well, and some of them handsomely. He could
talk to them in their own language and exchange
professional pleasantries with them. To some, in his
own way, he was the friend as well as the employer.
But it was not on them that he loved to lavish. Those
who grew grey in his editorial service were rarely in a
position to retire on stately terms. The road to fortune
on the great scale at Carmelite House was not editing

or writing, and so well was this understood that some
clever and adaptable men deliberately left the journalistic for the business side of the newspapers. There
Jupiter descended in immense showers of gold. Almost
splendid fortunes rewarded the gifted buyer of paper,
the born getter of advertisements, the adroit deviser of
ways and means, the successful manager of men. It
may have been a little jealousy that made Northcliffe,
speaking generally, a rather grudging patron of the
more creative elements of his staffs. He could write
in a sharp emphatic style, saying rather obvious things
in a rather obvious way. But he never, truth to tell,
got far beyond the " business " stage of intellectual
development, and while he liked the university note in
his personnel, he sincerely hated all that could emanate
from the old seats of learning beyond social aplomb
and ease of deportment. He seemed always to resent
any kind of knowledge which he had not found it easy
or had not thought it worth while to attain. With
his business men, of course, he could sniff a double
incense. They respected his practical *flair*, so often
proved right in face of their expert judgment, and they
naturally exaggerated his powers as a journalist—his
genius as a director of journalists they could not
exaggerate. On the other hand, not being versed in
the minutiæ of business, he naturally thought more of
their virtuosities of accountancy and organisation than
a man bred in these mysteries might have done. The
work of a writer or an editor, which to be good must
be readily understandable to anybody, must be very
understandable indeed to a tolerably well-informed
employer. On this side Harmsworth was a merciless
critic, though generally a discerning one. But he took
also, I think, an impish delight in playing on the
weaknesses of the journalist. Fleet Street is inhabited
by a race of men who, with many admirable qualities,

are inclined to be a little vain and not a little quarrel-
some. It was great fun to set them at loggerheads.
That Harmsworth did consistently, partly, no doubt,
on the principle of " *Divide et impera*," but largely also,
I think, because he enjoyed it. To create uneasiness
in the apparently established, to promote ambition in
the unestablished—this, of course, is common form in
all kinds of big-business organisations. It makes for
" efficiency " to remind every commanding officer that
there is growing talent and every subaltern that his
commanding officer is mortal. " Remember, young
man, the future is what you like to make it. Your
chances are literally illimitable. You may think your
road to success is barred by the commanding figure of
Mr. Blank. That is the case at present, I agree.
Mr. Blank is an exceedingly distinguished and able man.
But he is no longer a young man. A false step before
a motor-omnibus, a trifling obstruction in some little
tube in Mr. Blank's none too fit body—and a new era
opens before you. And, in fact, Mr. Blank, to be
quite candid, is even now showing a little the wane of
energy and initiative. My advice to you is to make
yourself quite ready for greatness, should greatness
come your way." Lord Northcliffe was an adept in
this art of leading people to expect more than he
actually promised. He contrived to make the most of
his editorial people jealous of each other, as well as a trifle
uneasy about themselves. Many of them lived very
long, and even outlived him, but none without being,
at certain times or to a certain extent, threatened.
There were often three or four kings at a time in the
Carmelite Brentford. The dictionary would probably
define an editor, on the archidiaconal precedent, as a
person performing editorial functions. But there were
sometimes men, defined as editors, whose editorial
functions were for the moment in abeyance, and there

were men, not defined as editors, who did perform
editorial functions.   Byzantium was a child to Tallis
Street.   The results were sometimes amusing, and—
in a small way—wasteful.

Let us take an example.   It is quite imaginary, but
within the limits of formal truth.   A country correspondent, let us say, sends a brief telegram to the
effect that a child was found to suffer from asthma
whenever brought within smelling distance of asparagus,
but that the ailment was at once exorcised by making it
stroke a cat.   The important person known as the
chief sub-editor, who is judge at first instance of news
values, naturally welcomes this as an item to gladden
the public, but does not regard it as of any great importance.   So next morning it appears as five lines
under the heading: "News in brief," "Much in Little,"
or whatever it may be.   But there is another official,
the news editor, whose function is constructive.   Searching the papers next morning for something to develop,
he seizes on this gem.   He instructs certain reporters
to consult " distinguished Harley Street physicians,"
wires to the country and to Paris and Berlin, and
perhaps cables to New York.   In the evening the
results of these activities reach the sub-editor.   He,
poor man, has on his mind a revolution in Portugal, a
crisis at Westminster, a battle in Ruritania, and an
earthquake in the West Indies, to say nothing of a
" society romance " and a thrilling murder or two.
Therefore he conceives that he cannot spare much
space for this matter.   But trouble has been taken, and
he hesitates to throw the thing away forthwith.   So he
hands it to a subordinate to cut down to thirty or forty
lines.   But subordinates do not always see the point,
and when the thirty or forty lines reach the chief
sub-editor he finds they are dull beyond all endurance.
One point that seems to stick out he marks with a

blue pencil and tosses the manuscript to the gentleman who exercises his ingenuity on " items." So yesterday's item becomes, from a new angle, an item again. The item gets into print and finds its way in proof to one of the persons discharging editorial functions. Discerning in it beautiful possibilities, he telephones to the chief sub-editor to " work it up," getting such fortifying material as may be gathered at short notice. With outward deference, but possibly with inward rage, the chief sub-editor agrees that something should be done, and grovels in his waste-paper basket for the mangled remains of what he has received from the news editor. Taking one of his brightest men off something else, he directs him to deal enthusiastically with the cat-and-asparagus business. This is done with the cool dexterity of an artist, with the result that a most engrossing column reaches the proof stage. In this form it dawns on the consciousness of Editor Number Two, who cuts it down. But Editor Number Three fancies it so much that the " cut " is restored. Then, when the page is hard on going to press, comes Editor Number Four, clothed in white waistcoat, mystic, wonderful, fresh from the table of a Cabinet minister. He, though possibly on the verge of being told that he must really take a three-months' holiday, can still assert himself on an appropriate occasion. He finds this occasion appropriate, condemns the whole thing as " perfect rot," and decrees its complete disappearance.

There was more of this sort of thing on Harmsworth's papers than on Pearson's, probably because money was more plentiful. On the other hand Pearson's men were much more prone to make the public pay for mistakes or misfortunes. If " Our Special Correspondent,"

I

by bad luck, happened to be a day—a day in this connection may be only a question of minutes—behind the news agency, his despatch might still be printed, though readers yawned. Harmsworth's men would have thrown the whole thing into the waste-paper basket, had it cost five times as much. This distinction held good in great as in little things. Pearson hesitated to acknowledge failure, still less to cut his losses ; it was probably without the smallest pang, either to his pride or his sense of money, that Harmsworth liquidated his unfortunate experiment of the woman's *Daily Mirror*. It was designed as a penny paper for moneyed women, and the moneyed women would not pay the penny for it. Its first number sold probably a million, but in three months or less the circulation had dropped to something, I believe, less than thirty thousand. Clearly this cock—or, more strictly, this hen—would not fight. Every device had been tried ; every conceivable talent had been enlisted ; at one moment the sub-editors' table, with the late Kennedy Jones at its head, must have represented a combined salary list of sixty thousand or so a year. All to no purpose. The mistake was one of strategy, and no tactical brilliance could remedy it. Once that was clear to Harmsworth, he acted with the swift and audacious decision of genius. At a time when the machinery of newspaper illustration was in the most rudimentary state, he decreed a half-penny picture paper. Nobody had yet succeeded in printing half-tone photographic plates on coarse paper by a rapid rotary machine, and it would not have done to plunge at once into an enterprise so uncertain and of such delicacy. The model at first was, therefore, the strange kind of weekly illustrated paper at that time popular among the masses—the paper in which highly imaginative artists produced exciting pictures of how

a man might look being sentenced to death, or how
a battleship would appear turning turtle. Things were
not depicted as they were, but as they should be if
destiny had a proper sense of drama. The strange race
of men who did this kind of work has, I imagine,
almost completely disappeared, conquered by the
camera. But they must have had a glorious time during
the first few months of the picture *Daily Mirror*, before
the experiments in printing photographs had revealed
the practicability of producing " half-tones " on a fast-
running machine. They invaded the scene like the
hosts of Alaric. The distinguished female staff disappeared in the twinkling of an eye. Gone was the
majestic lady whose word was final on all that related
to *chic*, gone was the knowing social expert who
occasionally complained of " the fatigues of a journey
to Bayswater," gone were the various attractive young
women who were presumed to know exactly what
duchesses want for their light reading. Nobody now
cared a dump for duchesses. With the ladies went
their belongings. On the Saturday morning the old
office in Whitefriars Street was still a colourable
imitation of a Mayfair flat, with its' Queen Anne
chairs, its gate-leg tables, its inconvenient but picturesque bureaux, its convex mirrors and silk curtains.
When Monday dawned Sheraton and Chippendale had
been replaced by bentwood and deal ; and where
beauty had so lately reigned, Bohemianism smoked and
joked and drank much beer.

Now such a complete acknowledgment of a mistake
and such a drastic rectification were not Pearson's way.
Palace revolutions might not be unknown in his offices,
but they had a way of ending in weak compromises.
He could not be coldly logical. Personal feeling stood
in the way. He might himself like some feature which
demonstrably deterred readers. People outside could

get at him and infect him with their fads. Or he might like some man who was obviously not fitted for any work available for him. Harmsworth, I have noted, had a deep-seated hatred for irrelevant cleverness. Pearson did appreciate cleverness, and sometimes the more when it was of no great use to him. He might be sometimes irritably conscious, in his efforts to modernise the *Standard*, of the massive conservatism of a man like the late S. H. Jeyes, a very Ajax defying the "brightening," who had been on the old *Standard* time out of mind, and never concealed the fact that he preferred it to Pearson's *Standard*. But Pearson liked Jeyes and admired his talents. It might not be very important that Jeyes could, if necessary, have written a leader in Latin with very little more trouble than in English. But Pearson was rather proud to have such learning under his patronage. He could delight in the wit and wisdom of Sidney Low, who would probably have irritated Harmsworth. But this amiability and comparative catholicity were, on the whole, a handicap. While he had a far more consistent political objective, Pearson never knew, as Harmsworth did, exactly what he wanted to make of his papers from a more general standpoint. He neither knew where exactly he wanted to go or where exactly he was going. He would listen to one set of arguments from the conservatives, and find much in them. Then he heard another set of arguments from the iconoclasts, and was perhaps still more impressed. But, liking equally both the stolid people and the brisk people, he could never quite make up his mind with which side to declare himself finally. Generally he compromised so as to make the worst of both worlds. It was a pleasant part of his character that he was not in the least jealous of his writers, and was usually most generously appreciative of any kind of brilliance, and, truth to tell, of much that was not brilliant at all. But his zest for cleverness sometimes led him to excessive indulgence of the kind of cleverness that is too clever by half. Harmsworth, with his natural hatred of intellectual subtlety, loathing the smallest suspicion of paradox, regarding with horror a joke that might by any possibility be taken in earnest, distrusting every idea that might estrange a suburban clerk, either subdued clever men to his purpose or excluded them altogether. All of which was a very good thing for himself and for the clever men who were excluded. With the doubtful exception of the late G. W. Steevens, none but second-rate reliable persons were entrusted with the things that really mattered. While the *Daily News* was weekly printing articles by Chesterton, Belloc and Gardiner in their young prime, the *Daily Mail* was well content with pedestrian ideas and newsy compilations. It was not accident, or want of discernment, but policy. Harmsworth, so far as concerned matters of general appeal, knew what he wanted, and got it. And he was right in judging that it was what the public, or at least a great public, wanted also.

Again Pearson, while enjoying power and newspaper distinction, enjoyed much besides, and dissipated his energies. He was fond of exercise. He enjoyed society. He liked entertaining. He relished " good " people, good wines, pretty good conversation. Harmsworth, I think, enjoyed very little but himself. He had a certain interest in what are called the pleasures of the table, and it was amusing to watch his progress from Sweeting's in Fleet Street to commanding heights of connoisseurship further west. He had, moreover, a certain disinterested reverence for expensive food. He loved to see news items about delicacies, and I think it gave him pain if one of his staff, honoured by an invitation, declined a plover's egg or a spoonful of superb caviare. His easy chairs were the easiest ever made, perhaps a thought too easy to be perfectly comfortable, and there was a note of his own rather feline nature in the general softness of his lodgment. But everything looked as if some man of taste had been paid to get together the very best that money could buy. Even at Sutton Place, delightful as it was, something lacked that can be found in any small manor-house—the sense of an owner to whom all of it means something. For sport, in the ordinary sense, he cared nothing, though he made attempts now and then to persuade himself that he did. An early enthusiasm for cycling had left him an interest in everything mechanical that ran on wheels or flew on wings. He was among the earliest motorists. He was the most generous and discriminating of the patrons of infant aviation. But he could not even pretend to play at being the country gentleman, and I do not think he liked squires. He accumulated a considerable but curiously assorted library, and assumed rather the pose of being a reading man ; certainly such pretension has been put forward on his behalf. But the one author whom he seems really to have known was Dickens, whom he admired intensely for two easily surmised reasons : Dickens had, in a different way, his own grasp of the average mind, and had also much of his own sturdy contempt for official inefficiencies and official arrogances. Harmsworth's dislike and distrust of the official were, like Dickens's, useful to the public, and, with all his mistakes, he merits recognition as having prolonged a little the general resistance to bureaucratic encroachment. But to return to the point, he can never, whatever his inclination, have found much time for other than newspaper reading, and he was too skilful a skimmer to have any great interest in the kind of books which must be genuinely read. Society in the ordinary sense, as we have seen, bored him, and society in his own peculiar sense was merely an extension of business. Thus he had little to distract him from the main enterprise of his life. Pearson had a great deal.

But quite apart from his personality, Harmsworth possessed an enormous advantage in that he could command the help of two remarkable men—his brother Harold and the late Kennedy Jones. Jones—to deal first with the less-indispensable influence—was much of a failure as a working journalist. So far as he made any impression in that capacity, it was that of a man of very moderate ambitions which still more moderate talents failed to realise. There was a time when he reached the very shabbiest kind of Bohemianism. He was in the position to which men descend not through unprofitable devotion to some artistic ideal, but through mere failure in bread-and-butter efficiency. He himself has left on record how he once went into a sausage-shop in Fleet Street and ordered a meal without having the money to pay for it. Fleet Street is, no doubt, a stony-hearted stepmother, but seldom so harsh in her treatment of ordinary competence. An indifferent workman, however, may make an excellent director of work, and incapacity to do small things is quite compatible with ability to conceive large things. Jones, having achieved a directorial position on the *Evening News* as a reward of his services in acquiring that paper, quickly justified the kindness of destiny. His manners were rough, his methods harsh. He believed in terrorism, and had large talents for terrorising. But he had also clear-cut and (so far as they went and from a certain point of view) sound ideas of what to give the public, and a sense of his mission which, in so very materialistic a person, was just a little comic—and pathetic. He really believed, or at any rate he used to say so in his moments of expansion, that he had

been put in the world to give the people cheap newspapers. By what high and discerning synod he never
suggested. In many ways he was not a bad fellow.
He had little " side." He never forgot that he had
been poor. He had uncommonly little respect for
pretenders. People might have cultivation, grace of
manner, distinction of birth, a " pull " in society, and
Jones was ready to pay well for all these perfections
if they contributed to journalistic efficiency ; otherwise
he had no " use " for them. Despite his failure on its
creative side, he knew all the tricks of his trade. His
mind was easily accessible to new ideas, but he was not
fascinated by mere novelty, and on the whole he was,
in matters of journalistic policy, of the Left Centre,
thus being a valuable corrective to the Harmsworth
audacity. He could value good work, and even
(within limits) good writing, and could make allowances
for a mistake, though never for a slackness. His
language was free. His occasional rages were terrific.
But he was on the whole a just master, and a very
faithful servant to the great man he introduced to daily
journalism.

Even Jones, however, was a less important element
in the success of the Harmsworth Press than Harold
Harmsworth, now Lord Rothermere. I doubt whether
Lord Rothermere himself could have erected this vast
organisation and brought it to its present position. His
difficulty would have been to interest himself sufficiently
in what was at first the vital matter, the journalistic
side of the problem. On that side he has neither the
swift intuition nor the impetuous decision of his
brother, whose career was built up on instantaneous
perception and swift invention—second sight and first
action. The strange certainty with which Alfred
Harmsworth, whose actual contact with the " man in
the street " cannot have been large, could penetrate

the reserve of the very ordinary mind and express to himself in clear terms what was mistily there, the rapidity with which he could devise means of establishing connection between that very ordinary mind and his own very extraordinary one—these were the late Lord Northcliffe's peculiar gifts. One does not feel that Lord Rothermere shares them. He may arrive at an opinion, sound or unsound, rapidly or slowly ; but it is reason, and not the guess of genius, that brings him there. But it is certain that, if he could not have done the thing alone, the thing could not have been done in the same way without him. His qualities were exactly those that Alfred lacked, and found most useful. He was at once the brake and the fly-wheel of the vast machine. He was a security against over-driving and a guarantee of continuous energy. Certainly not a less generous man than his brother, he looked more closely at money in business. Both were men of the most complete integrity in affairs ; but one would say that it is chiefly Lord Rothermere's work that has made the credit of the *Daily Mail*, through shine and shower, vastly better than that of the British Government. Pearson, on the other hand, had no business genius himself, and had no such business genius to his hand.

On a smaller scale the late Sir Edward Hulton was a combination of the two Harmsworth brothers. He was an excellent business man, and he had a distinct journalistic *flair*. His mind was masculine, and in some ways nearer akin than Northcliffe's to the average Englishman's. I might put it not unjustly that, while Northcliffe knew better than Hulton what people were saying in the tea-shops, Hulton knew better than Northcliffe what they were saying in the bar-parlours.

What handicapped Hulton was a provincial " nearness "
and caution that prevented him going " full out " either
in business or in national policy. He did greater
things with smaller expenditure than any of his journalistic contemporaries. But he lacked that little more
of audacity that might have made him as worthy of
detailed consideration here as either of his rivals. As
things were, he lies rather outside the period; the
great development of the Hulton Press took place in
the second decade of the century. The first ten years
saw only the small beginnings of its bid for a national
as distinct from a provincial standing.

TREE AND ALEXANDER

At the beginning of the twentieth century Irving was still alive and still acting, and certain traditions associated with his reign at the Lyceum were to dominate the English theatre for many years to come.

But, when all is said, he was a survivor from another epoch. The conditions in which he had always lived were passing. Irving belonged to the old company of players who were an empire within an empire, if not a world to themselves. On the boards it had been their affair to entertain the public which paid so many shillings or pence for seats in stalls or gallery, but when the curtain was lowered after the last act relations between themselves and the rest of mankind were severed. They went their ways into regions from which the general public, high or low, was normally excluded. They themselves appeared among ordinary mortals on set occasions only. The records of solemn meetings between Irving and Gladstone suggest encounters between potentates from China and Peru whose interest in one another was mainly philosophic curiosity.

Long before, the Puritans had set a ban upon the stage, and under it the players had achieved liberty and fraternity. To the very last Irving stood for the independence of Bohemia. Every out-of-elbows mummer resting in the byways of the Strand was nearer to him than was any distinguished acquaintance outside the Profession. In middle life and afterwards he would say, with evident complacency, that the need had passed to apologise for the actor's calling, and he was glad of his knighthood as an honour to the theatre, but he believed always in the advantages of splendid isolation.

The actors of the generation that followed him had no such idea.   In Lady Tree's biographical sketch of her husband there is no more significant passage than the one in which she writes : " We knew everybody and went everywhere."   Tree's devotion to the theatre was doubtless deep, and to his own theatre almost passionate, but there was nothing in it of exclusive insularity.   He was an actor, just as another is a barrister or a physician, but he was also a man of the world, and, if more precision be needed, of that section of the world which the French call fine.   He was friendly with two Prime Ministers, but such friendships are, of course, largely matters of chance.   What was really notable was that he could be at home and happy in every sort of smart society that was neither dull nor stupid.   It may be that he had an actor's face and that there was a flamboyance about him which betrayed the habit of donning strange costumes nightly and of courting attention with a speech or posture.   Wherever he went, perhaps, he took a suggestion of the stage with him.   But into the theatre he took much more that had hitherto been foreign to it ; the atmosphere of a society that was quite polite, cultured at the periphery, and wealthy to the core.   And Tree, when Irving died, was indubitably head of his profession in England.

Tree, wrote one of his critics, was " a glorified amateur."   Used of any of his great predecessors the words would have had an insulting meaning, but applied to him they scarcely carried the touch of censure. They were a plain statement of fact, and it would not have been very hard to persuade him that they contained a compliment.   The truth was he had never served

any very rigorous apprenticeship. Irving, before
London knew of him, had spent ten years in the
wilderness with stock companies and had appeared in
nearly six hundred characters. If he had been taught
little, he had learnt a good deal. Forbes-Robertson
had been trained by Samuel Phelps in the classic school.
Coquelin and all the stars of the French theatre had
been drilled at the Conservatoire, and if most of their
performance was the result of native talent there was
behind it a hard background of discipline. Tree, on
the contrary, as a young man in easy circumstances,
lightly attached to his father's office in the City, had
begun by amusing himself with amateur theatricals, and
his earliest professional engagements had often been
in more or less important London productions. In
half a dozen years he sauntered into the part of the
Rev. Robert Spalding in *The Private Secretary*, and
invented it anew as he rehearsed. From one point of
view that juvenile success was fatal.

Thenceforward, Tree " created " all his own parts.
Sometimes the results were admirable and surprising ;
sometimes only surprising. His Shylock and his
Svengali were not the personages of the comedy or the
novel, but it was arguable that they were better.
Again, when he appeared in *The Enemy of the People* he
displayed a character not to be discovered by close
reading of Ibsen's text, but who will say that he was
wrong in his attempt at " livening up " the Norwegian
drama ? On the other hand, his inability to interpret
literally, to act to order, after the manner of the technically proficient player, put an unusual number of parts
beyond his scope, and compelled him to hide deficiencies
in his rendering whenever anything outside the gamut
of his own feelings was required of him. Irving may
have smothered Shakespeare with his *mise en scène*, but
himself he never smothered. Men and women went

to the Lyceum, if not to see a play, primarily at least to
see an actor. At His Majesty's it was not play or
actor that counted most, but the spectacle. Tree's
Antony and Cleopatra, with all its costly mounting, not
to mention its vanishing Sphinx (from the old Egyptian
Hall) and its music (from a Port Said *palais de danse*),
would have gained if the whole company had employed
dumb-show exclusively.

Because Tree could not depend upon himself, he
put his trust in stage properties. His faith was, of
course, by no means new or peculiar. Mr. Vincent
Crummles, whose own histrionic abilities probably left
something to be desired, had, it may be remembered,
great belief in the virtue of " a real pump and two
washing tubs." Tree would have made it the River
Nile flowing into the Mediterranean Sea, but the
difference was of quality, not of kind. In brief, it is
hard to resist a fancy that Tree as a manager was
Crummles reincarnate, but translated from provincial
" smalls " to the West End and with the cash at
command to execute ideas hitherto dwarfed by circumstances. And there is no doubt whatever that
the recipe of " a little ballet interlude " appealed to the
one as strongly as the other.

Thus it seems that there was not one Tree, but two
Trees. There was Tree the actor, an accomplished
amateur of remarkable though erratic talent, and there
was Tree the manager, a consummate man of business.
To Tree the actor the theatre never ceased to be the
holy of holies it appears to the stage-stricken youth.
Always he resented suggestions that its sacred art could
be taught. Natural capabilities, he would admit, could
be improved, or, rather, developed by practice, but he
was far fonder of talking about inspiration, improvisa-
tion and the like, all of which your true professional in
every profession mistrusts more than a little. Genius

he used to call " an infinite faculty for not taking pains."
His failures to learn the mere words of a part were
notorious, and significant of this frame of mind.
Playing Wolsey in *Henry VIII* he used to say the scene
of the cardinal's fall might last for twenty-nine minutes,
or for thirty-nine : it all depended on which of two
persons was the prompter. And there was a wider
sense, too, in which he never learned a part. Tree
was the only actor, amateur or professional, who could
not give an imitation of Tree. He had many moods,
swift emotions, and the state of his spirits, not to
mention his temper and digestion, was rarely hidden
from the audience. To the same *rôle* he would give a
variety of renderings to which the only certain limitation
was the number of nights for which the play ran.
Critics who visited a hundredth performance were
baffled to find that though Tree, whom they had
praised or blamed upon the first night, was still there,
his original Caliban or Nero had been transformed.
A piece of business, an emphasis, a gesture that he
interpolated on the spur of the moment would often
draw the loudest applause, but the odds were rather
against its repetition. In twenty-four hours he would,
perhaps, have forgotten all about it, or, it might be,
had omitted it upon principle. That mechanical
efficiency which had hitherto been recognised as the
very basis of the actor's art was disdained by him as
rather vulgar. As his brother Max has written, the
theatre was always romantic and marvellous to him,
and " knowingness " about it jarred his sensibilities.
He hated play-house slang and would not use the
technical terms for the appurtenances of the stage. At
rehearsals there had always to be somebody to translate
his orders into the vulgar tongue. It hurt him to give
the signal for dawn as "Two reds, back stage, O.P .side,"
and nothing could have persuaded him to command the

shades of night with so horrid an invocation as " Biff
your number threes."

To the uninitiated he seemed a dilettante and
nothing more, and he had no objection of that notion
of himself gaining currency. Always excepting his
performances in certain Jewish *rôles* (Shylock, Svengali
or Fagin), he was at his best as the artistic lounger, as
a being who wins the sympathy of the audience by a
pathetic silliness that in real life would soon exhaust
the patience of the saints themselves. And that was
how he liked to appear, not only when playing before the
public, but also, for example, when rehearsing in the
presence of an author. On such an occasion the
hapless playwright would be utterly confounded. The
whole theatre seemed abandoned to a masque of anarchy
in which Tree figured as the lord of misrule, incapable
of understanding a suggestion made in words of more
than one syllable or of getting anything done on his own
account. Generally, the playwright would conclude
that there was no likelihood of his piece ever being
produced, and that if produced it could only be a dismal
fiasco, so he might as well stop bothering about it.
That, of course, was exactly what Tree desired. There
was vast method in his feigned imbecility. When the
harmful if necessary author had decamped in despair,
Tree, with all the strings quite firmly in his hands, and
with a stage-manager who understood all his nods and
becks and cryptic gibberish, had everything his own
way. Almost mournfully he would sometimes boast
among his intimates that he could do all the jobs in
the theatre better than any of the individuals salaried
to perform them, and the boast was not quite idle.
Casual as an actor he might be, but as a manager he
knew better than to leave any detail to chance. Productions at His Majesty's were too costly for that.
And when Tree gave evidence before the Commission

on the censorship, he made his avowal. He asked to be considered as two persons. He asked to speak as an artist who objected to the censor's trammels, and also to say a few words as a man of business who saw the censor as a useful guardian for those who had money in theatrical enterprises.

Those who fancied Tree as a dilettante first and last were mistaken. The plays of which his authors despaired invariably were produced at the appointed date and hour, elaborately magnificent, and, apart from Tree's usual aphasia, complete to the last gaiter-button. Assuredly they had not produced themselves, and he had never given anybody else any chance to produce them.

Beyond question Tree was a great manager and producer. His Falstaff might be far from "bully Hector," his Richard II fall somewhere short of the "figure of God's majesty, His captain, steward, deputy-elect," his Mark Antony be impossible to conceive as "the triple pillar of the world." There was a certain daintiness, not to say femininity, in his style that he could never overcome, and in such parts he either failed deplorably or achieved a success that was tantalisingly partial. But as a man who could present what was crudely but correctly called a "show," he was, in his own way, superb. Errors of taste might be detected in it, and in Tree's later years, when Reinhardt and Granville Barker were giving their "shows," critics began to jeer at His Majesty's as a home of the ostentatious and the commonplace. But in his heyday he gave the public what it demanded, and not meanly in commercial fashion, but generously with both hands. Always he could have contented his audience with something less than he provided, but he loved to furnish on the big plan, to cause sensation, to surpass himself. Tree was always Tree's most

K

dangerous competitor. And whatever was amiss with his theatre was amiss with his age. The mania for pageantry, which it reflected, was everywhere as part of the reaction against the drab asceticism of Victorian times, and lavishness in display of wealth was but one aspect of it. Again, the size of his production was eminently characteristic of a period that reverenced bigness, whether in sticks or empires, as an end desirable in itself. Tree was not of those who make history, but history made him what he was.

The common reproach against him that he did nothing for the drama, only alternating Shakespeare in travestied versions with the trumpery of journeymen playwrights, was not altogether fair. It had been made against Irving also, and with no better foundation. As a matter of fact both actors had striven valiantly in the cause of contemporary poetic drama. Irving put Tennyson on the stage, and Tree did as much for Stephen Phillips. If Tennyson had no dramatic faculty, and the world soon tired of Phillips, the actors were not to blame. As to their treatment of Shakespeare, a hundred faults may be found with it, but the right treatment has yet to be prescribed. The critics wring their hands if Shakespeare is neglected, and wring them a little more at almost every Shakespearean revival. The real truth, that Shakespeare is better read than acted, is rarely admitted. Of course, Tree was wrong in mixing the immortal bard with haberdashery and circus, but he would have been wrong whatever he had done, unless he had had the supreme courage to leave him entirely alone.

Where Tree did, perhaps, neglect his duty was in paying practically no attention to the particular type of play that contemporary authors were aptest to provide. The Edwardians liked pageantry and heroics for occasional diversion, but for their staple fare, in the

theatre or out of it, they required social comedy with a
pretence at least of naturalism. The supply of the
article they demanded was ample in quantity, and in
quality at least promising. Shaw was hard at work,
and so was Barrie. Before the end of the period,
Galsworthy, Hankin and Barker were under discussion,
whilst Arnold Bennett was waiting for encouragement
all the time. But Tree did nothing for any of these
writers. His theatre was not the place for their work.
Plays which did not lend themselves to elaborate and
costly mounting were not wanted at His Majesty's.
By building so sumptuous a temple for the drama,
Tree had put an additional limitation to his activities.
It would have seemed, and indeed been, wasteful to
use his stage for productions in which the most orna-
mental scene was, perhaps, a middle-class drawing-
room.

But at the St. James's Theatre, where George
Alexander ruled, modern comedy could be admitted.
Alexander could have claimed that he was the godfather
of modern comedy, for once upon a time he had produced *The Importance of Being Earnest*. Like Tree,
however, he was a manager first, and an actor in the
hours he could spare from management. It was rarely
that he appeared in any part that would have put a
strain upon him, and, unfortunately, he had a public
that did not expect him to act. In his early days he
had established his position as the matinée idol, and
there was no dethroning him whilst his handsome
presence could be advertised by picture-postcards. As
a rule he was content to give skilful impersonations of
himself in clothes which did credit to his tailor, but
had certainly been made for a gentleman of leisure and
not for a person whose trade it was to exhibit all sorts of
human emotions and activities. Now and then, when
the fortunes of romantic drama led him out of Bond

Street into Ruritania, and gave him a chance to doff his stiff collar and confiding waistcoat for the sake of, say, fighting a duel, it would dawn on people that his theatrical talents might not be negligible, but it was always to Bond Street he returned.   *Otium cum dignitate* was his motto for the stage.

The playwrights who were knocking vainly at the best stage-doors at the start of the century owed a good deal to Wilde, but did not want to own it. They adopted his literary manners, but carefully avoided his social *milieu*. If they were his disciples as regards sparkle in dialogue, they took an independent line by refusing their characters any sartorial smartness. Consequently, they had nothing into which Alexander could step without efforts that would have disturbed the set of his tie and the crease in his trousers. Also, their plays demanded a mental exertion that he could not spare, and involved risks he would not take. It was not only that management was his prime affair. Along with all his other colleagues who were asserting the players' right to walk with head erect outside the confines of Bohemia, he had more parts to play than could be acted on the boards. He rode ; he shot ; he played golf. He was, whatever that may entail, a liveryman of the Turners' Company. For a while he was an industrious member of the London County Council, representing St. Pancras in the Moderate interest. If in all this some of the actor was lost, it was not wonderful.

So, though the St. James's was the home of the modern comedy, the modern comedies in which Alexander played there were, apart from Wilde's, of no great moment. Pinero, Sutro and Bernstein provided him with such successes as *His House in Order*, *John Glayde's Honour* and *The Thief*. They were made, or adapted, perfectly to his measure. They had long runs. The fashion for them having passed, they will not be revived. Indeed, Alexander was even less an adventurer than was Tree. He, too, had in early life been in commerce, and its habits clung. His much admired taste in dress had no doubt been formed in days when he had interests in clothes beyond wearing them, and the rudiments of his celebrated charm of manner, which was to mean so much in the way of box-office receipts from the feminine three-quarters of the playgoing public, had, it may be, been first acquired when he was learning the mystery of the draper's trade. But, anyhow, there was in Alexander none of that vagabond temperament which once meant the undoing of so many actors and the making of so much art. As soon as big money began to come his way he established a fund, never to be touched for theatrical undertakings, on the interest of which he proposed to retire whenever its size and his own humour should make a farewell to the stage desirable. It was a sensible thing to do. It was a thing that is frequently done by other men in other professions. In the theatre, however, it was a new departure. It was a clear announcement that the Profession had ceased to be anything but a profession like any other.

When Bancroft died it was written of him that he had raised the status of the actor. Tree and Alexander shared the honour with him. The work he had begun they completed. If the result was attained at some expense to their art, the blame was theirs also. But, after all, there was no help for it. It is hard for an artist to be a man of business : harder for him to be a man of fashion. There is no possibility of him being the three at once, save in an imperfect way.

ALFRED LYTTELTON

It was on a dull afternoon in the year 1903 that I was given, quite casually, a considerable lesson in the power of personality. The business transacted itself in what is ordinarily a rather sobering place—one of the Chancery Courts—but, as it happened, a case unusually lively for this division of the High Court of Justice was in progress. It contained all the richest and rarest ingredients of a newspaper best-seller—society, sex, money, superstition ; and as counsel learned in the law are by no means immune from the taste for scandal which they reprobate in the mob, the benches reserved for the Bar were crowded.

Attracted, no doubt, by the common desire to see something of the personalities in a case of the moment, a tall, spare barrister, with rather prominent eyebrows, came in and took his seat in the place reserved for King's Counsel. Immediately the whole neighbourhood was one smile of welcome. The testy old silk who was cross-examining would have muttered a curse on anyone else guilty of never so light an interruption ; for this visitor his hard face wrinkled into a gracious little grimace. The red-faced leader on the other side, who had the reputation of " doing " himself as well as he did hostile witnesses badly, for once beamed affability. As the visitor shifted in his seat to look round, the junior Bar grinned and nodded their delight to be noticed by such a hero. Even the judge seemed to convey in some mysterious manner his sense of pleasure in merely having this person in his neighbourhood; it was much as if a sudden glory of sunshine had come into that gloomy place. In fact it was a burst of sunshine, and the name of it was Alfred Lyttelton.

If I had never seen this fortunate person, if he had remained for me but a name from *Wisden's Cricketers' Annual* and the newspaper reports, I should have been absolutely astonished when, some months later, I read that the Hon. Alfred Lyttelton, K.C., had kissed hands as His Majesty's Principal Secretary of State for the Colonies, in the place of the Right Honourable Joseph Chamberlain, resigned. As it was, astonishment was relative, if not quite non-existent. With a personality like Lyttelton's, the difficulty was not in getting to be something; it was merely in deciding what it was worth while to be. He was bound to go through life being offered all sorts of jobs; Recorderships and such things would be proffered to him as one hands a cigarette to a caller; a judgeship or a seat in the Cabinet might be looked on as only just a little more serious— the difference between a "gasper" and a choice Havana. And anything he took he would accept in the spirit in which it was offered, with a charming smile and a general air that it was only what was to be expected. Further, any job he took he was pretty sure to do, if not very well indeed, at least respectably, and in an exceedingly pleasant, airy and gentlemanly way.

For Alfred Lyttelton was above all things gentlemanly. He was the public school boy at his best, with all the public school virtues in exquisite balance, all the public school defects in admirable check—the latter a mere vague background against which the former could "stick fiery off indeed." He was the just Etonian made perfect. Nobody could claim Arthur Balfour, or George Wyndham, or even George Nathaniel Curzon as perfect products of the public school. Eton, of course, worked in them all, and for all their lives ; but there came to be other things as well. They grew. They got new ideas, new standards, other values. With Lyttelton it was otherwise. He remained all his life Eton pure and simple, very pure and quite simple—if we accept a certain quality of canniness and main-chance vision which, after all, does not sin against the highest public school standard.

Youngest of a family of twelve, motherless from infancy, the whole of his early childhood had been a preparation for Eton from the day when an elder brother went to him in the nursery with a big paper-knife and with it showed him how he should hold a cricket bat. He went to Eton with a feeling that his serious career, of which the chief aim was, naturally, to play in the match against Harrow, had at last begun. " Never," his wife has written, " was a boy born more absolutely fitted to enjoy and to profit by a big public school," and Lord Curzon was in later years to declare that " no athlete was ever quite such an athlete, and no boyish hero was ever quite such a hero as was Alfred Lyttelton." When the time came for him to leave, we are told he had a fancy that his career had ended ; everything else would be anti-climax. In some sense he was right. After-life was tame in comparison. He had been, in the language of his fellows, " a swell," and, except for hours he was still to spend on the cricket-field or the tennis-court, he was never going to be so completely and so splendidly " a swell " again. Those who descend in the world, even though the descent be slight, are apt to think always in terms of their greatest days, and there is nothing so hostile to growth as this tendency to look, with a gentle melancholy, backward to what one has been rather than forward to what one may be. After nineteen Lyttelton did not grow, chiefly because it might well appear to him that all growth was a travelling away from the best. Eton, as all mankind has learned with due if vague reverence, has something called " Pop," and it is further understood that the laws of nature require " Pop " to have a leader. Lyttelton was perhaps the best leader of " Pop " that " Pop " ever had, and though I would not care to be called on to define precisely what is the mental and moral equipment of a perfect leader of " Pop," I feel sure that Lyttelton retained it to the end.

Judged by ordinary standards, and without reference to his charming personality, Lyttelton's qualifications for the Colonial Secretaryship might be thought slender. He had done moderately, but no more than moderately, at the Bar, and there was no great promise of his doing conspicuously better. True, he had a fortunate name. A fifteenth-century ancestor had composed a treatise on Tenures which, attracting the criticism of a great legal pedant, had achieved a singular kind of immortality ; and Lytteltons since have in almost every generation achieved some sort of rather easy eminence. But not his warmest admirer could have pretended that he was likely to be more than a good, sound, humdrum lawyer. It was the same with politics. Though eight years in the House of Commons, he had made no name there. He had never been in subordinate office. He had not even been a Parliamentary private secretary. Once, indeed, he had done some official work in South Africa, and at another time had presided over an arbitration in Newfoundland, but for the rest there was nothing that could be said about him to the crowd, unless it was that he would be popular with the Australians because he had played against them in the first of all test matches. Actually, of course, there were stronger reasons for the appointment. He had real brains of a sort, good if not the best kind. He had a character of the very best in its kind. It was not then, as it is now, the one recommendation of a minister—to be proclaimed, as it were, with the blast of many press trumpets—that he is honest. Nobody thought of insulting Lyttelton, or the chief who chose him, by saying that, whatever he might or might not be, he was at least a man of spotless integrity. There was still a widespread belief that all ministers were, roughly speaking, straight, as there was a considerable presumption that most ministers were reasonably educated. The papers did not protest with passion that in no circumstances could Lyttelton rob a till, or infer from the fact that he could hammer out an average Latin author with a certain degree of pleasure that his mind was specially endued with " *gravitas* " and " *pietas*." Something was taken for granted in a ruling caste. But Lyttelton was in truth something more than a merely honest man. He was good as few have been since the primal fall. He was a good man, however, in precisely the same way as he had been a good boy. Everybody who knew him at Eton testified to the moral influence he had exercised in the school. He had stood for the straight life not less than for the straight bat. When he passed into the larger world he did not change. But it should be noted that, whilst his ideas of virtue were, as always, absolutely definite, vice remained to him as something vague. Throughout his life he fought against it, as many fight in their boyhood, instinctively and in half-darkness ; he never saw it as a duellist sees his enemy. This innocence of his was an asset to the Government, though not, perhaps, to the country.

If anything could have opened his eyes it would have been his mission to South Africa. There he acted as chairman to the committee appointed to examine the concessions granted by the South African Republic to a number of wealthy corporations and individuals. Kruger and his subordinates had been exceedingly amenable to arguments of the clinking kind, and the cosmopolitan magnates had been lavish with their gold. That much was practically on the surface, for the Boer view had ever been that the Uitlander, since he could not be excluded altogether, must at least pay his footing. But when Lyttelton had dealt well and firmly with the corruption on the surface, he accounted his work done. It did not occur to him that the smaller jobberies might sometimes be revealed to draw attention from the larger, nor yet that some who protested most against the briberies of the past were smarting because their own bribes had been rejected as insufficient. It never struck him that since the outside of the cup was so dirty the inside must almost infallibly be dirtier still. Indeed, he shrank from letting it strike him. Because of the healthful life he lived, because of his hearty cheer, because of the shape of his jaw, people were deluded into the belief that Lyttelton was a strong man. In truth he was weak, and weak chiefly because with him to be good was to be fastidious. One of the most sincerely religious men of his generation, he could not probe into his faith. He hated to probe far into anything lest he should come upon the disagreeable ; and he who will not know the worst of life cannot well make the best of it.

He could not be suspected of being moved, in entering the ministerial career, by motives of self-advancement. The Government he joined was already under sentence of death. Little was to be gained from taking office, and, in Lyttelton's case, much was to be risked. With only modest private means, he was dependent on the Bar for his income, and he had no great reputation such as would ensure that solicitors would remember him after an interruption in his career. Politics, in fact, had always involved him in sacrifice. His seat in the Commons had meant giving up the best part of his practice—that which lay at the Parliamentary Bar. Moreover, where politics were concerned, he had little confidence in his own ability. But it had been urged on him by a voice as authoritative in his eyes as that of a cricket captain that it was his duty to take part in public life, and he worked for his country in the same spirit as he had played for it, though with less personal enjoyment. If the captain put him on to bowl it was not his to reason why, even though inwardly conscious that wicket-keeping was his proper business. And if the captain were Arthur Balfour, he would even go to the crease with alacrity. Like all the best boys of all ages, Lyttelton was an idolater, and the Conservative leader, a man about as unlike himself as any human being could be, chanced to be his idol.

His chief job at the Colonial Office was a queer one for a man of his character. Following the annexation of the Boer Republics there had come a great cry from South Africa for more labour for the mines, without which, it was said, the prosperity of the territories newly added to the Empire could not be recovered. Black labour in sufficient quantity was then unobtainable. White labour was obtainable, but it was dear, and its introduction on a large scale would imply political complications. An influx of unskilled whites meant the arrival of Labour with a capital " L," and Labour with a capital " L " would perhaps pool its inevitable grievances with those of the conquered Dutch, and in combination might make matters extremely awkward for the authorities. Consequently Lord Milner added his voice to the voices of the Rand magnates and demanded an adequate supply of yellow coolies. Chinamen were to be indentured for a certain number of years, kept in compounds, and at the end of their term of service compulsorily returned to Asia.

No doubt had Joseph Chamberlain remained at the Colonies he would have vetoed such a proposal as certain to cause trouble at home. But the Balfour ministers were for the most part happy about it. Had Lyttelton trusted his generous instincts, he would no doubt have said " No." But the idealist of the public school often suffers from a fatal handicap. He does not like to be what is called " stuffy." It was so with Lyttelton. He was distrustful of his own convictions, and under an impression that they must be subordinated to other considerations whenever anybody pronounced the formula " economic compulsion," in a sufficiently grave tone. In the company of men of the world he was apprehensive of seeming a prig. He persuaded himself that the whole thing was, in words subsequently used by the Archbishop of Canterbury, a " regrettable necessity," and he acceded to it. When he had arrived at this conclusion, another schoolboy characteristic came into play. He had to do his very best for his side, to keep up the wicket.

As far as he was concerned, that would have been the end of the matter had he held any post in the Government other than that of Colonial Secretary. As things were, he had not only to agree that the Rand magnates should be supplied with the cheap, semi-servile labour they demanded, but to supply it himself. He had to plead for it, to contend for it, fight all the beasts in Ephesus on its behalf. By birth and breeding he was a Liberal. He had remained in the Liberal party long after the secession of the Unionist minority, and the break had finally been made with pain and hesitation. There was, of course, in him not the least element of Radicalism ; going to the root of things was foreign to his nature. The Liberal flavour of his mind gave an unpleasant taste to the Chinese business ; but he did not go below the surface. He seems to have had no notion of the abomination the indenture system might imply. In innocence he entered on the transaction, and with some distaste ; but when the great campaign began against it, he simply stood up to the bowling. Nothing then mattered but his duty to the team.

All this is the more curious because of the nature of his mind and the degree, singular in his profession, and still more singular among politicians, to which he was dominated by ideals of right and wrong. Lyttelton at the Bar had been more esteemed as an arbitrator than as an advocate. He had his cricketer's passion for fair play. Given a brief, he had never been able to make much of it without a conviction that right was on the side of the party for which he acted. And, perhaps because he had excelled at so many other games, the political game had in itself small attraction for him. He did, it is true, throw himself in later years with might and main into the fight against the Welsh Church Bill, which to him seemed in truth an effort to despoil God and to dethrone religion. For another Bill, to check sweating in English industries, he battled zealously. The best speech he ever made was his contribution to the Marconi debate. But when the contest did not seem to him to be obviously between good and evil, he was, as a rule, apathetic. When the tariff controversy was at its height, he was at once perplexed and uninterested. Yet on this question of Chinese labour he not only fought strenuously, but with a certain glee. Though he could have scarcely fancied all the angels were on his side, he contrived to be the resolute protagonist, the complete partisan, and even the happy warrior.

What sustained him was, doubtless, the presumed

hypocrisy of his adversaries. Labour "manacled by indentures" had in the past been no appalling spectacle to Liberal Governments, and Lyttelton had not the mind to draw distinctions between one set of manacles and another. Moreover, questions of taste were involved. Lyttelton had the public school conscience which bids men do the right thing and make no great say about it; indeed be a little shamefaced and embarrassed when detected in saintliness. Across the floor of the House, on the other hand, were men accustomed to testify to righteousness. Any scruples he may have had about the Transvaal ordinances departed when the Opposition began to cry "slavery." It was not in his nature to make allowance for the exaggerative language which is common form in political debate, and, imagining himself and his friends the objects of a bitterly calculated misrepresentation, he hardened his heart.

The situation was full of irony. To friend and enemy alike, Lyttelton was "the embodiment of everything which is good, and honest, and straightforward."[1] Before all else he was a man of principle, yet he was standing for a policy that offended ordinary, easy-going people, and could only be justified ultimately on grounds of somewhat base expediency.

Among the assailants of that policy were many unpleasant human beings, intent on little but personal and party gain. But on the whole the truth was with the liars, and the nobility of purpose with the ignoble. "Chinese slavery" cost the Conservatives many votes. Probably, but for Lyttelton, it would have cost many more. There were people who could not believe that he could have battled for anything that was not fair and clean.

[1] From a letter written by Major Seeley, published in Lady Edith Lyttelton's *Memoir of A. L.*

Lyttelton was not a success as a Parliamentarian. He was in the wrong atmosphere in an elected assembly. He was one of those men who are said to know everybody. When he was at the Colonial Office, a private secretary remarked that everybody called him Alfred. He was, in fact, a man of many friends and of still more relations. Mr. Gladstone was his uncle-in-law. Mrs. Asquith was his sister-in-law. Through his second wife he was connected with Balfours and Cecils, and with Arthur Balfour he had a lifelong friendship to which one key was a common love of music. His intimacy with Lords Curzon and Midleton dated from Eton and was never relaxed, though the mortal quarrel of the two made it utterly impossible to enjoy their society together. But if no man was ever more at home in the inner circle of politics, few can have been more hopelessly lost in the outer circles. He knew so many people who were somebody that he had no notion of what was in the mind and heart of the millions who are nobody. Until 1906 he was member for Warwick and Leamington, but he was never in close touch with the voters, and he was depressed and puzzled, small blame to him, by elections with all their appeals to prejudice and their noisy simulation of enthusiasm. Probably he thought that things were better done at Eton, where, too, he had helped to rule. At Evans's he had belonged to "the Library," and also, of course, to "Pop," both governing bodies whose members were never compelled to appeal for votes, but simply arrived by some process of self-election which nobody had the faintest desire to dispute. Lyttelton was not a snob; he was on terms of good fellowship with the early Labour members. Also, he was a philanthropist, with a sympathy for the poor that grew keen when some fragment of their suffering was revealed to his astonished mind. But no born Whig

ever became a democrat ; not even a Tory democrat.
As minister under a benevolent despotism Lyttelton
would have done well if served by capable and honest
officers of intelligence. As things were, he was always
the right man in the wrong place. In later years he
had at least one stroke of good fortune. When
Warwick rejected him, St. George's, Hanover Square,
gave him a political asylum. He must have known
a goodly number of his constituents in advance, and,
as the suffrages of the rest were equally assured, he
had to court none.

Lyttelton's life had always been exceptionally sheltered. He had known bitter grief, notably when his
first wife died after a very brief period of married life,
but he had been spared worries of the vulgar kind.
Because of the fame of his elder brothers he had
escaped those rough passages which the small boy
has normally to traverse on arriving at a big school,
and subsequently immunity from the rough and tumble
which is supposed to mould adolescent character was
the reward of his own athletic achievement. In the
toil that success upon the playing fields normally implies
he took the least possible share. He was a born
cricketer, and never seemed to need the practice
requisite to others. Without the responsibilities of
wealth, which to a man of his stamp would have been
distressing, he knew nothing of the restraints of poverty.
Enough work came to him at the Bar to secure him a
competence from the first. Always he was intimate
with the right people ; not merely with those who were
great in the eyes of the upper world, but with those
yet more influential personages whose Christian names
are scattered in diaries and letters and of whom the
crowd has no more precise knowledge. He delighted
in social intercourse, in all sports, in music. He had
a taste for all the decent luxuries : a little soup, a bit of

L

fish, a bird and a sweet were all, as he has left on record, that he really required for lunch. One need not be an anchorite to yearn for nothing more. Never was he forced to deny himself the thing he wanted. It would be easy to say that life had spoiled him, but more probably he would have been spoiled by any other sort of life.

His wife has described him on visits to France and Italy as being " like an unwilling child at a party " and as " trying fitfully to be interested." Quintessentially he was English ; a model of the English gentleman as envisaged by Dean Inge and such admirers of the type. A peculiarly privileged member of a class that had been long privileged, native of an island for centuries sheltered from the world's storms, he lived, it may be, thirty years too late. In the beginning of the twentieth century such as he still had a sort of prescriptive right to high place in politics, yet already they were obliged to adapt themselves to altered circumstances. But Lyttelton never understood how much the world had changed since his father drove about Worcestershire cracking a whip at all and sundry. True, he had himself no inclination to whip-cracking, but it may be doubted whether he ever quite understood that a time had come when one really must not crack whips even in joke. His handling of the Chinese labour business showed his ignorance both of the new proletariat and of the new plutocracy. He never visualised the cool, good-humoured, implacable resolve of Big Business to make a profit, without regard to any old-fashioned ideas of patriotism, religion or morality. He never grasped (as Joseph Chamberlain did) how English workmen would regard the thing as a preliminary to an attack on themselves. Such suspicion he regarded as fantastic. Those who entertained it were, he thought, simply befooled by agitators.

None the less, Lyttelton had his moments of insight.

When he and his were routed, and the enemy had come to power, there was no reversal of the yellow ordinances. Wherever else he had been wrong, he had been right in his idea of the hypocrisy in official Liberalism. After his party's fall, the new Liberal Government did not stop the supply of " slaves " demanded by the Rand lords, and one of its members admitted that " slavery " had been a terminological inexactitude.

ROBERTS AND KITCHENER

In the period between the Boer War and the Great
War, Lord Roberts and Lord Kitchener were the only
two soldiers of whom the English public spoke or
thought much, and they were mentioned always in the
order given. One said Roberts and Kitchener just as
one said Oxford and Cambridge. Roberts was put
first, partly because he was the elder of the pair, partly
because he was liked, while Kitchener was only
respected.

At this date one has to reverse the order. Time
has made it plain that Kitchener was altogether the
bigger of the two. Whether he was the greater
soldier is a question best left for argument to those of
his profession. What has become clear is that he was
the greater man ; possibly the greatest man who has
commanded British troops since Marlborough, almost
certainly the greatest since Wellington. This is not
to say that Roberts deserved less honour than was
bestowed in his lifetime, but rather that Kitchener
deserved more honour than has ever yet been yielded
him. The veteran of Kandahar was purely and simply
professional ; ". every inch a soldier," with all the
limitations that eulogy implies. Taken out of his
environment, it is quite likely that he would have been
accounted just a nice little man, without any special
significance. Kitchener, on the contrary, was bound
to make his mark anywhere and in anything. In his
last days, indeed, he puzzled and troubled those of his
colleagues who had been misled by the myth of his

supermanhood. He was found fallible. He was found human. Illusion after illusion disappeared. But he passed, nevertheless, the supreme test of greatness. Even those who felt that he had blundered here or there, and blundered sometimes very badly, could not rid themselves of the feeling that, after all, there was that in him which was bigger than the sum of his qualities. It was possible for his critics to say that he was fortunate in the opportunity of his death, that such work as he could do was done, and that the work that remained was better in other hands. But the most flippant of these critics could not but admit that, of all the British soldiers concerned in these vast transactions, he was still the only one who could, by any stretch of language, be called great.

Kitchener's life-story was quite unlike that of the average British officer. It was from the start unconventional to the point of being romantic, and that, perhaps, was why he wore before the world the air of an ultra-rigid precisian. Compare him with Roberts. The latter, with all his personal courage, hero of innumerable adventures that might have been specially enacted to please the boys of a preparatory school, lived from the cradle to the grave within the four corners of King's, or Queen's, Regulations. And because his whole life had been so essentially ordered, his heart was always full of romance, and he dared wear it on his sleeve at times. Kitchener could not risk that luxury, even had he wanted. For Kitchener had actually done those things which, according to what rankers call " the little red book," he ought not to have done, and therefore Kitchener was all iron and buckram. The men who tell have rarely kissed. The men who have kissed do not tell if they are men, and the rule of Venus holds good of Mars.

In the very year he received his commission in the

Royal Engineers, Kitchener had offered himself as a volunteer to Chanzy and the army of the new French Republic, struggling against the German invaders on the Loire. His connection with that forlorn hope seems to have been terminated only by illness. That he received nothing more than a scolding for his conduct was lucky for him, for he had certainly offended against the Foreign Enlistment Act. Probably his good fortune was due to the fact that the branch of the British Army to which he belonged had rather less conventional traditions than those which prevailed in, say, infantry or cavalry. All sappers, it is said, are either mad, married or Methodists, and young Kitchener's spirited indiscretion was probably excused on the first ground.

His next adventure was even stranger. For an account of it we must go to Mr. Churchill's book, *The River War*. Kitchener, when employed on the Palestine survey, had made himself proficient in Arabic, but knowledge of that language was not then a specially valuable asset to an officer. For practical purposes of promotion, it appeared that he might as well have learned Choctaw or Anglo-Saxon. But then came the year when Arabi was threatening trouble in Egypt, and Kitchener availed himself of a leave to hurry to the one spot where his linguistic talent would be of use to himself and to the Service. The storm, however, did not burst at once, and there was no likelihood that he would obtain more time. Consequently, he cabled for an extension of leave, adding that if he did not receive a refusal he would consider his request granted. In due course the refusal was despatched, but Kitchener had made arrangements that it should not reach him, and his plan succeeded. Alexandria was bombarded, every officer who could speak Arabic was wanted, and Kitchener, who was on the spot, though unofficially, got his chance, being one of the original twenty-five British officers who were set to work at the reorganisation of the Egyptian army after the collapse of the rebellion at Tel-el-Kebir.

These two stories of his early life show that Kitchener was made in a different mould from most soldiers, and even from so distinguished a soldier as Lord Roberts. Everybody remembers his appearance, and many will recall the vivid verbal portrait painted of him by G. W. Steevens when he was fresh from the triumph of Omdurman. Erect, six foot and more of flesh and bone, but mainly wire, tanned and moustached, yet with " no body but to carry his mind, no face but to keep his brain behind." It is the final words that have real meaning. Kitchener had not only a brain—many other British generals are reasonably endowed in that particular—but he had rather a peculiar sort of brain, and one worth concealing ; one, perhaps, that had to be concealed because it did not always work on strictly orthodox lines.

At the start of the century Kitchener was fresh from battles which, for one reason and another, had made a great impression on the public. We, with our memories of the Marne and Ypres, may smile at the old boasts over Atbara and Omdurman. We may also reflect that the campaign against the Khalifa had been undertaken, not (as was alleged) to deliver the Sudanese from a grinding tyranny, not (as was generally believed) to avenge the death of Gordon, but mainly because the Italians had lately been worsted in Ethiopia, and it was part of Lord Salisbury's diplomatic game of working hand in hand with the Triple Alliance to make a counter-move in the neighbourhood. We must not, however, be overwise after the event. Kitchener's battles had been rapturously applauded at home, and Kitchener was a hero of the hour. He set the fashion in strong, silent men. "There is no man Herbert Kitchener," Steevens had written, " but only the Sirdar, neither asking affection nor giving it." Talents he had, Mr. Churchill had said, "which will never be fettered by fear and not very often by sympathy." All this suggested to the great public a rigidity which, in fact, was non-existent. Kitchener was not the least a Prussian. As a soldier he had, no doubt, the insensibility proper to that character, and, being a greater soldier than most, he was probably less regardful than others of the eggs necessary for the making of his omelettes. He was not in the smallest degree either the *beau sabreur* or the military sentimentalist. It was remarked of him that he was never known to speak to a private soldier. Even in his own family he inspired awe rather than any warmer feeling. As a military leader he was terribly logical, recking nothing but victory. But the notion of him as only a " mechanical automaton," with no mind except for the problems of his profession, is belied by the mere facts. Kitchener had emphatically a talent for statesmanship and diplomacy, and that implies sympathy and a wide range of understanding. He could deal in what soldiers and sailors call " eyewash." He could estimate, in other words, the value of the imponderables. His very pose was a practical appreciation of such values. If it helped to be regarded as the stern and terrible human machine, it was worth while living up to the character.

There was, however, another reason for his iron reserve. The secret of his taciturnity was long kept, and almost to the end of his life it was fancied that he did not speak because he had nothing to say, because he lacked entirely that gift of tongue in which Roberts had a share, in which Napoleon and Lee were masters. But, in fact, he put so strong a curb upon himself because he was conscious of the necessity. So far from being without the gift of expression, he had it in excess. Lord Esher's memoir of Kitchener's last months makes it plain that once he let himself begin to talk he babbled, and there can be small doubt that in this matter he knew his own infirmity. Strict abstinence is the only thing for a man conscious of the passion of drink ; strict silence is necessary for one who knows that if he talks all will out. Kitchener, there is reason to believe, had a suppressed liking for oratory, and, aware of the dangers of that disposition, took the only effective means of averting them. The officers who formed his immediate entourage were devoted to him. Of this there can be no doubt. But it was a devotion of a quite peculiar character. It had nothing in common with the love Roberts inspired. It was not human in character, for to all human loves and friendships there are limits, and implicit in them all is a demand for reciprocity. Those who loved Roberts knew quite well that Roberts loved them. Had Roberts shown himself selfish, indifferent, exacting save where the needs of the Service were concerned, their sentiments would have been modified. With Kitchener it was different. No man lived who could say to himself with conviction that he was loved by Kitchener. But Kitchener could command anything that any officer of his possessed, and was offered it without question or demur. If he wanted a particular officer's charger, the animal was yielded him at once, and he accepted it as his due ; no thanks, in more than the formal sense, were given or expected. He was as near a god as a white man can be to white men, and it takes a considerable and a rather peculiar man to serve in that capacity. It takes a still greater and still more peculiar man to accept such worship and still retain intelligence and flexibility of mind. There Kitchener succeeded. Incense did not blind or intoxicate him.   If he was curt and brusque with the worshippers surrounding him, he could be diplomatic with others.

Twice at least in his career he gave evidence of extraordinary skill as a negotiator.   His treatment of the Fashoda affair was masterly.   One type of British officer would have thought it the right and John Bullish thing to bluster with Marchand's little band of interlopers ;   another would have fallen into the opposite error of gushing over them as heroes and imagining that all that was needed to conciliate was an embrace and some flatulent compliments.   Kitchener knew better. He knew how, according to French tradition, an English gentleman behaves.   By simply being *très correct* he kept the peace between the two nations.

When it came to peace-making with the Boers he triumphed again.   He chose Smuts as of all the Boer leaders the most open to reason, gripped him by the elbow, and led him out of the room where the rest were arguing in a circle with England's chief civilian representative.   Alone in the darkness the two talked together, and Kitchener stated his opinion that a Liberal Government would soon be in power and would grant a constitution to South Africa.   " That," said Smuts afterwards to Lord Shaw, " accomplished the peace."   Not many soldiers, one imagines, even possessing the same grasp of the political situation, would have ventured on the discussion of home politics with an enemy still in arms.   Almost all would have accounted such words as dangerous, if not seditious, and, anyhow, as beyond their province.   The incident is one of the rare glimpses we get at Kitchener's real mind, and we see that it was a mind without the usual professional boundaries.   With another professional soldier—Marchand—it had been right to be simply correct.   With Smuts, an amateur soldier who was

politician to the core, mere correctitude would have
been ridiculous.

Vereeniging was Kitchener's triumph in South
Africa. English arms won few laurels in that campaign, and the rare spectacular successes were gained
under Roberts, who had an aptitude for such things.
When Roberts departed, apparently under a delusion
that the end was in sight, it was left to Kitchener to do
all the hard, inglorious work. He was not quick about
it. According to Steevens, he was " never in a hurry,"
and Lord Esher has written that the " slow processes of
the Orient were burnt into him by the Egyptian sun."
But he was tenacious and ruthless, and another in whom
lurked some notion that it was a soldier's business to be
brilliant and chivalrous might have taken longer. In
the end, his reputation was neither increased nor
lessened. Roberts had had such plaudits as more or
less serious people could spare for South African achievements in generalship. French, as a cavalry leader,
had made a name among the specialists, and the crowd
had, of course, huzzaed for Baden-Powell. But
Kitchener was in no way damaged because the stubborn
struggle with the Boers had brought him no glory.
He was a firmly established British institution, and
the public had had too much to criticise to be in the
mood for superfluous criticism.

In India again Kitchener was to be severely tested,
and again the results were to be in a sense indecisive.
His reorganisation of the Indian army was largely
a technical business, and only to be appreciated by
technicians, but amongst them there seeems to be an
agreement that his reforms were wise. That he was
often obsessed by the idea of a Russian attack, and,
even after the Japanese War, rated the Russian power
too highly, must be admitted. That he was in the
wrong in his quarrel with Lord Curzon is certain. He

wanted power for himself, knew himself equal to wielding it in the country's interest, and probably realised that he was not a good collaborator. But he either could not see, or did not reck, the ultimate consequences of such concentration of authority. His claim to undivided control of things military in India meant placing on his successors duties and responsibilities beyond the ordinary general's capacity. Kitchener was an egoist without conceit. He knew himself capable of tackling big tasks. Later, when he was at the War Office, it was hard to persuade him that there might be any task he could not accomplish singlehanded. But there is no reason to think he was over-rating his own capacity in the Indian days. The fact was that, in one sense, he was too modest in his self-confidence. It seemed no miracle to him that he should perform a big job alone : why should such a job be impossible to other people ? I should say that Kitchener never thought of himself as a genius. Very probably he would have jeered at the use of such a word in regard to anybody. At any rate, his attitude towards others suggested that he did not realise the difference between men of very ordinary clay and himself. He made few allowances for physical weakness ; none for mental or moral weakness. Because he insisted on high standards, there is no doubt that he obtained better results than did those whose requirements were lower. But at the root of his Indian mistake, and of more serious mistakes in later life, can be espied his failure to recognise the shortcomings of men as facts beyond a certain point unalterable. Mr Churchill has written that, after Atbara, Kitchener being cheered by his troops " was quite human for a quarter of an hour." That quarter-hour did not often recur.

One occasion on which it did recur was unfortunate.

In 1910 there was a strong movement to secure his appointment as Lord Minto's successor in the Indian vice-royalty, and his candidature was not only hotly supported by King Edward, but favoured by the Prime Minister. The silent soldier of the legend could have had the post, but at a dinner with Lord Morley the suppressed Kitchener broke loose, talked at large, was copious in indiscretions, and horrified the prim and philosophic Radical who ruled the Indian Office. " Never, never shall he go " was his host's verdict. Morley himself often talked, and sometimes wrote, pretty considerable nonsense ; but it was always expressed in the ordered pomp of an impressive library style.   He could not, as a man of his own special type, tolerate the aberrations of a type quite dissimilar ; probably he did not understand that Kitchener was having one of his rare holidays.   Kitchener's inner tastes, Lord Minto once wrote, were more artistic than military, and this dictum, so startling at first sight, possessed an element of truth.   This generally un-suspected " temperament " was a strength and a weakness.   Kitchener, as I have said, fully understood its dangers, and so deliberately kept it in the back-ground.   But it was this very temperament which, while at rare intervals it stood in his way, raised him so far above the level of the ordinary professional soldier.

Kitchener's return to England, unemployed, in the midst of the turmoil caused by Mr. George's Budget, the House of Lords question, and the revival of Home Rule as a practical problem, was, in some quarters, regarded as an event that might have political im-portance.   " It has set going," Lord Morley wrote, " a tremendous chatter which may possibly swell." On many lips were the words " Strong man ! the man we want."   Hot-heads were already talking in terms of the civil war for which definite preparations were soon to be made in Ulster, but Kitchener was not to be drawn.

There is no suggestion that he was in the least affected by any of the temptations which seduced other soldiers. Yet he was, in the deeper sense, a far more politically minded man than any of his army contemporaries. He, alone of them all, could be imagined as playing the part, if things had come to the appropriate pass, of a Cromwell or a Napoleon. One is conscious in him, indeed, of something of the quality of the Cromwells and Napoleons. Had constitutional government really broken down, had " these grave matters " been fully " put to the test," such a general as Roberts would, perhaps, have played the part of a Schomberg. That is to say, he would have carried out the orders of something he regarded as a Government. He would have still been, in his own view, the instrument of the " civil authority." And when the whole thing was over (assuming success for his side) he would have retired on his pension and grant in the gracefullest and most self-abnegating way. One feels that Kitchener, while he had more scruple in the beginning than some of the soldiers, would have had less scruple at the end. He had a more logical brain than these good people. A revolution is no less a revolution because its sponsors move in the best society ; and a soldier must not lightly traffic with revolutionaries. But if the appeal to force really comes, then let force decide, and let him who can command the most force keep things in his own hands. If two sets of politicians cannot settle affairs without calling in a soldier, what is the sense of deciding the quarrel between them and then retiring quietly in favour of one set ? We have no right to assume that Kitchener would have consented, except in the gravest extremity, to act against constituted authority. But we may be pretty certain that

he would not have made war on the Asquith Cabinet
merely to replace it by a Carson-Smith combination.
Duty to king and country was one thing. Subservience
to a political junta, one imagines, would seem to
Kitchener quite another. His determined aloofness in
this emergency was no inconsiderable testimony to
the bigness of a man who could be imagined, in certain
circumstances, as a great military adventurer, but in
no circumstances as a small military intriguer.

Further, it is worth noting that Kitchener was not
to be drawn into the movement for compulsory military
training, in which Roberts was the leading spirit. A
proposal to enforce conscription of the Continental
kind might, or might not, have had his support. His
hesitation to advocate the system when war had actually
commenced throws no light on what his attitude might
have been in time of peace had proposals to that end
been seriously advanced. But the Roberts scheme of
universal but elementary soldiering, a little rifle-shooting
for everybody, a nation forced into the Volunteers by
Act of Parliament, does not seem to have appealed to
him. In Australia he had seen how that kind of thing
worked, had complimented the Australians on " the
natural military qualification " of their youths, and—
had then reminded them that they must rely on the
navy as their first line of defence. From Japan he
had put on record his wish that the spirit of our people
was more like that of the Japanese. Since, however,
the Japanese model was out of the question, he had
evidently no wish to see the Australian adopted.
Strict logician that he was, he could not be lured by
half-way houses. It may be that the dash of French
blood in Kitchener prevented him from sharing the
ordinary Englishman's liking for a compromise.

Roberts, " the happy warrior," loved soldiering, and
was sincerely sorry for the millions who were not

soldiers. To all those who could not, or would not, join with him in what he reckoned the most glorious of all vocations, he held out his hands appealingly, begging them, in effect, if they would not be his soldiers, at least to come and play at soldiers with him now and then. He was sure it would be good for them. He was certain they would enjoy it. And, from the national point of view, he believed that a man who had received some fraction of a soldier's training was more valuable than a man who had received none.

There is no indication that Kitchener had any of these sentiments. One would say he did not think of soldiering as a particularly joyous trade, but he did think of it as a trade, and he had the highest contempt for anything less than full mastery of the trade. There can be no doubt that he distrusted the man who was a quarter trained or less. Rightly or wrongly, when the War came he virtually ignored the Territorials.

Morley, who had an affection for Roberts that he could not extend to Kitchener, and yielded, as did all men, to the former's extraordinary personal attraction, wrote once of his " curious belatedness of mind." His vision of India was always the India of the Mutiny. His conception of Europe and a war in Europe may have been no less archaic. The history of the nineteenth century shows several cases where highly trained troops were held or worsted by forces of technically inferior quality in which patriotic enthusiasm and ability to hit the mark with a bullet compensated for other deficiencies. As late as 1870, the French irregulars had given more trouble than had the imperial veterans to the conquering Germans. The case, however, was altered by scientific armament and what not. Later events, which Roberts did not live to see, proved conclusively that imperfectly trained troops are a positive encumbrance to an army, and that it may be quicker to prepare raw recruits for the field than those who fancy themselves already fit for war.

But whatever errors of judgment Roberts may have made in his later years, his services to the country were great even in that period. Though Government and public would have none of his compulsory service, his advocacy of preparation for war was by no means futile. Junior ministers might scoff, and even reprimand him for panic-mongering, but in the inner circle of the Cabinet there may well have been a feeling that he was doing good work in accustoming England to thoughts of wrath to come. Also, he was a useful recruiting-sergeant for Lord Haldane's " new model." People had a genuine fondness for " Bobs " ; most heard him gladly, and at least a fair minority was always ready to do what he asked them. In a small war of the old-fashioned kind, when every soldier had the chance of a look, if not a word, from his general, he would have been an ideal commander, always given an adequate chief of staff. In the Great War, even apart from his age, he could have scarcely counted. No amount of individual charm could have permeated the vast organisation which the British army then became. All that could reach the millions was a sense of trust in a leader magnificent but unknown, partly magnificent because unknown. In the beginning Kitchener filled that part, though his place was at the War Office, not at the Front. By virtue of his aloofness from the common run of men, he could be ranked as a demi-god, and those who would have pulled him from his high niche, whatever plausible excuses they may have had, were doing bad service to the State, for there was no other British soldier to stand where he had stood, to be substituted for him as the figure of a legend. No other British soldier was, in fact, found. In the repository of military confidence a first qualification was to be,

M

somehow or other, incomprehensible, and our other generals had little to conceal.

There was never a shade of mystery about Roberts. Lovable, kindly, courageous, devoted to duty, simply and sincerely religious, but easily misled when he ventured off his own ground, and with more pertinacity than discernment, his qualities and defects were all obvious. Prince Hal's words of Percy fit him well :

> " I do not think a braver gentleman,
>   More active-valiant, or more valiant-young,
>   More daring or more bold, is now alive."

But Kitchener was complex, and all about him was secret. The most certain thing about him was that he allowed none to understand him, but whether he himself knew the answer to the riddle of his own personality is doubtful. There were streaks of genius in him, and there were streaks of what people not stupid were often tempted to call stupidity. But it was, at any rate, not at all a common kind of stupidity, and nobody could quite decisively say that the so-called stupidity was not itself a kind of genius. Kitchener sometimes seemed to employ the wrong kind of men, and employ them at the wrong tasks, yet he forced good results from them. He seemed as unimaginative as Wellington, yet Gordon was the one soldier who inspired him with interest. He sometimes appeared to ignore facts when they ran counter to his pre-possessions, yet he, who of all British soldiers was most separated from his circumstances from Europe and European ideas, set about preparing troops for " three years or the duration of the war " when generals who had closely studied the Continental situation were talking of a short campaign and an early peace. He never showed a sign of having thought of anything outside the limits of his calling, and yet, of all British soldiers since Marlborough, he gave most hint of capacities not military, and there was always a suggestion that these capacities were at bottom more important than his professional proficiency. One sees " Bobs " marching on Kandahar and Pretoria, and chatting pleasantly in clubs and drawing-rooms ; one cannot see him much otherwise. But the imagination is wholly unfettered as regards Kitchener. We know something of what he was, and much of what he did. But as to what he might have been had the circumstances been different, we have the widest choice of speculation. He is one of the few British soldiers whom it would be ridiculous to label " an officer and a gentleman." He was very much more than an officer. And his lonely inscrutable figure suggested something of such enormous and universal potentiality that the most ordinary sense of congruity would shrink from attaching to him a label common to all the magistrates, sheriffs of the county, and small respectabilities of these islands.

WILLIAM HESKETH LEVER

On one side William Hesketh Lever, afterwards Baron Leverhulme, had marked affinities with the old Victorian type of self-made man. There was a good deal of the Smiles hero about him; it might almost be said that he caricatured the Smiles hero.

Mr. Lever had none of that resolute humility, that shrinking from self-advertisement, which distinguished so many of the very rich men of his day, here and in America. Privately he admired himself heartily, and found no reason against doing it in public. He loved to talk rather piously about his ideals, faiths and enthusiasms, and one was constantly reminded that if he had not been so very busy in organising soap it would have taken very little to make him a lay preacher. He like to sermonise, and the burden of his sermons was that there was nothing like leather— or rather Lever. He was fond of recalling to reverent interviewers his early difficulties and triumphs, in such sort as to suggest that he regarded self-denial for strictly business purposes as on the same level as Christian virtue.

All this and much more—the narrative enlivened with much shrewd comment and many amusing stories — Lord Leverhulme, grown old, would tell those he took over his great house at Hampstead or the wonderful city of Port Sunlight, which so signally illustrated his genius for organisation. In this naïve relish of himself and all his doings he reminded one that he was born as long ago as 1851, and shared the intellectual simplicity of his class in that age.

But in all other respects he was ultra-modern, and there was no better example of many of the qualities necessary in the " big business " of the twentieth century. Though he created much he was not eminently creative. He did not invent soap. He did not perhaps improve soap to any remarkable degree. His name will not go down to posterity bracketed with those of men who were inventors as well as manufacturers, who enriched mankind by pushing forward the frontiers of knowledge and opening up quite new sources of wealth. He organised and developed ; he economised and unified ; he did not originate.

Yet within its limits his work was vast in volume and achievement. It is true that before his time the British soap trade was a great and flourishing industry, already engaging a vast capital. Its technical methods were reasonably efficient. It earned a large profit. It was rather specially notable for its enterprise in advertising and its skill in the art of popular appeal. But it was still far from perfectly organised. Side by side with the few big and well-managed concerns were a vast number of tiny enterprises, shaky in their finance, backward in their equipment, and content with scarcely more than a local trade. The industry depended for its raw material on resources largely undeveloped and somewhat precarious. Its markets abroad were not systematically mapped out and worked. There was no common cause among the members of the trade, and, though great in the bulk, their individual operations were comparatively peddling and uneconomic. All this Mr. Lever changed. He made the British soap industry almost one of the Great Powers. By the time his schemes were completed its travellers were found on every road, sea and river. Its agents were in every capital. It practically governed large tracts of territory. All land and ocean yielded it tribute.

William Hesketh Lever started life with few advantages in the accepted sense. True, the stock from which he came, though humble, was sound. His father was a small grocer of Bolton, pious in the old Puritanical way, thoroughly honest, thrifty, unadventurous, intensely respectable. William was one of nine children, seven of them daughters. The mother seems to have been one of those gentle, religious-minded women who, without possessing themselves any great force of character, are so often found capable of forming character in their children. The lad had thus made a wise choice of parents. But otherwise his handicaps were great. He had no education but that of the local school, and he left at fifteen for the paternal shop at a wage of one shilling a week. His first work, as he used to delight to recall, brought him into contact with what he was to make and what, in return, made him. It was cutting up bars of common soap.

The boy had hardly developed into a youth, when he agitated to be put on the road as his father's traveller ; and he used to say he looked on a certain afternoon at a wayside station as the turning-point in his career. This station had so far represented the *ultima Thule* of his traveller's round. But it happened on that particular afternoon he had an hour and a half to spare through the awkwardness of the time-table. Should he waste it ? If not, how should he employ it ? How could it be put to profit ? Now it happened that the next place of any importance was Ince, and there was a convenient train going there. Young Lever decided to put in his ninety minutes at Ince. He succeded in doing a little business, and henceforward Ince became a part of his regular round. Then he ventured further. Grimy Wigan began to beckon alluringly. To Wigan he went; there he did business, then more business, and still more business, until at last the possibilities seemed to justify him in setting up his own establishment there.

At Wigan, then, he settled as a wholesale grocer in a small way. It was not before he was thirty-five that he decided to make soap as well as sell it. He had always had an interest in soap, had read various works on its manufacture, and had experimented in an amateur way in producing it. It was therefore natural that when a small and badly managed soap concern came into the market he should be impelled to make the venture which was to lead to such enormous results.

The business began to prosper, and after a time Mr. Lever felt justified in deserting the grocery trade and entering on a larger soap enterprise at Warrington. In a very short time this began to flourish mightily, and the name of Lever Brothers, cleverly advertised, soon won a more than local fame. There was, however, some danger in his position. The greater Mr. Lever's success the more he was liable to be crushed by competition before he could consolidate it. He eked out his small capital by returning to the business every penny beyond what was necessary to live; denying himself not only luxury but even the comforts to which an ordinary man would think his position fully entitled him. Something he had to borrow for purposes of development, but he could not be easy with overdrafts at the bank, and he would not—to his credit—" float " anything that he could not honestly offer the public as a safe investment.

At last the business reached a position of solidity, and the next question was expansion. Walking one Sunday along the banks of the Mersey, Mr. Lever, now a man of something over forty, came across some rough fields with a big frontage to the river. Here, he thought, was the ideal place for his extending enterprises to find their final home. There was ample room for any degree of expansion. There was every convenience for water carriage. The rail was not far off. The whole resources of the busiest manufacturing region of England were within easy reach.

Even then, also, the romantic side of this very practical man was touched by the idea of a model industrial town away from the smoke and filth of the ordinary working district—a town in which he could put into practice all the notions of order and organisation natural to him. He bought the ground, and on those rough fields rose the vast working hive of Port Sunlight.

The years went on, and the house of Lever grew into the biggest soap concern in the country. The restless and aspiring spirit which had led the young grocer to Wigan, which had pushed him thence to Warrington, which had urged him to the grandiose design of Port Sunlight, now suggested a larger integration. In it, no doubt, the Mr. Lever of those days was encouraged by the instinct of thrifty orderliness which was a dominating passion from his earliest years. Waste and disarray were always anathema to him. His first recollections, he has told us, were of arranging, at the age of four, some books on a bookshelf, putting the tallest and thickest on the left hand and working with exact precision to the smallest and thinnest at the right. Such was his instinct for order. His instinct for economy may be judged from the fact that when he was making fifty thousand a year at Warrington he still lived in a house rented at less than fifteen shillings a week.

To a man of this disposition the waste involved in the competition of many soap firms, great and small, may well have seemed not merely foolish, but positively immoral. Take advertising, for example. Lever Brothers knew all about advertising. There were never more clever announcements than those which asked plaintively : " Why does a woman look older than a man ? " By answering that the reason was simply washing-day, and that Sunlight Soap robbed washing day of its chief terrors, the manufacturers enlisted sentiment on the side of good business. All that was chivalrous in England was ranged on the side of the future Leverhulme peerage.

Yes, undoubtedly Levers had little to learn on the subject of advertising ; was not the very name of Sunlight Soap an inspiration ? Nevertheless advertising was very expensive. It was a waste unless it was necessary. Under competition it was, of course, necessary. But why should there be competition ? Why not eliminate competition and substitute understanding ?

From these thoughts, germinating in the mind of a man of enormous energy, will, perspicacity and business acumen, rose the great soap combination of the first decade of the present century. Its early history was complicated by the fierce hostility of the powerful newspapers controlled by Lord Northcliffe ; and the litigation which ensued, though ending in a decisive victory for the Levers, involved their plans in a publicity which was doubtless far from welcome. Mr. Lever had to defend his projects for the grouping of a vast number of concerns under one control, and he did so on the ground that this virtual unification was actually in the public interest. He could take up this position with the utmost sincerity, for, as already noted, the bias of his mind was altogether towards organisation, and there was an almost quaint contrast between his theoretical passion for extreme individualism and his practical hostility to individualism in being. Intellectually he belonged to the school which believes in giving the freest possible scope to effort and securing it the utmost possible reward. For nationalisation and State enterprise he nourished the sturdiest contempt ; all that was " the most absurd gospel in the world " ; " the English," he said, " have pushed their fortunes never by the aid of the Government, but, on the contrary, almost always in the teeth of Government opposition." He scouted as mere nonsense the notion of the British workman being a " wage slave " ; opportunity, he held, was open to everybody ; and he proclaimed ceaselessly, in a world given to much vague self-indulgence and self-deception, the sturdy old doctrines of thrift, self-help and self-denial.

Yet in his own business he instituted a paternal form of rule which, by all analogy, should be unfavourable to the reproduction of the types of which he was so shining an example. " It is a splendid sight," wrote an admirer, " to see him at Port Sunlight, where he sits in a glass room, with a thousand clerks on his right hand and a thousand on his left." He boasted that system, such as he had instituted, is everything ; you got your system, and all went on then automatically. But that, surely, is the claim of Socialism also— Socialism, the favourite bugbear of Mr. Lever.

His full success had not come during the first decade ; it was not until the second had ended that he could point to no fewer than one hundred and thirty companies or firms within the orbit of Port Sunlight. In contriving this great combination the future Lord Leverhulme fulfilled two of his chief aims. He built up his own business on foundations of adamant. He brought all the other businesses within his influence. His third great aim was the last to be realised ; it was to achieve full command of the sources of raw material.

Even when the Levers were comparatively small people they took long views on this question ; in later years it was almost their main preoccupation. Soap is dependent on fat or grease of some kind. Lord Leverhulme decided that the supply of fat and grease must not be left to chance. He devoted the foresight and dexterity of a Richelieu to the great problem of ensuring the constant feeding of his industry, and wherever there was fat or grease, animal, vegetable or mineral, there were his agents at work. He put his hands on every available supply of animal fat, from Smithfield to China or Chicago. The Congo, British West Africa, the Solomon Islands supplied him with copra and palm oil produced on his own or associated plantations or concessions. He controlled the Southern Whaling Company, which fishes the Antarctic Seas. He had cattle ranches and cocoanut groves, dense tropical forests and grassy pampas, depots in the northern snows and under the vertical sun. Every kind of black and brown man laboured to supply the ever-hungry vats.

The subsidiary concerns of the Levers included firms engaged in land development, marine and land transport, building, gas production, pulp-board making and engineering ; and the obscurest of these enterprises had its due share of attention from the rather corpulent little man who sat among his two thousand clerks at Port Sunlight, showed his old masters to visitors at Hampstead, romped with the children of his workmen, and slept all weathers in a small iron bedstead under an awning not extensive enough to save his very pillow from the invasion of an occasional flurry of snow.

The first maxim of Mr. Lever was economy and efficiency in manufacture—getting material as cheaply as possible and working it up with a minimum of cost. The second was economy and efficiency of salesmanship. Here the training of the grocer counted greatly. He took over concerns built up on clever advertising, and, while decreasing advertisement, trebled their turn-over by dexterous and well-organised salesmanship. In the soap world, indeed, competitive advertising practically ceased. The chief object of a soap advertisement was latterly rather to tell people to go on washing than to adjure them to wash with any special soap.

There is a story which well illustrates the Lever combination of the Czaristic temper with theoretical reverence for the tenets of an old-fashioned Liberalism. Once, when a new road was to be made to his house at Thornton, the surveyor came to him with elaborate plans, showing contours and gradients with many windings. Mr. Lever took a pencil and ruler and drew a straight line. "That," he said, "is how the road is to be made." And "that" is how Port Sunlight was made; the place was the emanation of his will, just as much as that Hampstead bathroom of his, furnished with a tap that "enabled the bath to be filled in fifteen seconds"—so that there should be no waste of time!

This directness was at the root of the man's character. He would have gone less far if he had not gone straight in every sense of the term. A hard man in a bargain—"there is no room for philanthropy in business" was one of his favourite sayings—his successes were solid and honest successes. He built up his vast wealth, not by stock-manipulating deftness, but by sheer capacity working on a basis of sheer integrity. His morality was a limited thing, no doubt, but within its limits was absolute.

Mr. Lloyd George said of Lord Leverhulme that he could not work with other men; Lord Leverhulme retorted that he had been working with other men all his life. Yet there was some justice in the charge. He worked with men only as their master, and if a benevolent despot, a despot he certainly was. About him there was room for every talent of the subsidiary kind, but it was he, and he alone, who must do the thinking and the willing. Port Sunlight might be the creation of a theoretical democrat, and in the kindliness and common sense of its rule it was quite English. But not Krupp or Stinnes ruled with a firmer hand, or exercised a more all-pervasive influence.

Such was the man who, starting at scratch, found England, even in days when the Smiles tradition had considerably waned, so rich a land of opportunity. It may be interesting to quote his own view on the chances still open to ambitious poor in the third decade of the century.

" In England," he once said, " there is a ladder by which an office boy can rise to be chairman of the company. But it means innumerable acts of self-denial, the giving up of picture-shows and all sorts of allurements, and devotion through a long life to the service of the public and the study of business."

In other words the gold is no longer on the top. The days are gone when men lucky enough to " strike it rich " could shovel up what they wanted, and then retire to enjoy their good fortune. Success is now chiefly a matter of scientific deep mining, which brings greater results but also means the dedication of all the energies. Modern business is a kind mistress to the successful wooer. But she is jealous, and will brook no rival.

TARIFF REFORMERS AND FREE TRADERS

IF the Tariff Reform controversy was not the most important event of the early years of the century it was certainly the most noisy ; it had a lasting effect on the public fortunes and on the careers of men ; and most of the statesmen of the period are to be considered and appraised chiefly in relation to it.

It was very characteristic of Joseph Chamberlain, with his acute but far from long-sighted perception, that he should have so exactly guessed, not the truth indeed, but a fraction of it.   England was not, as the event proved, ready to abandon the economic system under which she had enjoyed a lopsided sort of prosperity for the greater part of the Victorian age.   But she was quite ready to cheer anybody who proposed to " make the foreigner pay."   The foreigner is seldom popular in these islands, and he was rather exceptionally unpopular just then.   Memories were recent of the threat of a Continental coalition.   The Potsdam telegram to Kruger had not been forgotten.   Neither had the affair of the Bundesrath, in which peace was saved only at the expense of abject submission.   The brutal cartoons in the French press still rankled.   Russia was regarded with deep suspicion.   It seemed impossible that France could ever be a friend.   In the feeling regarding Germany a slight tinge of apprehension—it was, as yet, no more—mingled with resentment that the Prussianised Empire should be so ungrateful for all our good offices as to range itself, however tentatively, on the side of our enemies and critics. Nor was America more popular. There had been a spectacular invasion of England by Transatlantic capital. It had bought our ships. It had bought our tobacco companies. It had set about electrifying the London Underground. For the moment things looked black. Englishmen, of course, never would be slaves. But was there not a possibility of their becoming the servants of avaricious Yankee trusts ? And if the operations of high diplomacy and high finance disturbed the patriot and the business man, the clerk was incensed to find himself, the master of no language but his own, threatened by a horde of polyglot Germans, willing to work for half his wage.

The mass psychology, therefore, was favourable to Mr. Chamberlain. When he asked " Are we down-hearted ? " there might be more volume than conviction in the thundered " No." But when he proceeded : " Shall we take it lying down ? " there was no trace of dubiety in the answering " Yes " of the populace. He was appealing less to reason than to passion, and according to Disraeli men are greater through their passions than through their reason. A little later reason's turn came, and here Mr. Chamberlain was not so successful. It was all very well to say we should not take it lying down. But how were we to take it standing up ? In other words how were we to make the foreigner pay ? How were we, in practice, to distinguish " dumping " from fair exchange ? How were we to tax food without making food dearer, making dearer also articles produced by people who ate that food, and therefore handicapping ourselves in the world's markets ? What was " raw material " which should still be imported without let or hindrance, and what were " finished goods " which should be made to pay toll ? Was not the finished article of one trade often the raw material of another ?   If a door ready to be built into a cottage was to be regarded as a finished article, why not include in that category the shaped timbers of which the door was made, and in fact go backwards until we insisted that the pine hewn on Norwegian hills should come over without a branch touched by the hated foreigner ?

These were the questions Mr. Chamberlain had to meet, and he was not well equipped to meet them.   His direct and rather shallow mind could comprehend a limited proposition, but, feeling no need of a general philosophy, he had never troubled to acquire one, and he was quite hopeless, as events in other fields had shown, in the presence of any problem of real complexity.   When cornered, he began to footle.   One can only call footling those calculations of his about the farthings the working man would save in one direction and the farthings he would lose in another by the adoption of his policy.   One can only call footling his later " personal pledges " (in conjunction with Mr. Balfour) that food under Preference should cost no more—as if any human being could control such matters.   There was one—and only one—argument which Chamberlain could have used against the Free Traders.   He could have quoted against them Adam Smith's famous " Defence more than opulence," could have arraigned them for their one great crime and folly, the sacrifice of British agriculture, and could have built up a case more on a qualitative than a quantitative basis.   This, however, he was not qualified to do.   If he were an idealist, it was one of a very matter-of-fact kind, and his main complaint in essence was, not that there was too little farm and too much slum in England, but that there would be too little even of slum for its expanding population unless the means of making more slum were found.

But what he was eminently qualified for he did.

He brought over to his side all the vague resentments of foreign commercial success and enlisted that type of patriotism the main inspiration of which is dislike of other peoples. On the other hand he omitted the unpleasant duty of telling the British people its faults and impressing the truth that, after all, only its virtues could save it, and some little responsibility attached to him in relation to the disposition (which dates from his time) of trades in trouble to look to the State.

It was a natural consequence of the character of its leader that the Tariff Reform party was, on the whole, much stronger in invective than in argument, and was finally guided almost entirely by passion. Much excuse may be found, however, for a body of men so bedevilled by their party chief as these men were by Mr. Balfour. I suppose the last day will have arrived before it is exactly known how far the philosophic doubter really accepted the Chamberlain plan. That he did not believe in " Cobdenism " we may reasonably gather ; that he would have adopted Tariff Reform if the country as a whole had rapturously welcomed it may be inferred ; but that he simply played with Chamberlain, as an angler might play with a fish hardly less strong than himself and very much stronger than his tackle, until the fish tired out—the exhausted angler fell in shortly afterwards—is certain. I personally believe that Mr. Balfour deserved better of his country than of his party ; that he must be considered during the Tariff fight rather as a statesman with an eye to the great European problem than as a fiscal sceptic ; and that things would have gone much more happily for the country had his Gallio-like spirit triumphed sooner over the Chamberlain enthusiasm. But one can believe all that and yet preserve some sympathy for Chamberlain in his tragic failure, and sympathy still

N

stronger for the army which was so often marched up the hill only to be marched down again.

Nor were the Conservative Free Traders inclined to complain less bitterly. Ritchie is generally branded by the Tariff Reformers as the villain of the piece, and indeed he was a commonplace person of no great personal charm. But Ritchie had just cause to resent the way in which he was jockeyed out of the Cabinet in 1903. So had George Hamilton, the most interesting of the Free Trade martyrs—interesting because nobody had ever suspected him of the stuff of which martyrs are made. So had the Duke of Devonshire, whose yawning inattention momentarily put him in the position of " letting down " people who had put their trust in him. Winston Churchill was too early in his appreciation of the situation, and too logical in his acceptance of it, to protest that he had been betrayed. But Hugh and Robert Cecil were as well entitled as any of the Tariff Reformers to regard themselves as wounded in the house of a friend—and in this case of a kinsman.

On the Liberal side Mr. Asquith was undoubtedly the greatest figure. He has had three " best periods." There was this Tariff Reform episode. There was the constitutional struggle of 1910-11. There was the first year of the Great War. I will not attempt to compare them, but I think it cannot be denied by any candid critic that his intellect was never engaged to better advantage than between 1903 and 1905—and that without belittling in the least the marvellous display of skill and patience which disarmed the House of Lords (which he intended), and also in the long run destroyed the Liberal party (which, it is to be presumed, he did not intend). His advocacy of Free Trade was superb in its force and its economy. If, as Chamberlain said, he talked like a barrister from his brief, it was just the forensic touch that the case wanted. On the Tariff Reform side there was room for rhetoric, more room for rhetoric than for anything else, indeed. For that case was, if winnable at all, only to be won by appeals to something greater than economy. On the other hand, nobody could be got really enthusiastic over Free Trade, if only that it was the creed in possession, and therefore to be held responsible for anything that was amiss. Asquith was not the man, as he showed afterwards, to inspire a beaten party with the spirit that wrenches victory out of the jaws of defeat. But he was fitted as no other man for the job that fell to him in 1903. The brief was one which he had read—contrary to his ordinary practice—with more than a transitory attention. He had digested its substance long before, and it needed only to get up the topicalities. The argument was just the sort that suited him, with his cold intellectualism, his love of the exact word, his dislike of sloppiness and rant. He could smash every advocate on the other side. His brain was equally fitted to deal with the crudities of Chamberlain and the refinements of Balfour. And though his case was negative, there was a very positive enthusiasm in its presentment ; the man whom a strange fate had marked out not only to live through revolutions, but to cause them, was philosophically the incarnation of *laissez faire* and *quieta non movere*. I should say he resented Chamberlain much as Fidgety Phil's father disapproved of that restless young gentleman. Why *couldn't* he sit still at the well-filled Free Trade table ?

It is curious that the greatest of the latter-day defenders of Free Trade should have so considerably resembled the minister through whom Free Trade triumphed. Asquith was Peel without Peel's intense industry, his haughty shyness, his ungenial character. But he was, like Peel, a very great Parliamentarian,

and, like Peel also, mingled with a rather cynical view
of politicians as individuals a reverence for the House
of Commons that amounted almost to a religion.
Peel founded a school which was represented in minis-
tries almost half a century after his death. Asquith's
young men include names which can be mentioned
without absurdity in comparison with any but Gladstone's. Peel was the more juicy orator, but he, like
Asquith, spoke always for a definite end, and, that
achieved, cared nothing. Possibly for this reason,
that by the economy of their utterance they gave the
impression of having much more to say than they
actually said, each inspired some excess of faith, and
ultimately paid the penalty of being too implicitly
trusted. But there was a still more fundamental
similarity between them. Peel, the consummate Parliamentarian, abandoned two positions to which he had
clung with tenacity, and which he had defended with
every weapon of strategy and eloquence, and ended
by reducing his party to impotence. Asquith, a consummate Parliamentarian, and certainly as convinced a
Liberal as Peel was a Conservative, left to his sucessor
a task no less appalling than that which confronted
Derby and Disraeli. Like Peel, he confused values.
An individualist in philosophy, he tolerated dabblings
in Socialism ; a Liberal Imperialist, he allowed his
Little Englanders to do and say much what they
liked ; a stern opponent of woman franchise, he
bestowed his blessing on the measure which gave a
vote to every female over thirty. If later it was hard
for a Liberal to say what Liberalism stood for, if to
many Liberals it seemed no great matter to go over to
Labour, if other Liberals found as little difficulty in
embracing the Tory creed, much of this mental bewilderment might be justly laid at the door of Mr.
Asquith. Yet he himself has changed very little in

mind since Gladstone picked him out, at forty, to be
Home Secretary. The change has been in other
directions. When he became Prime Minister those
who had been afraid that he might prove too rigid
began gradually to find that in many important matters
he was not rigid enough. They discovered, bit by bit,
that love of ease, liking for friends, desire to avoid
disagreeables, dislike of personal friction made him
prone to compromises of a kind which he could not
have endured had he been, as he sometimes seemed,
only an embodied intelligence. But in the early years
of the century this side of his character was not generally appreciated. He was the cold, hard, remote, inflexible, " direct " Asquith, the man of great brain and
not much heart. He could even suggest, on the part
of a highly intelligent writer perhaps not then too much
in love with him, an analogy with Cromwell.

If Mr. Asquith was at his best, or not far from his
best, in the middle years of the first decade, Mr. Lloyd
George was very nearly at his worst. He had become
a considerable man before the Chamberlain scheme
was launched. People had begun to see that his
attitude in the Boer War, at any rate after the first few
months, had something more than mere factiousness in
it. He had shown in his opposition to the Education
Bill a most unusual command of Parliamentary tactics.
But, as I have said elsewhere, the Tariff Reform controversy limited rather than advanced his pretensions
to great office ; and it was possible for an intelligent
and well-informed Radical writer to assign him a
position—that of the Duchy of Lancaster—inferior to
those indicated for Mr. Herbert Gladstone, Mr. Sidney
Buxton, and even Mr. John Burns. In the first place
the brief was a defensive one, and Mr. George is best
in attack. Free Trade was on its trial, charged with
many high crimes and misdemeanours—iron gone,

cotton going, shipping threatened, and so forth. Clearly the best way to secure acquittal was to smash the indictment count by count, as Mr. Asquith, King's Counsel fashion, actually did, leaving as little as possible for the other party to get hold of. Mr. Lloyd George, on the other hand, was always trying to prove too much. He laid stress on the social misery to which the Tariff Reformers pointed — it was the Free Trade case that the country was doing well. He proposed to deal with that misery on lines of State interference, whereas it was the Free Trade case that State interference aggravated the trouble it sought to relieve.

There were great landowners among the rebels against the Chamberlain domination ; Mr. Lloyd George was full of new burdens on land. He could, it is true, make very good jokes. But even the jokes were generally with a point against his own case. The fact was that his mind was as much confused as Chamberlain's about the pith of the whole matter, and his feelings were divided—there was a hatred of " Protection " as connected with his dislike of the landowning classes and an aversion from pure *laissez faire* because of his Social Reform enthusiasms. His colleagues must often have wished him out of the arena, where his fireworks were perpetually disconcerting them in their serious sword-play.

Of much more account fiscally was the young— then very young—Winston Churchill. I shall not attempt here an exegesis of Mr. Churchill's economic professions. I seem to remember that someone once persuaded him to turn his attention to Plato. But he speedily gave up that respectable philosopher because he found—I love him both for the substance of the declaration and for its frankness—that as a boy of fourteen he had fully thought out the problems so inconclusively handled by the Greek. Assuming the truth of this story, I imagine he had never digested the far less succulent exponents of Cobdenism. But he had evidently dipped into them, and it is not easy to avoid a suspicion that he never even dipped into the extensive but rather deterring literature of Tariff Reform. Therefore, notwithstanding later ministerial departures from the true faith, I shall assume that Mr. Churchill had his convictions, and that about May 1903 he was seriously troubled by the heretical tendencies then declaring themselves in the Conservative party. Whether haply a party chief of kindliness and prescience could have found some balm for these wounds is another question into which I need not enter. No balm was offered; instead, Mr. Churchill was treated cavalierly enough. And he was so constituted as to be incapable of even that squealing, kicking, railing loyalty that kept the Cecils within the party fold. I once heard Mr. Churchill say a very illuminating thing. It was said jokingly, but proverbially a true word may be uttered in jest. "Not for us in politics," he said, "is money or the reverence of men—but we do get a little fun." On the Conservative side he had not met much fun. There had been, it is true, a delightful little interlude of pro-Boer baiting; but that had passed, and Mr. Churchill, despite the portentous gravity with which he sought every occasion to distinguish himself, was still not particularly distinguished. The Tariff Reform business gave him an opportunity to get fully in the limelight and to keep there. In his party, while his allegiance lay in the balance, there was more concern over the one lamb that wobbled than over a hundred sturdy wethers indubitably sound on their legs. And when he went over he enjoyed all the distinction belonging to the notable recruit.   I suppose William of Orange was more gracious to Mr. Churchill's great ancestor than to most of the Whig squires and peers who had been in correspondence with him for months. At any rate the Liberals chieftains were most cordial to Mr. Churchill, and he fully repaid their discriminating courtesy.

He could be as witty as Mr. Lloyd George, and he knew enough of what he was talking about to make sure that his jokes were not two-edged.   I seem to remember him going down to Manchester and saying perhaps the smartest thing of the whole campaign. He spoke of the statue in that grim city to Cobden, " the man who gave England cheap bread," and suggested that side by side with it should be erected another monument to Chamberlain, " the man who gave England cheap consols."   His defence of pickles and jam—Chamberlain had sneered at their alleged progress while deploring in elegiac strain the decay of sugar—was a delicious piece of satire.   His gay audacity in Birmingham, the Tariff Reform holy of holies, testified to his courage in one way.   His attack on Mr. Balfour proved it in another—though here his usual good fortune left him, and he exposed himself to a deadly volley of what Lord Morley (who had experienced it) called " polished raillery . . . new, effective and unpleasant."

Altogether Mr. Churchill, despite his immaturity, was Asquith's most effective aid, and his reward, when the Liberal party came into power, was not an excessive guerdon for such services as he had rendered.   In office for some years he did not quite realise the hopes formed of him in opposition ; and I should say that, though a most vehement Radical warrior, he was never quite a happy one.   I imagine it was during these years that a natural tendency was confirmed in him. From the first he had been a rather lonely figure in politics ; during his Liberal years the habit of solitude grew. He could have little in common with the Liberal and Radical respectables, and there were things—including certain legacies of John, Duke of Marlborough—which sharply differentiated him from the livelier members of the party. One is conscious in all this time of a certain strain, in its way not less wearing and formidable than the strain of his early allegiance to the Tory party. In fact, Mr. Churchill was never either Liberal or Conservative, but, like Mr. Bob Sawyer, a kind of plaid. Creeds, fashions and disciplines mean for him little. He has to recognise their existence, for sometimes they must be used and sometimes they must be dodged. But the chief virtue of a party is that it requires clever men as leaders ; and as Mr. Churchill, with all his talents, has never possessed that of getting a following of his own, it is natural that he should be a little contemptuous of the whole Party system. Probably nobody was more sincerely sorry when the Coalition broke down ; that system suited him exceedingly well, and promised a comfort which mere reabsorption into the Conservative body could hardly bring. Within a Coalition Mr. Churchill could be himself ; within any party he must be, by an annoying fraction, more or less than himself. I suppose nobody even to-day would be bold enough to prophesy exactly where he may end, and it is curious to note that even in his most raspingly Radical days an observer like Mr. Gardiner, not then prone to suspicion of his party chiefs, could indulge speculation as to whether he had found his final resting-place in the Liberal party.

The other protagonists in the Tariff fight may be

classed as men who had passed their zenith or men who had not yet attained it.   On the one side were the bewildered Devonshire, the now feeble Harcourt, Ritchie and Hicks-Beach, the Fowlers and Morleys and such.   On the other side was one figure to become considerable, Bonar Law, but it was not until some time after he had become leader of the party that his full stature was apparent.   Perhaps, however, I may take a little notice here of two men less interesting and significant (in my opinion) than those considered under separate headings.   But, in fact, they had very little part in the Tariff Reform controversy, neither of them being well qualified to shout arguments on an intricate subject from public platforms.   They were both rather men of the study than of the arena, and while both held important administrative posts it cannot be said that politics gave either his chief title to distinction.

Mr. Birrell we have, happily, still with us.   But a young man of letters who should address some note to this distinguished essayist should be excused if he forgot to inscribe the envelope with a " Right Honourable." Yet round about 1906 Mr. Birrell's position in politics was such that *Punch*, without being ridiculous, could depict him as a knight in armour, the one dependable champion " C.-B." could find to send to the Irish Office.   He had failed with an Education Bill, but in the manner that wins as much respect as victory. Ireland was destined to prove his political grave, but even there, for some years, he contrived, thanks to some luck, much good humour, and a gift of effectively snubbing critics, to make things comfortable for himself and not unpleasant for other people.

He was helped by his physique, which expressed what Pope called a " strong benevolence."   There was something at once burly and kindly that freed his arguments for letting well alone from the suspicion of cowardice or mere bewilderment. And he was the master of a kind of satire which, polite in form, was deadly in effect. Bonar Law once charged him with obscuring truth with a shower of epigrams. " Epigrams—surely the Right Honourable gentleman means platitudes," interjected Birrell. Surely modesty was never more irritatingly contemptuous. Mr. Birrell was, in fact, rather easily moved to contempt, and despite a decided gift for humour was very far from the tolerance which generally goes with it. I mean, of course, tolerance of individual stupidities and insolences. His patience with collective offences of the kind was infinite and on the whole wise. He was continually being urged to do drastic things in Ireland, but steadily refused. True, at the last he came down badly, but even yet it cannot be said with assurance that he was not wise, for the greater part of his tenure of office, in refusing to see the things he did not want to see. His policy was really non-government, or at least the minimum of government. It provided no solution for the Irish problem, but it did at least make possible that afternoon on which John Redmond offered England the Irish sword against Germany.

A less interesting figure, though on much the same plane politically, was James Bryce, who, after being " a transient and embarrassed phantom " in Ireland, was sent to Washington as ambassador, and there won all American hearts. The character of Lord Bryce, and the way his generation treated him, has always reminded me of another distinguished and learned Scot—that Sir James Mackintosh who is the subject of one of the less successful of Macaulay's *Essays*. Both were very learned. Both were very lucky. Both had enormous chances of which they failed to take full advantage. And both enjoyed a degree of consideration which the most brilliant success, in action or speculation, might not have ensured. " He distinguished himself highly in Parliament," says Macaulay of Mackintosh, " but nevertheless Parliament was not exactly the sphere for him. . . . His luminous and philosophical disquisition on the Reform Bill was spoken to empty benches. Those, indeed, who had the wit to keep their seats picked up hints which, skilfully used, made the fortunes of more than one speech. But ' it was caviare to the general.' " Mackintosh, I suspect, had more in him than Bryce, and certainly he possessed a happier style ; but Bryce was a man of the same fulness, the same proneness to elaboration, the same tendency to exhaust his hearer. Macaulay says again of Mackintosh : " His mind was a vast magazine, admirably arranged. Everything was there, and everything was in its place. . . . It would have been strange, indeed, if you had asked for anything that was not to be found in that vast store-house. The article which you required was not only there. It was ready. It was in its own proper department. In a moment it was brought down, unpacked, and displayed. . . . He did not find but bring." Compare Gardiner of Bryce : " Across the field of vision flit the shadows of the past—warriors, statesmen, sages—and the famous figures of the present. Perhaps you mention, let us say, the *Civis Romanus sum* speech of Palmerston and instantly the whole story of Don Pacifico's bedstead is unfolded with all its bearings on European politics. . . . He has taken the world for his province, but he has taken it only to make you a freeman of it." And so forth and so on.

All this admiration is for powers of mind admirable so far as they go, but perhaps scarcely worth such fervency of worship. Rapid comprehension, a strong memory, and some taste often give an impression of an intellectual vigour which, in fact, is rarely associated with those qualities in their exaggeration. Macaulay was surprised to find that in Mackintosh's *Fragment of English History* the narrative was " better executed than the disquisitions." In fact it was not surprising in Mackintosh, and it was not surprising in Bryce, about whom the remark might with equal truth have been made. The mind which accumulates so much fuel has generally little fire, and one who has not sufficiently considered the difference between absorption and creation understands with difficulty why it is that men extolled for their vast learning are often so trivial and obvious and unoriginal (and above all so prolix) in their reflections.

Mackintosh founded his life on a lucky youthful book, the *Vindiciæ Gallicæ*—a Whig counterblast to Burke's *Reflections* on the French Revolution. It was not nearly so good a book as Burke's, but it was, naturally, more sane, and it met a distinct need as no other Whig writer seemed able to do. Bryce was equally fortunate. *The Holy Roman Empire* is not a good book. It is written with a bias that would have damned it had it been published fifty years later. But it also happened to meet a need. It filled a blank in popular reading. Before it was written the subject it dealt with could only be followed through a number of works various in everything else but their generally forbidding character. So *The Holy Roman Empire* has gone through a multitude of editions, and remains, most improperly, the popular authority on the subject of German relations with Italy—improperly because the worship of all things German which pervades it is definitely misleading. Yet, such as it is, *The Holy Roman Empire* gave Bryce a European reputation. His *American Commonwealth* gave him an American one ; and enabled him to be, on the human side at least, a highly successful ambassador. As to the other side, even his biographer seems to be in some doubt.

A last parallel. Mackintosh, the Whig of the Revolution, lived to oppose the Reform Bill, and to speak against Catholic emancipation. Bryce, in his study of post-war democracy, seems to have become almost a Conservative.

LORD STRATHCONA .

I MET Lord Strathcona but once, when I tried to interest him in a certain artistic scheme. It was, of course, his money I wanted. Mildly interested, he expressed a willingness to give two hundred and fifty pounds. I wanted ten thousand pounds. Very gently he put aside any such idea. " The thing, if done at all," he said, " should be done by corporate effort. I could, of course, contribute the sum you mention. But I should prefer only to play the part of an ordinary citizen in a matter which is, if an interest at all, the interest of all citizens." The result was that he did not part even with the two hundred and fifty pounds.

But when that matter was disposed of he went on talking about things in general, and especially on the fleeting nature of everything. " My chief impression of life," he said, " is how short it is." He was nearly ninety at the time, with a stirring past behind him and a present full of quiet bustle. But in a calm moment he was one with the old sages. Life, at its fullest and briskest, what is it ?

Those who saw Lord Strathcona and Mount Royal only in public would not have suspected him of contemplating, as Mr. Pecksniff would say, " the silent tomb." During his term of office as High Commissioner of Canada in London, he was one of the best-known figures in the social life of the capital. No public function was complete without his venerable and commanding presence. But it was as a figure only that he was known. While all spoke of him reverently, yet it was always in language of picturesque and mythological vagueness. He was an Empire builder ; he was the very archetype of the self-made man, the perfect hero according to Dr. Samuel Smiles ; he was the ambassador of Our Lady of the Snows ; he was the Grand Old Man of the Dominion. For the stranger who wanted to learn how he had built the Empire there was the one definite piece of information—that he had linked ocean to ocean by causing the construction of the Canadian Pacific Railway. There would also be mentioned the fact that during the South African War a regiment of horse, which bore his name, had been raised by his munificence.

Further inquiries were, as a rule, fruitless. Lord Strathcona, as I found during my solitary interview, was not averse from talking, and full ready to fall into the reminiscent manner, particularly for the benefit of young men who had their way to make in life. Recalling his own distant youth, he would speak of the value of hard work and thrift, and, again, of the importance of a mother's influence in moulding character. Listeners went away with the impression of a massive simplicity and guilelessness. Here was " colonial " virtue incarnate : the stout heart, the sane and healthy mind, the strong nerve, the Puritan cleanliness—Miles Standish without his sword. He brought with him the keen fresh air of the open spaces, which (and not the stove-heated sickliness in which Canadians spend so much of their lives) is pictured as the special privilege and delight of those new British nations which are presumed to have none of the guile of our older, more complex, more frousty civilisation.

Such was the first and prevailing impression. But even in his moments of personal expansion, there might occur a fancy that he was maintaining certain decent barriers behind which none might spy. " Lord

Strathcona," wrote an ex-viceroy, " has always shown a reticence regarding his personal experiences, and a dislike to recording his own performances." One of his biographers, after a gallant struggle with scanty material, has made apology to possibly disappointed readers with a remark concerning his hero's " unconquerable modesty " and " aversion to publicity." And perhaps I may more conveniently acknowledge here the heavy debt I owe to Mr. W. T. R. Preston, author of *The Life and Times of Lord Strathcona,* for the details of many transactions which would have been obscure without him.

Yet the white-bearded veteran of the London dinner-tables had behind him a career scarcely less interesting than that of Cecil Rhodes. Donald Alexander Smith, a native of Forres in the County of Elgin, was born in the year 1820. At eighteen, having obtained a junior clerkship in the Hudson Bay Company through the influence of an uncle, he left for Canada, or, to be more precise, for the bleak peninsula of Labrador. Details of his life for the next thirty years are scarce. His devotion to duty seems to have been considerable, and the hard work he was afterwards to eulogise no doubt was the foundation of his later fortunes. That he practised stern thrift is not strange ; in those sub-Arctic regions there was small scope for any but senseless extravagance, and nothing Smith did was senseless. Gradually he won the Company's esteem. " However poor the post might be," it has been said, " Donald Smith always showed a balance on the right side of the ledger." From being a clerk he rose to be a chief trader in the Company's employ, and then to be a chief factor. At forty-eight he was selected as head executive officer of the Company in Canada. Thus far he had lived an arduous life. He had been under an iron discipline. He had known the pains of

o

cold and hunger, and the horrors of solitude. Any ordinary man of his age, with such experience behind him, would surely have begun to think of a time when it would be possible for him to rest and be thankful. The money he had earned was sagaciously invested. There was no further promotion the Company could give him. What better than to hold for another ten years or so to the well-remunerated, responsible and dignified position he had won, governing an area as large as four or five of the larger European countries put together, and thereafter to retire on a handsome pension ?

But for Donald A. Smith at forty-eight life was just beginning. Great changes were toward in British North America, and he was one of those fortunate beings who always see how something can be made out of every opportunity. For a long time the Company's territorial sovereignty over vast stretches of land had been resented by patriotic Canadians, but the resentment had been tempered by a belief that, after all, these regions were just a frozen wilderness. The Company had kept its secret well. White strangers trespassed at their peril on its domains, for the Indians had been taught by its agents that any " paleface " who was not a Hudson Bay agent was an enemy to their kind. Thus of the actual and potential wealth of the north-west territories little was known, except to the few who had been managing them and had already begun their exploitation. And, of course, nobody knew quite as much as Smith, the head man upon the spot.

When the Dominion Government did acquire sovereignty over these lands, the sum paid in cash was but a million and a half dollars, and shareholders in Canada and England talked of confiscation. Of the immense value of the blocks of land which the Company was to hold as private property, neither they nor the Government were remotely aware. All but everybody immediately started to sell Hudson Bay shares for anything they would fetch. The exception was Donald A. Smith, who bought and bought and bought. Naturally, his name did not appear in the transactions, but during the period of panic he was able to obtain holdings that gave him a controlling interest. Thenceforward he was no longer the Company's first servant. He was its master.

Of the Riel rebellion that followed transfer to the Dominion of the north-west little need be said, though in the stirring events of the time Smith was deeply concerned. The Indians and half-bloods flew to arms because it had always been impressed upon them that save under the Company's protection there was no safety for them. Various officers of the Company may even have been as foolish as to continue propagating this notion after the negotiations for sale had been completed. But Smith was assuredly not of their number. In due course he received the medal awarded to the chief agent in the suppression of this mad rising. His honour and his interests alike would have prevented him from countenancing a folly which disturbed, and threatened to postpone, the tranquil consummation of a a deal to which he was the most successful party. Donald A. went forward to the Canadian House of Commons as first M.P. for the new west. Riel fled the country, to which he was to return only to be executed as a malefactor.

Some two years after the future Lord Strathcona entered Parliament a first-class political scandal was revealed at Ottawa. It was found that Sir John Macdonald, the Conservative Premier, had promised to grant a charter for construction of the Canadian Pacific Railway to a wealthy shipowner, by name Allan, and in return was to receive large sums of money for the party chest. The Liberals, of course, made all possible capital out of the affair, but as the means by which the incriminating correspondence had been brought to light were rather shadier than the affair itself, it seemed probable that the Government would survive the shock. Whilst one side cried out on bribery, the other retaliated with talk about suborning private secretaries and stealing private letters, and the party ranks were at first unbroken. They would have remained unbroken but for Donald Alexander Smith.

When the matter was under debate in the Commons, Mr. Smith rose quietly in his place among the Conservatives, and began in the approved style with an earnest denunciation of those who had violated confidences. With every sentence he spoke the Tory cheers grew louder, and Liberal hearts sank. Then, after a single " But," he changed his note. He threw party considerations on one side. He rose superior to attachments and prejudices. His condemnation of the corrupt Government he had theretofore supported was cold, terrible, deadly and, because there was no taint in it of partisanship, utterly damning. Without waiting for a vote of confidence, Sir John Macdonald resigned.

The subsequent elections resulted in a Liberal victory, and among supporters of the new Government none was more influential than the man from the west who had overthrown the Conservatives. No more, of course, was heard of a railway charter for the unlucky individual who had financed the beaten and discredited party. Mackenzie, the new Prime Minister, was, indeed, resolved that the line should be built by the State itself, and the public as a whole was with him. Governments, however, move slowly, and whilst Smith was busily increasing his fortunes by speculations in the United States, repeating his Hudson Bay coup

over the St. Paul and Minneapolis Railway, construction
of the C.P.R. was delayed. British Columbia threatened secession if the link with the rest of Canada was
not provided, and many efforts were made to hustle
the Liberals into sanctioning the undertaking as a
private enterprise. Smith himself, as an influential
member of the party, tried to persuade his leader that
the work should be handed over to a syndicate, but
it was all in vain. Mackenzie insisted on his policy of
hurrying slowly, and antedated the Earl of Oxford with
advice to wait and see.

The Conservatives, on the contrary, were for immediate action, and giving a chance to one or more of
the capitalists who were so anxious to assist in the
great Imperial task. But their ban on Smith was
absolute. When another general election was toward,
vast sums of money were at their disposal for expenses.
Much came from persons believed to be interested in
railway building. But there was not a Tory candidate
who would not have lost his seat rather than touch a
penny from the man whom they execrated as a renegade.
Smith, for his part, stood again as a supporter of the
Liberals, and was once more victorious, but this time
he was one of a minority. The Conservatives were in
power once more, and their first business would have
to be completion of arrangements for construction of
the C.P.R. by a syndicate.

There were at least two tenders between which the
Government could, in theory, choose. But, in practice,
the Government was not free. The contract less
favourable to the Dominion had to be approved because
the syndicate presenting it had come to an understanding
with the party leaders before the polls, and Sir John
Macdonald could not face a second exposure. When
ratified, the agreement provided for payment to the
contractors of a twenty-five million dollar subsidy, a

land grant of as many acres, a monopoly in the western territories for twenty years, and exemption from taxation for a like period. But the contract, as it was presented to Parliament, did not bear the name of Smith. Only when the last possible concession was thought to have been extracted from the Government was it made known that " Donald A." was the head and centre of the syndicate. " By reason of his own express wish," says one of his reverential biographers, that interesting fact had been suppressed till the eleventh hour and beyond it.

Not for the first time his " unconquerable modesty " had stood him in good stead. He had kept in the background during the Hudson Bay panic, when a single boast from him about the property he was acquiring would have halted his advance in fortune by putting a thousand competitors against him. He had kept in the background again over the C.P.R. negotiations, when one sign of his secret exultation would have put a full stop to the whole affair. With grim tenacity he had worked for his stupendous triumph. Thanks to his intervention the Tory Government had been stopped from carrying out its bargain with Sir Hugh Allan. Afterwards, it was his syndicate with its power of the purse that helped the Tories back to power when the Liberals were refusing all dealings with private contractors. Years later, when Lord Strathcona was High Commissioner in London, special confidence was reported in him because he was a non-party man. Truly, he had belonged to both parties, and for a time at least, whilst sitting and voting with the one, his bounty had been showered on the other. With rare tact he had concealed from the recipients its source, and his example suffices to show how false may be the saying that success all depends upon advertisement.

But in the hour of his triumph Smith was beset by sundry troubles. First, there was an election petition in which he had to defend himself against a charge of corrupt practice. At the first trial the verdict was in his favour, but unfortunately a local journalist discovered that the successful litigant had a while before lent the judge the paltry sum of four thousand dollars, and, when an appeal was made to the Supreme Court, Smith lost his seat. Standing again as an Independent, he was defeated. Then arose difficulties regarding the railway. European investors were shy of what they imagined a " wild-cat " scheme, and the Canadian Government had to be approached once more for pecuniary assistance. The difficulty was that Macdonald and the Conservatives had not forgiven Smith his original apostasy. Indeed, their rage against him had only increased with years. " Ratting " had been bad enough, but since ratting he had made them his marionettes. What chance had the C.P.R. syndicate, which had obtained so much from them already, to obtain more now that Donald A. was known to be its moving spirit ?

None the less, with grey top-hat in hand, Donald A. had to wait upon the Conservative Premier with a humble prayer for aid in a financial crisis. Sir John Macdonald was too much a statesman to refuse him. It would have been ruinous to Canada if the famous railway enterprise had had to be abandoned for lack of funds after it had once been started in earnest. It would have been ruinous for the Conservatives if the syndicate to which they had entrusted the enterprise had crashed into bankruptcy. So Sir John agreed that the Government should rescue it with a loan of thirty million dollars. One condition, however, was attached. Smith was to stand for the House of Commons, in a Montreal constituency, and on the platform in Canada's chief city was to give testimony to his unbounded confidence in the Conservative leader whom he had formerly denounced for dishonesty over the Allan scandal, the Conservative leader who had shouted in the House of Commons : " That fellow Smith is the greatest liar I ever met."

Donald A. Smith did not recoil. But it is not surprising, as Mr. Preston, the biographer already quoted, notes, that when in time to come he sought a house in Scotland, he selected a site commanding a view of Glencoe, where once upon a time so many of the Macdonald clan had been butchered, nor that when he was named for a peerage he expressed a wish that Glencoe might be the title !

The loan, however, relieved him and the syndicate from their troubles. Work upon the famous railway was continued at top speed, and in 1887 he had the satisfaction of driving the golden nail into the final rail of the track which joined east to west at last. With termini at Montreal and Vancouver, crossing the Rockies at over 5500 feet, having a total length of nearly 3000 miles, it was one of the greatest achievements of the century, and, in the words of another Canadian statesman, it owed its completion and success to " the indomitable pluck and energy and determination, both financially and in every other way, of Sir Donald Smith." The farmers of the west for a while grumbled at its freight rates (twenty-eight cents per bushel for wheat from Winnipeg to the nearest lake port, about 600 miles away, when Smith's American railroad was carrying American grain at less than half the cost), but then farmers will always grumble. That the C.P.R. brought Smith colossal wealth need scarcely be emphasised, though it has been denied by persons anxious to show how millionaires flourish on their losses. The total value of his personal estate at death was proved at over four and a half millions, and this did not include a holding of one million in the Anglo-Persian Oil Company, which, with some other stocks, he had doubtless distributed during his lifetime. " Simple, honest, clear-sighted, practical as a plumber, stable as the hills " was Mr. A. G. Gardiner's verdict on him, and he is quoted by the same writer as saying : " I would rather be a very good man than a very rich man." He had, perhaps, one weakness : it would seem that he was never quite contented.

Sir Donald Smith arrived as Canadian High Commissioner in London during the 'nineties, and received his peerage at the Diamond Jubilee. With the advent of the Laurier Government his recall was expected, for the whole weight of the C.P.R. had been used at the elections against the Liberals, but the new Premier was too shrewd and temperate to allow himself the luxury of showing malice. Lord Strathcona's record proved him to be a disturbing element in Canadian politics, and there were advantages in having him on the far-side of the Atlantic. In England, on the other hand, his presence made for the prestige of the Dominion. Only extreme old age was allowed to take him from his post when he had passed his ninetieth year.

And there is no doubt that Lord Strathcona did make England, or, anyhow, the part of England that mattered, think respectfully of Canada. With admirable candour he used to insist that Canada was no El Dorado, but a land where success was the reward of hard endeavour. None the less, just enough of his story was known to make people understand that, for men of the right sort, success was there in waiting. Perhaps for his successors and for the High Commissioners of other Dominions he created precedents that were hard to follow. At Knebworth, the ancestral mansion of the Lyttons, he entertained on a truly lordly scale, and there, where

Pym and Cromwell, men who, like himself, had known
how to combine politics and business, had once fore-
gathered, he was the right man in the right place.   His
conduct of Canadian affairs was by some counted
autocratic.   Canadians of whom for some reason or
other he disapproved found such favours as invitations
to coronations and royal parties hard to obtain.
Callers at his office, whose credentials were not obviously
of the best, were, too, sometimes treated in a cavalier
fashion.   Efforts to communicate with the Ottawa
Government save through his department were bitterly
resented.   But, when all is said, it would have been
absurd to expect mild complaisance from one who, like
Lord Strathcona, had fought and won in a long uphill
battle.   And from the English point of view, at least,
because he seemed to be Canada personified, his autocratic ways were more than pardonable.   With Chamberlain, Rhodes and Kipling he must be ranked as of
the four who made Empire popular in England.   Those
who remember his patriarchal mien will realise that he
did, too, what was beyond the genius of the others.
Kipling made men think of Imperialism as a gallant
adventure.   Smith persuaded even Little Englanders
that it was compatible with that most blest of combinations—moral austerity and a money-making instinct.

FIVE EDITORS

THE first decade was rich in editors, real, if not " great," in the sense that the adjective is dedicated to that rather boring celebrity Delane. The nearest greatness in that way was assuredly Mr. J. Alfred Spender, of the old green *Westminster*. Spender's reign extended from 1896 to 1922, but he was perhaps at the very height of his powers and his influence during the period under review. What is a great editor ? I should define him as a man who, without perhaps doing anything in particular, and certainly without interfering fussily with his subordinates, manages to imprint his personality on everything permitting of the expression of personality that appears in his paper. The great editor therefore must be to a very large extent an uncontrolled editor. He must have the last word in everything. Nobody under him must suspect that there is some lively intelligence in the background prompting or correcting him. The moment that occurs there is a want of coherence which the reader feels, though he may not be able to explain. " Just like a man with a tall hat and brown boots," a shrewd critic said to me, in relation to a newspaper which, while priding itself on its tone and traditions, was making frantic efforts to reach the populace. Such incongruity must always come of a divided control. If, on the other hand, one mind rules, things fall into their proper relation without much effort. The sort of man likely to take a sane and proportioned view of politics is likely to see the smaller things of life in a more or less just relation to the larger.   Sport will take its proper place and space ; finance will be treated rather in the spirit of the economist than in that of the tipster ; a film actor will automatically yield the *pas* to a statesman ; the best seller will not be always the book of the day ; advertising doctors and popular scientists will have to puff themselves elsewhere.   If, again, a newspaper is under the full control of a person with no kind of philosophy, but with an unerring instinct for " what the public wants," it will probably do very well indeed from its point of view.   The one certain failure from all points of view is the paper which lacks this unencumbered directing personality, and the heavy mortality of once great journals during the first fifteen years or so of the twentieth century was the result of foolish efforts to appeal at once to the excellent man who likes Gibbon, and to the perhaps not less worthy man who likes *Tit-Bits*.

I know nothing of Mr. Spender's relations with the people who found the money for the *Westminster*. Judging from the contempt he often expressed for the hirelings of the " syndicated press," I should imagine they were very enviable.   But, at any rate, he was enough of the autocrat to make his newspaper in every particular a faithful reflection of his own personality. I would not say he was as great a man as the late Lord Morley.   He was certainly not so great a writer.   But he was surely a far greater editor.   In fact, it is only a species of snobbery that has given Morley the reputation, still clinging to him, of an inspired conductor of a newspaper.   Really, he was a very bad editor indeed. He seems to have been regarded with more awe than affection by his staff.   But he could never make his staff do what he wanted.   He lacked altogether that power of influencing without acting which is the secret of most management, and particularly of this kind of management. He had, as his biographers admit, no interest in three-fourths of the matter that filled his paper. He had no " nose for news." He was quite without the journalistic instinct. He " looked with infinite contempt on most of the trifles that interest the British tomfool." All that was to be expected. All that might have been present, and Morley might still have been, in a certain genre, a great editor. But he did not even know his own particular business of keeping his policy straight. He admitted Stead to be his chief lieutenant—Stead who thought on almost every subject in terms impossible for the philosophic Radical even to understand. And when he was away Stead played the devil with everything Morley held dear—eulogised the Tzar, quizzed Morley's pet politicians, went after every kind of strange god. No; Spender was, no doubt, a little like Morley in his attitude to the British tomfool. He cared little for " news." There is a story, no doubt apocryphal, that during the days of the censorship the *Westminster* published in a mild form information on account of which another evening paper, elaborating and improving, was suspended. The next day, it is said, Spender was heard to exclaim : " We've had a narrow escape, and it must be a lesson to us. That's the first time a piece of news has appeared in the *Westminster*, and I'll take good care it is the last." But though he looked on his paper as more an organ of opinion than a news-sheet, he had, in a remarkable degree, the faculty of making his personality felt everywhere. It was extremely difficult to tell when he was on a holiday. He must sometimes have been ill. He must occasionally have been a-weary. Even so delightful a job as his must have palled at times. Yet for years the *Westminster* never varied. It remained always on the same high table-land of bland sanity, intelligent limitation and cultivated Philistinism. There may have been times when, as official Liberal organ, it experienced a doubt as to what was official Liberalism to-day and what might be official Liberalism to-morrow. But no trace of such trouble ever disturbed the urbane flow. There always emerged, to use one of Mr. Spender's favourite expressions, a perfect example of what people call (now, alas, sometimes with a tinge of disrespect) the statesmanlike utterance.

I have spoken of intelligent limitation. Mr. Spender's chief limitation was class bias. I remember he once wrote a charming article discussing what period an intelligent man would have liked best to live through. His fancy, I think, was the period extending from 1844 to 1914. The person born in the early 'forties would have come in for Free Trade and would have escaped the Great War. It was an illuminating statement. The seventy years in question were not wholly jolly for the mass of the working-class. Great numbers of the kind of people who were more or less independent in the 'forties had become proletarians and mere wage-earning dependents by the 'nineties. And of the wage-earners, whole masses lived far harder lives, far less secure lives, lives sweetened by far less of good things, material and intellectual, than is the case even in these profoundly unsatisfactory times. On the other hand, it may be doubted whether the aristocrat was better off in the last days of the century than he was in the 'forties. He could get better treatment if he broke his leg in the hunting-field. He was buried with as much pomp and respect if he broke his neck. He enjoyed a more varied table. He could be more comfortably migratory and perambulatory. But, on the other hand, such men enjoy power, and his power was less. Such men enjoy social pre-eminence, and his social pre-eminence was less. Such men enjoy the thought that they can hand

down to their children and their children's children an
undiminished birthright, and if his own future was not
seriously menaced, a certain threat always lay over that
of his family.   But the middle-class as a whole did
certainly gain during those seventy years ; and any
intelligent member of the middle-class could, at any
time during those years, look forward to much.   He
might even change his class.   Now, to Mr. Spender,
though he himself probably never realised it, the welfare
of humanity and the welfare of the upper middle-class of
England were very nearly synonymous terms.   His
vision of the perfect world was one of undisputed
middle-class hegemony.   The aristocrat was to be shorn
of his privileges chiefly that the middle-class, as the
brain and backbone of the country, might the better
direct its destinies, holding the lower orders in benevolent tutelage.   There should be no barrier, of course,
to exclude fit recruits from the masses ; even the
Janissaries were too wide-minded for that, and should
an English Liberal, Christian in morality if not in
dogma, fall below the heathen Turk ?   But what
was the use of being the son of a Bath doctor
and a Balliol honours man, to say nothing of having a brain first-rate in its way, unless these things
counted ?   It is, by the way, the cruellest satire
I have ever encountered on our system of high
education that of the Spender brothers Alfred, in-
comparably the most talented, did less well at Oxford
than Harold.   If Alfred had been a wayward genius
one could understand it ; but how the academic mind
in such perfection escaped the academic recognition
deemed meet for a much less exalted example of the
same kind of mind is frankly incomprehensible to me.
But to resume.   Mr. Spender, the Bath doctor's son
and the Balliol honours man, could see the Duke of
Somerset as a mischievous anachronism whom it was

desirable to exclude from political power and to tax out of existence. But he was probably rather further than the Duke of Somerset himself from any conception of a majority rule under which the majority should really have its way. He was all for Labour while Labour behaved itself. He was quite sure that Codlin and not Short was the proper depository of Labour's confidence. But it was clearly absurd that Labour should set up for itself, instead of finding its true blessedness under the leadership of the Liberal intelligentsia. And in this regard he contributed more than most men to a dangerous illusion from which the Liberal party is not yet entirely free. His rather rigid mind would not grasp the fact that the conditions of the late Victorian times were not inevitable and fixed, but accidental and transitory. Chance had made the first representatives of the working-classes look rather to the Liberals than to the Conservatives, and he concluded that it would always be so. He could not, apparently, understand that since Liberalism stood in essence for a fair field and no favour, it was an excellent creed for the expansive middle-class, but much less satisfactory for the masses, who, through the very success of Liberalism on its economic side, had reached a position in which only a very few individuals could possibly hope to better their status by competitive exertions, and must, therefore, rely increasingly on combinations to improve or even maintain their conditions. In proportion as they realised the true nature of the case, they must inevitably treat the Liberal, not as an ally seeking similar ends with a trifle less enthusiasm, but as an enemy to be extirpated—an enemy more dangerous than the Conservative himself.

With the Victorian scheme of things crumbling in this as in other ways, Mr. Spender suffered increasing discomfort. The Progressive found himself casting

pathetic glances backwards; the Liberal, in his intact
orthodoxy, became the one true Conservative. But in
the early years of the century this strain had not yet
grown painful, and Mr. Spender could still think of
himself as living in the world's luckiest era. On almost
everything there was a plausible case for him to argue.
He had a fairly definite ideal to defend, a fairly definite
enemy to attack. And there was probably never a
journalist better fitted to present a Party case. It was
not a matter of giving up to party what was meant for
mankind. For mankind there was hardly enough of
Mr. Spender to go round ; when, as in his *Comments of
Bagshot*, he deals with universal things, he is not at
his best. But in the service of a political combination
in which he genuinely believed, a combination with a
creed that, in its purity, entirely satisfied his intellectual
and moral being, he was emphatically in his right place.
He had every strength save that of passion, and every
weapon save that of humour.

Mr. Spender was a great editor. I should not apply
that adjective to Mr. A. G. Gardiner of the *Daily News*.
Yet he was in many ways a remarkable success in the
seat first occupied, during a few uneasy months, by
Charles Dickens. The *Daily News* had been rather
poorly served for some years when Mr. Cadbury, who
had bought the paper, decided on a bold experiment.
A young Blackburn journalist, who knew nothing of
London, and perhaps not too much of other things,
was suddenly translated to Bouverie Street. In some
ways the selection was abundantly justified. The paper
cast off at once all the dullness which it had accumulated. It throbbed with moral purpose. It sparkled
with cleverness. Its editor was emphatically a writing
man, and knew what was good writing in other people,

P

Nobody could have been in less intellectual sympathy with Mr. Chesterton. Nobody could have been further removed from the fundamental convictions of Mr. Belloc. Yet for some years these three brilliant people appreciated and co-operated with each other. Writing, Mr. Gardiner has always understood. Men and politics, I think, he has generally misunderstood. You read those admirable character sketches of his, and are charmed with their sheer dexterity, what I may call their instinctive virtuosity. Every quotation comes in as naturally and inevitably as if its place had been fore-seen before the pen touched paper. Every story, even if it be a familiar one, gets a new charm in the telling. You have the impression of somebody who, it may be, is not on dining terms with anybody or anything, but is on the pleasantest tea-drinking terms with all the world. Not an intellectual millionaire, as Disraeli would have said, but with an inexhaustible pocketful of sixpences. You go on—or at least I go on—in sheer delight until something occurs to you—or at least to me. And that something is that it is all wrong. The proportion is at fault. Fundamentals are mini-mised into incidentals. Incidentals are exaggerated into fundamentals. One lawyer on the make becomes a Liberal knight-errant. Another lawyer on the make is transformed into the very Satan of a malignant Toryism. Lord Hugh Cecil parades as a mediæval mystic. Lord Leverhulme is at bottom a merry little man who loves a romp with the children. King Edward is just a pleasant, bluff gentleman a little bored by unmeaning duties. Mr. Lloyd George at one time cares for nothing but the people, and at another for nothing but his career. Mr. Gardiner thinks too ill of a squire, and too well of one of the less pleasant members of the middle-class who had become a peer of the realm through cornering something. When this less pleasant

member of the middle-class happens also to be an
" old-fashioned Puritan " with a complicated " simplicity of life," and a tendency to ordain garden cities
for his employees, the enthusiasm becomes a little
tiresome. Less trying, no doubt, but somewhat tiresome is his excessive respect for the intellectual millionaire—the man who has amassed learning as the millionaire has amassed gold, and flashes it about. I can
hardly take seriously, of course, his famous tribute to
that highly amiable and respectable person, the late
Viscount Bryce. Bryce was a man of very wide
information, who had on the whole a great deal of luck,
in the way of friends as well as of offices and copyright
fees. Far be it from me to decry him. But I do
confess to feeling a certain animosity against Bryce when
I first came across the passage in which Mr. Gardiner
extols his conversational powers. Mr. Gardiner says
that the true test of a talker is whether you would like to
have him as a comrade on a desert island. " On the
whole," he proceeds, " the companion of my choice
would be Mr. Bryce, for with him he would bring the
story of the ages and the constant cheerfulness of a
mind filled with a radiance of its own. With such a
companion the days would pass as unwearyingly as the
nights with Scheherazade, and when the sail of the
deliverer appeared above the horizon it would be greeted
almost like an intrusion upon an unfinished and delightful talk." Now I will hold, under persecution, that the
natural and healthy man, on a desert island, would end
by killing anybody who talked, with cocoanuts and
breadfruit to gather and prepare, in the way which is
permissible and agreeable at a London dinner-table.
Even the " delightful and unaffected freshness " of
Viscount Bryce would not have saved him had he
invited one, in such circumstances, to " pass spiritually
into the universe with the most accomplished of guides."

But the introduction of Scheherazade is the real point. The vision it calls up of Viscount Bryce in his pyjamas soothing a thousand and one tropical nights with gay legends of the Hohenstaufen Cæsars and acute dissections of the American polity seems to suggest that Mr. Gardiner, with all his brilliant wit, has an uncertain sense of humour.

His strictly political work naturally gave less scope for his individuality. He was as middle-class as Mr. Spender, but drew the line somewhat lower, and his sympathies embraced also the genuine poor, though he was at one with Mr. Spender in thinking them the fit objects of " social reform " engineered by the Liberal party rather than the possible masters of their own destiny. He was not without that belatedness which is so common a " Progressive " characteristic. His democratic fury was chiefly roused by an order which even before the War was manifestly decaying. " The Dukes " were, for him, the enemy; Chamberlain's German-made tariff scheme was merely an attempt to return to the old Protection. But, after all, Mr. Gardiner is scarcely to be considered as a political thinker. His true distinction is that he has the most lively and graceful pen wielded on the Liberal side.

I have said that Mr. Gardiner's sense of humour is a little uncertain. The absence of this sometimes inconvenient quality is the first enormous asset of Mr. J. L. Garvin. He has a dozen talents, each of which might have made the fortunes of a lesser man ; but success so resounding and splendid as his could hardly have been possible, even with his gifts, had he been [cursed by a quality which, among other things, implies a capacity for ironical self-envisagement. Or, at least, though the success might have come otherwise, it would not have arrived in his particular way.

I suppose everybody knows that Mr. Garvin in his early days was a very wild Irishman indeed. On Tyneside there still linger memories of the gaunt young man, with intense eyes, who talked fiercely on Nationalist platforms about the Saxon oppressor. Parnell was his hero then, but he had nice things also to say about O'Donovan Rossa. I have sometimes encountered a dark theory based on these harmless facts. According to this view Mr. Garvin took in his youth an oath to destroy the British Empire, and his subsequent career can be explained on the assumption that he has ever since been trying to fulfil that vow. In his adolescence he was content with crude methods. Older and wiser grown, he has pursued more subtle ways of undermining the fabric of British power. Conceiving the Conservative party to be the one effective bulwark of the Empire, he has sought to subvert the Empire by subverting the party. And he has sought to subvert the party by giving it advice. Thus can be found a consistency in many apparent inconsistencies. Thus can be explained the disastrous counsel given in the Budget and Veto issues. Thus can be explained his efforts at one time to tie the party to some form of Home Rule and at another to deliver it, bound hand and foot, to the Carsonites.

Now I need hardly say that I reject with all decision this fantastic and sinister hypothesis. Nothing in Mr. Garvin's head, nothing in Mr. Garvin's heart, suggests the possibility of his being a life-long plotter in any cause, and whatever cause he may have espoused at any time, we may be sure that he espoused it in the fullest sincerity. He is incapable of guile. He is beyond all suspicion of artifice. He could neither speak nor act in bad faith or levity. His strange journalistic

Odyssey is to be explained on a much less far-fetched hypothesis. He is simply, I take it, one of those astoundingly clever men in whom the faculty of rapid comprehension is developed somewhat at the expense of the judgment. Such men see at a glance the implications up to a point of a new proposition. They grasp, with a swiftness which is the despair of less active minds, the possibilities of action on a new course. They can find at once justifications sufficient to convince themselves, and far more than sufficient to convince multitudes of others. But in this matter, as elsewhere, easy come is easy go. Caught by the new idea, such men discard without shame or regret all the ideas they held but a moment before. They turn to a new situation as a barrister does to a new brief, with a mind stripped of all prepossessions. But while that is the right way with briefs, which, by their nature, deal with a limited set of facts, it is less the right way with life, in which any fact may rapidly become relevant. It is a dangerous gift, this of being able to take an instantaneous glance down a long corridor of logical sequence, convinced that one has seen all that need be seen. It is as if a detective should satisfy himself by looking down the corridor of a hotel, without troubling about what may be hidden behind the locked doors on either side. This gift of rapid but imperfect comprehension, when combined with a generally high mentality and abounding vigour, has perhaps done more harm to the world than any other intellectual quality ; and part of the peril of the present time is that it is, of all intellectual qualities, the most apparent in our clever people. Mr. Wells is an example in literature ; every other statesman is an example in politics.

Mr. Garvin, then, has to begin with an unusual capacity of being attracted by a plausible idea, of thinking he has fully thought it out when he has but

imperfectly thought it in. Allied with this is a truly
magnificent fluency of expression, a superb mastery of
language that compels admiration, but also a delight
in it that sometimes carries him, as well as his reader,
off his feet. There is something further, not quite
easy to define. Mr. Chesterton once wittily said of
Frederick the Great that he was " something devilish
like a hero." I might do worse than adapt the image
to Mr. Garvin's case. He has something devilish like
earnestness. There can be no mistake concerning the
reality of the fever and passion he imports into his
writing. And yet the earnestness is not quite that of a
man who has slowly and painfully arrived at the final
heat of conviction. In his most complete abandon
there is still a certain reservation. The contortions of
the Sybil are genuine enough, but there is something in
the regularity of their rhythm that makes the cool
observer wonder whether after all the force that sways
her is something wholly beyond her control. Mr.
Garvin must feel, or he is the greatest actor of his time,
what he affects to feel in a moment of exaltation. Somebody has told me that he once declared, in tones that
left no possible doubt of his sincerity, that if putting his
right hand into the flames of the Constitutional smoke-
room fire would prevent the passage of the Parliament
Bill, he would make the sacrifice of that extremely useful
member. And yet how are we to account wholly for
that sudden change which would occasionally come
over him in his least-restrained days, when, the week
after he had been riding the Ulster high horse like the
fiercest galloper of them all, he would purr conciliation
for three mellifluous columns ? Was it something in
himself not himself that made for reasonableness ? But
if so, why did this mood declare itself, as a rule, when
there was no chance of conciliation, and why did it so
seldom arrive when the portents were really favourable ?

I give it up, only observing that whatever may be the explanation, it must be one which leaves no imputation against the least Machiavelian of all publicists.

That there is included in his queer complex of qualities a sort of sudden and profound wisdom which will break through at the most unexpected moments, can hardly be denied. Mr. Gardiner has made legitimate fun of Mr. Garvin's soul's need of hero-worship, and of his search for heroes in a world not too promising for such quest. But Mr. Garvin has undoubtedly an eye for a certain sort of man. He has an eye for a certain sort of book. He has an eye for the kernel of a situation. And every now and then he says something which really illuminates, not seldom something which truly helps. No man writing in the press can say a really great thing so greatly. But one result of his incapacity for self-criticism is that, while the great Garvin—who is great indeed—includes all sorts of little Garvins, he is never able to distinguish between his larger and lesser selves. To the great Garvin all the other Garvins are equally admirable. The least of them never brings a blush to the cheek of the greatest. And, really, that blush should have come more than once. It should have come when he raved against Mr. Redmond as the " dollar dictator " only a few weeks after he had been arguing for an Irish settlement which would have satisfied Mr. Redmond.

As he is in print, so is he in society, satisfied wholly with all the Garvins. It is not a vulgar self-satisfaction. Indeed, Mr. Garvin is, on occasion, a thought too humble. I once heard him apologise for his want of Greek to a company of rather dull academic men ; he went so far as to say he would give his left hand to be a competent Hellenist ; his right hand, as we saw, had already been contingently dedicated. But his mind apparently includes no machinery of censorship.

What happens to be there must come out. There is
no sort of check or sieve.. Most people are carried off
their feet by that conversational rush, and only remember when the occasion has passed that after all it is
given to no son of Adam to be quite so wise and omniscient as Mr. Garvin seems. Occasionally, of course,
he meets some person of warped or sceptical mind whom
he cannot charm. I shall always remember the expression with which a certain artist told me a story of
the eminent editor. " He came to my studio—alone,
mark you. He took up a jolly little Rembrandt
reproduction—Rembrandt's mother. We were alone,
I repeat, and I am an artist. ' Ah,' he said, ' this man
knew what it was to have a mother.' We were alone,
I say. If there had been any people of the kind who like
that sort of thing, I should have no complaint to make.
I should feel no sense of outrage. But to say that to
me, an artist, who knew that Rembrandt did it because
it was a nice bit of light and shade—really. These
things are not done."

Mr. Garvin is, in truth, a little given to such harmless
oblivion of the respect due to people of his own kind.
I remember him once calling an opposition editor an
" amateur " in political matters. It would have been,
of course, in order to stigmatise the poor man as a
ruffian and a traitor, but amateur—no. That is as
bad as Mr. Slurk's " ungrammatical twaddler." But
here is a more subtle instance of the same thing. I
heard Mr. Garvin once, at the luncheon-table, making
slighting reference to a poet of note who is now dead.
" That may or may not be," said a not undistinguished
man of letters who happened to be present. " But
at least he is a very considerable poet and I might almost
say a great one." " Not great," replied Mr. Garvin.
" Intelligent I would say, but not great. He has no
repose. You can't have greatness without repose."

And he went on, in his breathless way, to something else. Now I submit, with great respect, that this sort of thing is not fair in conversation. Indiscriminate indulgence in it would soon lead us back to primitive savagery. I have, of course, no manner of objection to a literary man saying, in print, that so-and-so " lacks the repose that goes with true greatness." It does not mean anything, but it comes in handily to round off a review in which one wants to convey that the author, though not so bad, is not so very good. After all, critics and such must live, or think they must, and with income-tax at present levels they find it at best a hard business ; it would be an impossible business were they always to take the trouble to say exactly what they mean. This about " repose " was the invention of some lazy, clever man, eagerly taken up by men less clever and still more lazy, as a formula of discrimination. To assert that Mr. Garvin as a writer is constantly saying such things is only to state that he is a busy, clever man, doing far too much. He can be excused all that in any case, and could be excused even more graciously were he not rich enough to afford a certain economy in *cliché*. The charge against him is simply his knocking down a fellow-craftsman, in a general company, with an old cabbage-stalk of this kind. I suppose the fact is partly to be explained on the ground that Mr. Garvin is not a writer pure and simple, and has caught some bad habits from his political friends. But the main reason, no doubt, why, despite the generally exquisite urbanity of his attitude towards a fellow-craftsman, he will occasionally treat one of his own trade as he would treat the general public is that incapacity for self-criticism to which I have referred.

Yet it is this automatic egotism, this surprising ease with which he accepts as final, and passes on as valuable, whatever may occur to a quick and brilliant brain, that

has contributed to his making. The mere volume of
his output has created an impression which a more
sparing and considered production might have failed
to achieve. Of course, sheer mass without quality
would not have sufficed. But always there is some
quality even in Mr. Garvin's hastiest writing. By
every calculation he should be wearisome, but he
contrives to escape being so—at any rate for long
together. I suppose it is because he enjoys himself so
immensely that he has so sensuous a delight in words,
so overpowering an intellectual pleasure in constructing
dilemmas, that part of his own feeling is communicated
to the reader. One has the same sort of gratification
in seeing a healthy boy at the tuck-shop or a pretty
woman at a modiste's—unless one happens, in the
latter case, to be paying the bill.

Besides, he is, in the genuine sense, a publicist, and
not a mere bravo. He loves his craft ; he sees dignity
in it ; he is didactic to the last fibre ; he really does
think of his paper as a pulpit and of himself as the bearer
of a message. And the wildness with which he can be
justly charged largely belongs to the pre-War period ;
to use his own expression, he has now more " repose."
But I often wonder what a Tory of the old school—
they still exist, and he must run across them at some
country-house or the other — really makes of this
brilliant Irishman as an exponent of the Conservative
faith.

Mr. Garvin is naturally dynamic. It was the tragedy
of the late St. Loe Strachey's life that he was not permitted to be as static as he might have wished. His great
misfortune was Joseph Chamberlain. Before that great
man, looking for an " issue " that should make people
forget the Boer War and the Education Act, first got

interested and then captivated by Tariff Reform, Mr.
Strachey's mind was unperplexed, his path clear.   It
was no rude or thorny way.   He had enjoyed everything that Oxford and Heaven—perhaps he might have
quarrelled with that order, and perhaps not—could give
him.   He had an excellent property in *The Spectator*.
It gave him reputation.   It yielded him a handsome
revenue.   A good many weekly reviews are maintained
on principles I do not profess to understand.   They
are kept by rich men who spend a lot of money on
them, but generally guard the secret of their pro-
prietorship as if there were a tinge of the disgraceful in
it.   I can understand the sacrifice, but not the attitude.
It may be pleasant to imitate on a small scale the
Emperor Hadrian, who maintained, along with his
gladiators and pugilists, a bevy of tame philosophers.
There may be something most attractive in being able
to say, in however small a voice, something that has a
meaning about things that matter.   So that I can readily
comprehend a millionaire saying : " There she is, the
beauty.   She costs me an unconscionable lot, but she is
well worth it."   What I cannot penetrate is the
mystery of secretive profusion.   Mr. Strachey enjoyed
a more rational satisfaction.   He was in the position
of being happily married to the mistress of his desire.
She was rich.   She was respected.   She gave him his
special position in life, and yet he was not simply her
husband.   For he was not just the owner of *The
Spectator*, or its editor ; he was *The Spectator*.   Few
people could think of *The Spectator* apart from him,
any more than they could think of him apart from *The
Spectator*.   There might be a few fogies here and
there who talked of the great days of Mr. Hutton, but
then there are always fogies to talk like that ; and no
serious critic could deny that the " traditions " of *The
Spectator* were being worthily upheld.   Its traditions

had always been enormously respectable. It had never had the flippancy of some reviews, the dubious commercialism of others. Moral conviction had always been its stock-in-trade. Rectitude was stamped on pages broad as the widest phylacteries. There was something in its very appearance, its exceedingly white paper and its neatly emphatic print, that emphasised the impression of its habitually decent and moderate style. Bibles and prayer-books are, I suppose, set up by compositors of the ordinary kind, knowing in the matter of racehorses, and printed by possibly profane machinists. But one never thinks of trouble over a " dirty " proof of Kings or a " pie " of the marriage service. So with *The Spectator*. One had, from the very " make-up," the illusion of something aloof from all human imperfection.

Mr. Strachey was eminently qualified to carry on the tradition. He was an excellent journalist in his way, with an eye for the " human " not generally developed in his bookish type. But one always thought of him as very much more than a journalist. One had the impression that he was not in the business, as they say, for his health. He was chiefly in it for the health of other people, and especially for their moral health. Mr. A. G. Gardiner, in perhaps his cruellest sketch, has made great play with Mr. Strachey's appeals to the " right-thinking man " ; and has not obscurely hinted at Pecksniffery. I should not say Mr. Strachey was ever in the least a Pecksniff. A man is only a hypocrite when he assumes a virtue he knows he does not possess. Mr. Strachey was highly conscious of possessing the kind of virtues which entitled him to speak in the name of the right-thinking. I imagine he never had a doubt concerning himself or *The Spectator*. He might admit a certain human imperfection in both, but he could hardly fail to think them, on the whole, the most

satisfying facts within the range of his acquaintance.
But he did have quite a number of painful doubts about
other things, and Mr. Chamberlain was the main cause
of the trouble.

Mr. Strachey was a Conservative with some qualifications ; he was one of those Conservatives anxious to
" do something," but something not too much or too
precise, and the father's playing with a sort of voluntary-
ism in Social Reform may have had something to do
with the son's whole-hog Socialism. But Mr. Strachey
was a Unionist without any kind of qualification. He
was also a Free Trader with as little qualification as
might be convenient. The Chamberlain business,
therefore, stretched him on the horns of the cruellest
dilemma. The one effective way to defeat fiscal heresy
was to join forces with the Liberals. But that meant
generally opening the floodgates, to use Sir Leicester
Dedlock's neat expression. Specifically it meant at
least a danger of Home Rule. It was a painful time for
Mr. Strachey, and some pang was mingled with every
partisan thrill. The Marconi affair was a great opportunity for the moralist and the practical politician.
Mr. Lloyd George could certainly be " improved."
He might possibly be destroyed. But if Mr. George
came down, and dragged with him the whole Government, Tariff Reform might not be a matter of " two
elections," but one of here and now. Mr. Strachey
understood as well as anybody the business of being a
man of principle. But he had somehow to contrive to
be a man of two principles, and it is no discredit to
his head or his heart that he cut a rather pathetic figure
during these agonised years. The just man made
perfect appeared as the man still just, but not quite
perfect, and in a terrible state of twitter and fluster.
Mrs. Micawber would never desert Mr. Micawber, but
she esteemed it a wifely duty to hint on occasion that

there was such a thing as a divorce court. It was
unfortunate. There is some sort of case for " My
party right or wrong." There is another sort of case
for putting opinion on a capital issue before party.
But the long strain of Mr Strachey's double loyalty
was no doubt excessive. *Amicus Plato, amicus Socrates,
sed magis amica veritas* may get one on bad terms with
those individuals. But one has the consolation, for
what that counts, of having sacrificed something worth
calling sacrifice for truth. But to declare that the
truth is above Mr. Balfour except when there appears
to be some small risk of setting Mr. Balfour below
truth is not the way of rendering the maximum service
to either.

Indeed, Mr. Strachey, to some considerable extent,
though to a less extent than Mr. Garvin, bore
responsibility for that Conservative habit of mixing up
fundamentals which allowed Mr. Baldwin in 1923,
without peril to " party unity," to propose Mr. McKenna
as his Chancellor of the Exchequer in May and to go
to the country on a policy of naked Protection in
October.

Last on my list is that very interesting figure, Mr.
Henry William Massingham. A man of brilliant
parts, he somehow just failed to realise himself. Possibly the reason was his sectarianism. Possibly it was
merely his defects of temper. But, whatever the cause,
though he did wonderful things at a very early age,
and maintained his intellectual vigour to the end, he
was more of a character than a force. Like so many
emphatic democrats, he was of a rather disdainful habit
of mind—intellectually superior, morally overbearing.
In one way he was as apt as Mr. Strachey to suggest
that he trod the paths of rather lonely virtue. " Moral "

was his weakness, as "right-thinking" Mr. Strachey's.
If Mr. Massingham agreed with you, you were happy
enough to appeal to him as a person of "unequalled
moral force"; he would give you credit for understanding "moral standards" and the "full moral
implications" of the "moral proposition," whatever it
might be; you would be one of the few who could
foresee and strive to avoid "moral disaster"; you
would be superior, in a word, to "existing popular
standards of morality." Less happy if you chanced to
disappoint him. Then you would be arraigned for
treason (supposing that you had been a Liberal) to the
"free conscience" on which you had been "suckled"
and to the "moral ideals" that you had absorbed. As
it somehow happened that almost every prominent
public man did end by disappointing Mr. Massingham, his judgments were somewhat fluctuating. He
could be fairly consistent with such a one as Sir Edward
Grey. But the Lloyd George of the Budget days,
perhaps his hero-in-chief, became afterwards his principal villain. On the other hand a former reprobate
might come strangely by grace; Lord Lansdowne
was the enemy of democracy in 1910 and its chief
friend in 1917—and that without much change
perceptible to a thick vision. President Wilson's
stock rose and fell sharply during some years. At
one time Massingham looked to Labour for a
"solid recruitment of wisdom." But he saw at another
time the working masses debauched, sunk in material-
ism, and "slaves to a spiritual tyranny imposed by a
few newspaper proprietors." Despite his enjoyment
in talking about spiritual values and his contempt
for material considerations, he had studied effectively the art of living, and there was little in the
lore of the table in which he was not versed.
Yet he strangely lacked the geniality which generally

accompanies such tastes. Possibly what he chiefly
suffered from was the refinement derived from his
Nonconformist origins, the Calvinistic contempt for
anything short of perfection, the Calvinistic refusal
to look with favour on more than one of the sorts
that make a world. With him " popular " was a
mere term of abuse, and with all his faith in the
democratic ideal I fancy he had an almost physical
loathing both for the masses and for the sort of
people who could appeal successfully to the masses.
This may have been an element in his tendency
to sympathise with foreign countries against his
own. Mr. Aldous Huxley, in one of his novels,
describes how an antiquarian squire, from sheer sense
of duty, went wearily through the routine of a
bank-holiday fête in his grounds. When free at
last he exclaimed how interesting it would all have
been had these people been dead five hundred years,
and were it only possible to reconstruct their doings
from some old manuscript. Undoubtedly there is, for
scholarly men a temptation to be somewhat too
disgusted with what lives, shouts, sweats, feeds, and
smells round them, and to be somewhat too partial to
people so long dead or so remote that they can be
studied only in the printed page ; and this may, at least
partially, account for the mixture of Casca and Pangloss
in Massingham. His charity began abroad and his
patience ended at home. Mr. Lloyd George once
complained of being " drenched with cocoa slops."
I should not call Mr. Massingham cocoa ; he was far
too brisk and spiritual, both in the English and the
French sense. But he might be compared with the
liqueur called " crême de cacao "—the same flavour with
a kick in it. Widely narrow, Quakerishly belligerent,
sometimes piously unchristian, he was at least never
uninteresting. It has been remarked as extraordinary

Q

that *The Nation,* which under him was so alive and individual, should have had a title so all-embracing and an outlook so sectarian.   But, after all, *The Nation* was in one sense most national.   One could not imagine it existing outside of England.

TWO ADMIRALS

ONE who ought to know, for he had had much experience, once told me that, while it was easy enough to run the War Office, it was the very devil to be political head of the Admiralty. "Generals," he said, "are like ballet-girls for vanity. Flatter them, and they fall to you, and the one you seduce can be depended on to down the others. But that solid block of admirals, all of one mind, and that mind opposed to yours—whew!"

And yet—even admirals are not all of the same kind, or the same mind. Some admirals can talk. Some admirals can hate. Some admirals will purr when you stroke, and scratch when you hustle them. Human nature remains human, however salted with spindthrift; and all the discipline of a king's ship will not make a naturally garrulous man taciturn or a naturally vain man humble. And, of course, it is necessary to understand exactly what discipline is and is not. On a certain page of Laughton's *Life of Nelson* it is written that in his (Nelson's) eyes " mutiny or treason was as the sin for which there is no forgiveness." But the page opposite records how Nelson, having received Keith's order to go to Minorca, " instead of obeying it, proceeded to discuss its bearings on the state of affairs in Naples and Sicily," and " determined to stay where he was." If we bear these passages in mind, we may perhaps be in a better position to appreciate a good deal in the naval history of the early years of the twentieth century.

"One iron rule at sea binds everyone," says a modern poet who has been down to the sea in ships, and a certain inquiry which made famous the order "On the knee, dog," showed that early in the first decade discipline in the navy could be indeed metallic, or possibly wooden. But does the iron rule bind everyone? It may not be improper to quote from that well-known authority, Captain Marryat. On board the *Harpy*, it may be recalled, the captain once explained to Mr. Midshipman Easy that everybody was equally bound to adhere to the articles of war. So far as he went he was speaking strict truth. "Everybody" on the *Harpy* was "everybody from the captain to the least boy in the ship." Had the *Harpy* been a flagship, however, the assertion could not have well been made without a mental reservation in favour of the admiral. For admirals, or, at all events, admirals who have achieved a certain degree of distinction in the Service, are, it seems, exempted by tradition from strict adherence to the common code of discipline. Easy, if he had but known, might have very nearly got his captain into a corner on this point. His captain, to get out of it, would have had to say that what was the unforgivable sin in others, might in the admiral be "zeal"; or, again, though there is no mention that he ever used the phrase, he might have said that it was "the Nelson touch." Strange, but true, the navy which takes obedience to superiors as the law and the commandments, and a good deal more important than either, has as its demi-god, to put him no higher, Lord Nelson, the most insubordinate person who ever sailed the sea or walked the land. The admirable and evergreen Marryat knew all about it. "We have two laws, that which is written and the *lex non scripta* . . . the articles of war cannot provide for everything." In other words, there is naval discipline, and supplementing it, occasionally contradicting, there is " zeal " or " the Nelson touch."

Now, in the long and glorious annals of the British navy there can never have been two officers more conspicuous for " zeal " than were Lord Fisher and Lord Charles Beresford. In most other ways, whether in regard to career or character, they were remarkable in contrast, but in display of this particular quality they ran neck and neck. Fisher was by five years the elder of the pair, and before his rival entered the Service had gone as a midshipman to the Baltic in the Russian War. However, long before the name of Fisher was known to the general public, Beresford was a celebrity. It would, of course, have been rather difficult for anybody with the name and blood of Beresford to avoid a measure of fame. He was of the kin of that " dashing Lord Waterford, reckless and rollicking," whose exploits are exalted in the Irish ditty. In early youth he developed a habit of bringing drowning comrades to safety and the newspapers, but had he stayed on dry land all his life he would have been doing deeds just as daring, though, it may be, less useful. Bred to the shore life, he would probably have been riding over the stiffest fences in Great Britain and Ireland. That was the sort of man he was. He was one of the family of the irrepressibles.

Indeed, had Beresford not been a sailor it is probable that yet more would have been heard of him, for during the greater part of his time afloat our navy was given few chances of distinction. One of the few was the bombardment of Alexandria, which, when England viewed it on the panorama, was esteemed a great feat of arms, but even that, by all sober accounts of it, was no very glorious affair, and as a national triumph was decidedly cheap—a mere bargain-counter piece. But though the plaudits for the pounding of Arabi and his rebels may have been rather embarrassing for most of those who did it, the special plaudits for Beresford's share in the business had been earned. When the guns of Fort Marabout began to annoy the armour-clads of our inshore squadron, Beresford, on his small gunboat, and at his own initiative, ran close under the guns and engaged the fort in manful fashion for an hour and a half. The signal of " Well done, *Condor*," which he received from the flagship, was well deserved. Not one of his crew took the slightest harm from the exploit, but had the Egyptian gunnery been a trifle more accurate the *Condor* would have been sent to the bottom. Beresford was brave and Beresford was lucky. The public, which gathered that much about him, and knew nothing whatever about any of its other sailors, elected him, in its warm heart, as the new Nelson.

Fisher's early years at sea brought him no such wide notability. He joined the navy as nominee of Nelson's last captain, and, after the Baltic expedition, did some fighting with Chinese pirates, but he had no influential friends, and, being extremely poor, no facilities for making them. He experienced hard times. The only sort of popularity that ever accrued to him was earned by taking the duty of other officers who wanted to go on land, when in port. Fisher, on such occasions, kept by the ship simply because he could not afford a good time on shore. Probably he did not always enjoy being a sailor. " And there shall be no more sea " is alleged to have been the Biblical text he relished above all others. But, pinned to his work when others disported themselves, he acquired a professional competence that earned him the notice of commanders and captains, and presently was to bring him to the attention of the highly placed. Not that the attention was always favourable. Jack Fisher knew his job, which was very good, but he also knew several other persons' jobs, which was not so good. Also, he had the sobriquet of " Radical Jack," and that was bad.

Lord Charles Beresford went into politics and Parliament on the Conservative side. He was a good electioneer, with a " Yo, heave ho ! " manner irresistible to voters, and he knew the ropes of the House of Commons, despite his engaging show of innocence. Fisher never sought a seat in Parliament, or, rather, waited until his services were rewarded with a peerage, and he made some profession that his only politics were the politics of the navy. But just as Lord Charles was a natural Tory, Fisher was a natural Radical. The one grew up finding the world every day more pleasant ; the other soon discovered it to be a rather dismal and unsatisfactory place, where impostors flourished and genuine men were depressed. The former was ready to keep most things as they were : the latter wanted to reform all but everything. Fisher's spirit might be indicated by saying that he was as enthusiastic a pro-Boer as Mr. Lloyd George or Mr. Belloc, but it is better illustrated by his attitude towards the compass. Every sailor who was, as the French say, *bien pensant*, revered the old Admiralty compass. It might have its defects, but one no more thought of criticising it openly than of reviling one's mother in a public-house. Fisher treated it with undisguised contempt. When he was asked at an inquiry whether the sacred thing was sensitive, he replied that : " You had to kick it to get a move on." On his ship he always carried Kelvin's compass, a new-fangled instrument, and was frequently reprimanded for his temerity. The " Old Salts," he wrote, called him a " d——d revolutionary." None the less he prevailed. Eventually the old Admiralty compass was kicked overboard, the Kelvin compass substituted. Which either showed that the navy was more friendly to new ideas than was commonly

supposed, or else that Fisher had superhuman pertinacity.

Unpopular in the navy Fisher most certainly was,
and for a while his " manias " retarded his promotion,
yet whilst he was still a very junior captain he was made
captain of the *Inflexible*, the biggest ship afloat. He
owed the appointment to Lord Northbrook, then First
Lord of the Admiralty. Long ago, then, in the early
'eighties, he had started on the path he was to follow.
If naval bigwigs loathed him and stood in his path,
there was a way round them on the shoulders of the
civilians. Not, by the way, on the shoulders of the
cheering crowd who carried Beresford through the
streets after electoral victories. Beresford, aristocrat
and believer in aristocracy, was adored by the mob.
Fisher, who would have been a demagogue if he had
not been a sailor, who on land shouted of liberty,
equality and fraternity, in select company was apter to
win the good opinions of great personages.

How did Fisher do it ? He had no social graces.
He was as far as possible from a courtier. King
Edward once had to say to him : " Would you kindly
leave off shaking your fist in my face ? " He was so
little a respecter of persons that one of his first and
fiercest agitations had for its intended victim the
brother-in-law of the Prime Minister then in office.
Before attaining flag-rank he collaborated with Stead
in producing *The Truth about the Navy*, of which the
result was larger estimates, and he could have committed
no worse offence in the eyes of the average politician.
Yet there is no doubt that he did possess the secret of
impressing politicians, and, in the long run, of making
them do pretty much what he wanted.

Part of the secret was, perhaps, that he was not at all
the silent admiral. He could talk, and talk well,
clearly and picturesquely ; he could not only say what

he wanted done for the navy, but explain just why he wanted it and why nothing else would do. Most of his fellow-seamen merely foamed at the mouth if their wishes were not anticipated. As a sea lord, many years before he was First Sea Lord, he was regularly the interpreter between his speechlessly indignant colleagues and the amiable but puzzled civilian who presided at their gatherings. Beresford, too, could talk, and volubly, but Beresford never quite learned that a Cabinet minister was not a public meeting, and always comported himself as if he suspected a Liberal Cabinet minister of having a cheque from a foreign finance minister in his pocket. Fisher would sometimes shake his fist, but was a fighter of the cunning kind that gives way on everything but essentials. And, being himself a patriotic Radical, he could think of other Radicals as possible patriots. Which flattered them immensely, accustomed as they were to very different treatment, and made them often forget in sheer exhilaration their election pledges of retrenchment.

All this had a deep importance when the 1906 elections brought the Liberals to power and office. Campbell-Bannerman had said at the Albert Hall, on the eve of the polls : " We want relief from the pressure of excessive taxation . . . we want money to meet our domestic needs at home." The new Prime Minister made it plain that he would endeavour to attain these two objects through cutting down expenditure on armaments. To the average naval officer the prospect was appalling—the blacker as a policy of " economies " had already been initiated by the Conservatives with Lord Selborne at the Admiralty, and if these were not enough, it was argued, then the plight of the fleet would be truly desperate. Fisher was perfectly calm, and it was assumed that he had decided to sell the pass. He had just been made

First Sea Lord when the Selborne retrenchments were announced. He remained at his post with no visible signs of discomfort when the Liberals arrived with their pledges to retrench yet further. Very soon he was to be marked as the chief villain of the piece.

Now Fisher may have been a Radical, but, being a man without illusions, he was as far as possible from being a "Pacifist" or a "Little Navy" advocate. Unlike, however, most sailors and soldiers he had traces of a financial conscience. The thought of money being spent upon the upkeep of ships that were not required for national defence positively hurt him. To Beresford and his kind any and every ship was somehow precious. To Fisher, on the contrary, ships which, as he put it, could "neither fight nor run away" were irritating and disgraceful, and he was well aware that the navy had always contained many such. Therefore, when a First Lord of the Admiralty was warned by a Chancellor of the Exchequer that his estimates must be reduced, Fisher was genuinely helpful. Immediately and gleefully he could point to a hundred and fifty so-called vessels of war that might, in his opinion, be scrapped without any hurt to the country and with much gain to the country's pocket. What were those vessels doing? In the blessed phrase, they were "Showing the Flag." And what did "Showing the Flag" mean? It meant that the officers of the vessels "were shooting pheasants up Chinese rivers and giving tea-parties to British Consuls." Fisher did not consider it his duty to give naval officers a good time at the public expense. He knew something of those tea-parties by not sharing them. He had been a worker himself, not occasionally, but always.

And when more serious economics came to be discussed he showed a serpentine wisdom. His own building programme was not modest. Very big ships that could be built very rapidly, would move at great speed and carry enormous guns : that was one of his ideas, and it could not be executed for a trifle. The *Dreadnought* was his child, and it was only the eldest of a long family of very big and terribly expensive offspring. Fisher had his eye on Tirpitz all the time. Instead of letting our best ships cruise in the Mediterranean, he brought them into the North Sea, where, he knew, they would one day have to fight, and that did not make him any more popular, for the North Sea possesses few amenities. But it did show everybody who was not too angry to think that his devotion to German interests was less complete than some of those " Old Salts " fancied. Only he had the wit to know that it was no good flying into a temper if there was a delay about *Dreadnoughts* in 1906, a check in 1907, and some hurrying slowly in the next year. He knew all about election pledges of economy. He knew that they simply must be honoured for a while, and then, as Burgess says in *Candida*, left off " grajally," like strong drink. Consequently, he did not unduly press demands which he knew could not be granted. Ministers, unused to such considerate treatment from their professional advisers, thought him the most reasonable of men, and later, as his programme lengthened, could be lured into acceding to it. With other people he might rant and roar. " The Kingdom of Heaven," he would quote, " suffereth violence," but he was well aware that Cabinets are carried by more subtle means.

From 1906 onwards a furious Campaign was conducted against him for his alleged compliance with the Radicals in reducing our naval strength. When the Cawdor policy of " four large armoured ships annually " was cut down to three because the advent of the *Dreadnought* had temporarily stopped building of warships abroad, there was an immediate outcry against

Sir John Fisher. One Tory journalist, with a passionate disregard of syntax, wrote : " We assert that more than any one man, the responsibility and guilt for those reductions lies at his door." Fisher's withers were unwrung. These critics, he wrote to Lord Tweedmouth, were " all capable of absolute pulverisation. Who were they ? A military correspondent lecturing the Board of Admiralty. . . . Admirals whose names were bywords of inefficiency and ineptitude when they were afloat . . . the Blackwood Balaam." But the campaign grew in force. *The Standard* branded him for " subservience " to the Government ; Mr. Maxse denounced his " tragic swagger " ; *The Spectator* deplored his " un-English boastfulness " ; *The Morning Post* hinted that the German authorities were somehow working through Lord Esher to maintain him in office. At drawing-room meetings held by the Imperial Maritime League he was attacked in more overt and less polite language. Mr. William Le Queux was quoted as a witness against him. Echoes of his misdeeds reverberated in the normally tranquil pages of *The Ladies' Pictorial.* Many worthy persons did hold, in perfect good faith, that he was the accredited agent of the Kaiser for the destruction of Britain. And about the time when suspicion of him was at its blackest he was lamenting to King Edward that the Prime Minister would not let him "Copenhagen" the German fleet at Kiel !

In the opinion of numerous landsmen, and of yet more landswomen, the blackest evidence against Fisher was the open hostility between himself and their idol, Beresford. Lord Charles was then in command of the Channel fleet, and in the event of war would presumably have been our admiralissimo, but there are sundry signs that Fisher's opinion of him was none too high. According to Mr. Maxse it was " jealousy

of the mud admiral for the sea admiral," but, be that
how it may, there was constant friction. On the other
hand, of course, Fisher's confidence in Fisher was
boundless. So one day, or perhaps one night, some
bluejackets were told to go up on the roof of the
Admiralty and there erect a wireless installation. When
the thing was done it was bruited about that the
Post Office had raised pedantic objection. The man
who really objected was Beresford. Thenceforward
every ship could be " manipulated from Whitehall like
a piece on the chess-board." Thenceforward Fisher,
in war or peace, would be master of the situation.
The commander-in-chief of the Channel fleet would
have to obey orders just as though he had been an
ordinary officer or man.

Beresford's ambition for supremacy in home waters
was baulked in other ways. He wanted unified command, but the Nore fleet, and the so-called Home fleet,
which was really a reserve force, were kept from him.
In return he agitated for the creation of a Naval War
Staff, which body should have as its prime function
the duty of limiting Fisher's autocracy. From time
to time there were " unpleasant incidents." At a levée
Beresford failed conspicuously to see Fisher's proffered
hand. A few months later " The Strange Occurrence
in the Fleet" became a standing headline in a certain
newspaper. Beresford, it was said, had signalled
orders for a manœuvre which must have resulted in a
collision, and Sir Percy Scott, on one of the ships
concerned, had received it with Nelson's blind eye.
Everybody knew what it all meant. Scott was one of
Fisher's " favourites." " It was he and he alone,"
Fisher wrote afterwards, " who made the first start
of the fleet's hitting the enemy and not missing him."
In 1908, the year of the " strange occurrence," the navy
was split into two factions, not on speaking terms with

one another, and each using its organs in the press for
mutual belittlement and abuse.

Into all that part of the quarrel that was technical
there is no need to enter, save in noting that Fisher
was ever the advocate of innovations from the compass
to *Dreadnoughts* and submarines. Some of his adversaries were honestly suspicious. They thought he was
on the side of the new thing because, as he used to tell
the politicians, it was the cheap thing. But that was
only his cunning. Mr. McKenna went to the Admiralty to cut down expenditure, and before long, with
Fisher at his elbow, was breaking records in the way
of spending. Then there were the people who hated
his innovations because they meant going to school
again or making a mess of things. Fisher used to hint
that he was the first person who had made a change in
the navy since King Alfred founded it. Poor So-and-so,
who had been brought up on a particular type of ship,
and had never dreamed that his grandchildren would
know any other, would wake one morning to find
Fisher had condemned his old coracle, appointed him
to a vessel he had never glimpsed in nightmare, and
was sure to break him if he could not get the perfect
" bearing " of it within about four-and-twenty hours.
No wonder certain gallant officers preferred Beresford
with his comfortable belief that " principles of sea-power
do not change." The youngest naval cadet could see
that Beresford was the better sort. He held, and
said, that the fleet existed for other purposes besides
a war. It was, he maintained, meant to carry " British
ideas of justice and good government to every corner
of the globe," and for that cargo any familiar craft
would do, and any officer, provided the officer was a
gentleman.

Yet it was Fisher with his everlasting preparations
for war with Germany who told the public to sleep

quiet in their beds, whilst it was Beresford and his supporters who engaged in making our flesh creep with prophecies of invasion. On both sides the inconsistency was more apparent than real. A sentence from the Latin primer, illustrating the ablative absolute, gives a key to the situation : *Nil desperandum, Teucro duce.* Fisher being *dux*, there was, in Fisher's opinion, no reason for despair. The Germans might be building, and Messrs George and Churchill might be doing their worst to limit our reply, but Fisher felt himself a match for the lot of them. Beresford, who in his heart believed that one English ship, especially if commanded by an Anglo-Irishman, ought always to beat two beneath any foreign flag, still felt it his duty to engineer naval panics. But then Beresford was not *dux*. All the talk about "betrayal" and "fool-gunnery" and the like could be interpreted very simply as "Put Beresford in charge." To him and to his admirers the thought of anybody sleeping quietly until the primary precaution had been taken was monstrously wrong-headed.

At last the long duel ended. Early in 1909 the Admiralty decided to reduce the length of ships' commissions from three to two years, and, as a consequence, Beresford was ordered to haul down his flag and to come on shore. On Portsmouth Hard, and again at Waterloo Station, he received a mighty ovation from affectionate crowds. Fisher had triumphed. Before the year's end he was raised to the peerage, and though within a few more weeks he was to retire from the office of First Sea Lord, the navy was by then unquestionably his navy. *Inflexible, Indomitable, Invincible.* Such were the names of the first three battle-cruisers of his Dreadnought type, and such were the characteristics of the man. England did not love him ; but, when the war came for which he had prepared, he was among the first men whose services England demanded. And at that time, for some reason or other, everybody forgot that such a person as Beresford existed. Of a sudden the *Condor* shrunk to the dimensions of a tom-tit.

HENRY JAMES AND MAX BEERBOHM

To most if not all of his contemporaries, Henry James appeared as the one eminent writer of fiction in our language who had no axe to grind.

He was not a moralist in the manner of Thackeray, and obviously had none of that zeal for righting wrongs which marked Dickens in his Radical phases. Such philosophic theories of life as were propounded by Meredith and Hardy are sought vainly in his volumes. Although an idol to the coterie of " The Yellow Book," he was too much a Puritan to be a decadent, but he was too consciously an artist to be a Puritan, except subconsciously. Again, comparing him with the younger men, he was neither Socialist nor humanitarian, neither Papist nor Imperialist. Indeed, it is easy enough to understand why he was judged the perfect Gallio of his time. His sole permanent interests seemed to be in the art of pure letters and the study of human character in certain restricted circles. For his occasional and timid expeditions about the borderlands of the occult, he would invariably apologise, as for breaches of good manners. But we who have survived him, together with the European War and sundry other cataclysmic events of history, may be able to see the truth about him more plainly. Henry James, like his yet more famous compatriot, George Washington, had his little axe. What is more, he used it, with a purpose. And there should be no doubt to-day that the purpose was defence of civilisation as a whole.

In the nineteenth century there were many causes for which men strove, as, for instance, Church and State, Free Trade, or the betterment of the working-classes. In the first years of the twentieth century, the causes were different, but yet more numerous. Only, despite the warnings of Matthew Arnold, very few realised that civilisation itself might be in danger and in need of defenders. Henry James was one of the tiny minority. In a childhood and youth divided between the eminently cultured household of his family in the United States and journeys to and about Europe, he had met a great company of English men of letters. Arnold had been of the number, and may not inconceivably have made a special impression upon the young man. But James's awareness of the menace was mainly due to the fact that he was an American. The Civil War had been the chief event of his boyhood. No young Englishman of his period had had any such experience. None of our English wars in that age had been fought near home ; none had even threatened to interrupt the normal course of life, or to check a progress that was thought to be a law of nature. The war between North and South had been of a different order. On each side there had been a definite belief that victory for the other would mean an overthrow of civilisation. The Confederates, though curiously enough James never came near to discovering their point of view, were fighting for the supremacy which meant the very existence of the gentlemanly, leisured class, without which, as they believed, civilisation must perish in America. To the Northerner, on the other hand, as James was to put it, Southern triumph meant that " history, the history of everything, would be re-written *adsum Delphini*—the Dauphin being in this case the budding Southern mind " ; it meant enthronement of principles which the rest of the world denied ;

it meant secession, not merely from the Union, but from humanity at large.

And although what the James family would have regarded as the worst did not happen, the success of their side entailed consequences that must have seemed to them only less calamitous. The violent overthrow of the Southern gentleman did not mean, as possibly they had fancied, transfer of influence to an enlightened aristocracy of talent in New England and its spiritual outposts. On the morrow of the conflict two other forces began to divide control of America, both, as a James saw it, quite uncivilised, a crude democracy, and an if possible cruder plutocracy.

From early days, therefore, Henry James understood much better than any Englishman of his generation how tender a plant civilisation was, how liable to be uprooted and trampled underfoot by the barbarians. He was without the average Victorian's superstition as to the inevitable and as it were mechanical tendency of mankind to move onwards and upwards. But if he were less satisfied about the present and less confident about the future than those with whom he came to dwell, he was, unfortunately, ignorant to an extraordinary degree about any past excepting the immediate past. Any French peasant, any English agricultural labourer made garrulous by a few pots of beer, could have told him more about the foundations of Europe than he ever managed to discover. Directly one begins to regard him as anything except a literary dandy who wrote wonderfully expressive and rather tiresome prose, one perceives him as a pathetic figure. The cause he had at heart was so enormous, so overwhelmingly important, and he himself so poorly equipped to be its defender.

In the first place, Mr. James had been educated very well but not very wisely. The European part of his education, in particular, had been somewhat futile. A corrective for sundry prejudices and misconceptions acquired in his adolescence upon American soil might have been provided by Paris or Oxford. The classics would have been beneficial to a young man steeped in modern culture from his cradle, and he needed the sense of history which is in the atmosphere of the old seats of learning, and is almost necessarily defective in every American. Even in a German university he might have found something to his advantage, had it been only some unpleasant, not to say brutal, reality against which he could have reacted strongly. Instead, he attended lectures at the Academy of Geneva, of all cities surely the most utterly divorced from the tradition and the fact of Europe. Whatever he learned there simply confirmed him in all the errors of his native judgment.

Of the false notions that took root in him during youth, none was falser nor more abiding than that civilisation and respectability as known at, say, Concord, Massachusetts, were interchangeable terms. Consequently, though he sometimes wrote of Christendom, the middle ages were too coarse for him. He left them out of his purview. Imperial Rome and the Renaissance were, because of their vices, equally beyond his scope. As a pilgrim wandering about Europe in search of culture for export to his own continent his steps were for a while dogged by sheer disappointment. When he crossed the Alps he soon found that Italy was more to his taste than the Italians. In a letter written from Florence to his mother he started by depreciating compatriots whom he met there, calling them " vulgar " and what not, but ended by talking of the Latins as false and feverish. Later, in correspondence from Paris, he returned to the theme of American " vulgarity," and for a while was pleased to be in the company of Daudet, Maupassant, Zola and others of their calibre, but the deadly seriousness of the French, their passionate *jusqu 'au-boutisme,* was more than he could stomach.

For James, England proved to be, if not the land of heart's desire, at least the land he could inhabit with most peace of mind. At first its expanding industrialism had frightened him, and his letters contain terrified references to Birmingham. His fears were, of course, based on American experience. In New York he managed to exist without the sullying contact of " down town " and business, but at the cost, as he realised, of living a Crusoe's life, of being a solitary, " alone," as he put it in one of his prefaces, " with the music-masters and French pastry-cooks, the ladies and children."

England, however, being an older, more sophisticated country, is more cunningly arranged. In England, he discovered, one could live for years in unconsciousness that there was any such place as Birmingham. Still more delightful, one could live in London, if one settled in Kensington, and only know just as much of London as one desired, all but without a suspicion that one was missing the essentials of the country or of its capital. If the English were, as Mr. Kipling was anon to affirm, " a business people," they had, at all events, the decency, or, it may be, the hypocrisy, to pretend that other interests beyond those of the shop were worthy of a man.

Mr. James's selection of an environment was, however, mainly decided for him by the English country-house. Here at last was the refuge for which he had been pining. As an American with a decent competence and reputable connections doors were opened to him at which an English writer without already founded celebrity might have knocked in vain. He had the advantage of being a foreigner but not the

disadvantage of speaking a foreign language. Ever-
body could understand him, and everybody had to be
polite to him. James was delighted. He met Lord
Houghton, Gladstone, Tennyson and many other
personages whom he described in one of his letters
home as of " high culture," whilst the country-house
itself seemed to him one of the " highest results of
civilisation." Readers of his novels know how largely
it loomed in his work. To its " old forms and pleasant
rites " he succumbed the more easily because they were
so entirely formal and ritual, so little significant. Had
they conveyed any definite meaning, it is probable that
he would have taken alarm at them. Rude Nature
abhors a vacuum, but a refined American loves it.

Henry James, writing of the English landscape,
declared its two great factors were the squire and the
parson. But there is no sign that he attached any
spiritual value to the latter. Visiting New York in
the later years of his life he did, indeed, deplore that
in that city of monstrous lay architecture the church
buildings had been dwarfed and lost. Europe had
accustomed him to the vision of spires, towers and
cupolas against the sky, and their sudden absence
shocked him, yet they had been no more to him than
" charming elements " in a world still tolerably full of
charm. From the windows of the country-house he
had seen the parson and noted his functions, of which
the first must have been that he gave a sort of consecra-
tion to the squire's presence. There is no reason to
fancy that in London, that is to say in Kensington, a
passing cleric would have inspired him with any feeling
whatsoever. The Church, apart from buildings which
might be meritorious anywhere, was to him just one of
the several important parts of country life. Its possible
relevance in the scheme of things elsewhere escaped
him.

With fraternal candour William James had criticised his younger brother's novels as "thin and empty," and Henry had explained that they were artistic experiments unsuitable for a big theme. Later, they were to be "fat and full," but the promise of growth was never quite fulfilled. Like his own Duncombe, he was "a passionate corrector, a fingerer of style." For years England provided him with refuge—Kensington, then Lamb House, at Rye—from the disagreeables. During the war between Spain and America he eschewed newspapers, for, he said, "One must save one's life if one can." Of some other matter he wrote once : "The facts were too abysmal for a permitted distinctness." Publication of his stories was often painful to him because of the company in which they might appear. When *The Death of the Lion* appeared in the "Yellow Book," he made excuses : it had been done for gold. Of *The Turn of the Screw*, a tale in which he had condescended to appeal to the common emotions of terror and pity, he would say nothing except that it was a pot-boiler. He read *Tess of the d'Urbervilles*, only to find its heroine "vile," whilst the energetic earnestness of Ibsen struck him as "bottomlessly bourgeois." On the other hand, in the shoddy romanticism of *Trilby* he noted "a charm and lovability to gild the whole day." In Stevenson he had a temporarily congenial spirit, but when that prose stylist went to live among Samoan "savages," and even mixed in their outlandish politics, James was profoundly shocked.

Yet it is not for one moment to be thought that James in his ivory tower did not know what was happening in the outside world. In fact, he knew much better than those who were themselves outside. When he refused to read newspapers it was because he knew by instinct everything they contained except the unnecessary details, and he knew also what they never by any chance did contain, the portent of the news. Long before his friends of the country-houses had scented danger, he realised the troubles that were brewing for them. In 1886 he wrote of the " damaged prestige of the English upper-class " and of its condition as " collapsible," adding that " the Huns and Vandals will have to come *up*—from the black depths of the (in the people) enormous misery." In the next year the Jubilee seemed to him " grotesque." Nor had he any firmer confidence in American solidity. " There are really two civilisations there side by side," he wrote at the time of the troubles over the Venezuelan frontier ; " or rather one civilisation and a barbarism." The civilisation, he thought, might prevail, but only " on condition of its fighting hard."

Born in 1843, James belonged chronologically to the Victorian era, but in his mental attitude he was entirely Edwardian. The Victorians all had beliefs and were, therefore, all more or less optimists. They believed in God or in evolution, in the people or in the Queen, in heroes or in education ; and without exception they believed in themselves. The Edwardians, or most of them, only had their disbeliefs. Mr. Shaw's plays are a series of negatives ; Mr. Well's novels a string of contradictions. Henry James was creedless, and so a pessimist. That civilisation for which he trembled, which he sought to embalm in art, because on all sides of him he discerned that it was decomposing, had, as far as he knew, no roots as long as those of the squire's oaks, no foundations deeper than those of the squire's mansions. He loved it without trust. It was a roof over his head, liable to fall, not a rock on which he or any man could stand. Delicate artist as he was, there are terrible depths of bitterness in his work. Human beings, as such, were to him " cats and monkeys, monkeys and cats." Comprehensively he damned and belittled mankind when he wrote: "The soul is immortal certainly—if you've got one—but most people haven't." If he believed in himself it was only relatively to his scepticism about others. He called himself a confirmed spectator, ran no risks, took no plunges.

The last fifteen years of his life (he died in 1916) were probably the happiest, even though each was bringing nearer the dissolution of society that he, almost alone among his contemporaries, had foreseen. But the nineteenth century, materially comfortable as it had been for him, had withheld from him its appreciation. The country-house people had been kind to him, but had they read his books? Almost surely they had not understood them, and quite certainly they had not bought them. True, the " Yellow Book " clique had raved about his art, but their raving could only have distressed him. He had put Wilde down as " feeble " and " vulgar," and rated Beardsley's work as " base," until some authoritative and intellectual Slav told him he must, absolutely must, change his mind.

In the new century James came into his own. He was decorated with the Order of Merit. Better still, he was recognised as master by a considerable group of young authors, whose manners, social and literary, he could approve. Harvard and Oxford gave him honorary degrees. And, in tune with the times, as incident after incident gave proof that the bases of society were weakening he ceased to trouble about anything not strictly personal to himself. Gently but firmly he could rebuke a friend who had written to him about Roosevelt. Of that " mere monstrous embodiment of unprecedented resounding Noise " he had been contriving not to think. So in a deliberately contrived serenity he remained until the outbreak of war, and on the very morrow of the explosion could write : " We can still . . . *make* a little civilisation, the inkpot aiding, even when vast chunks of it, around us, go down into the abyss." As always, a pathetic personage, he yet faced the end of his world with a certain courage. He was aware that the epoch of elaborate pretence had run its course, but he, at least, would go on pretending. On the same sheet of notepaper he wrote : " After all, *vive* the old delusion and fill again the flowing stylograph."

Henry James had imitators and disciples—far too many of both. Among them all, however, there was but one who showed any true promise of carrying on the torch of literary dandyism. I refer, of course, to Max Beerbohm. For various reasons, the influence of Mr. James on " Max " has been imperfectly acknowledged. Their names are, and were, seldom coupled. James was at once diffident and pompous. He was always deprecating his own productions, and always fuming because the world at large was so ready to agree. " Max," on the contrary, was impudent and in a permanent attitude of unbending affably. Of the latter, Mr. Holbrook Jackson once wrote : " He is civilisation conserving itself and laughing at itself." Of Henry James one could not, of course, write that, but the first part of the dictum fits him. He also was " civilisation conserving itself," only he had not the gift of self-derision. It is a gift rare among the English ; unknown among the Americans. Beerbohm was James plus an alien strain of humour.

One other critic, Mr. Bohun Lynch, seems to have come near a like conclusion when dealing with the parodies of " Max." When parodying George Moore or Bennett or Belloc, " Max " is superlatively clever, but there is a faint touch of hostility. On the other hand, he parodied James as he parodied himself, gaily exaggerating the tricks of style, pointing every absurdity

yet unable wholly to conceal his natural sympathy with
the original. But the point to note, the point noted
by Mr. Lynch, is that not only in parody has Mr.
Beerbohm "slipped into step with this—I might almost
say—with his—master." On many pages "Max"
may be caught falling into the Jamesian manner, and
then slipping out of it. For example, take this from
Zuleika Dobson on the Duke in love : " He had always
fancied himself secure against any so vulgar peril ;
always fancied that by him at least the proud old motto
of his family—*Pas si bête*—would not be belied." The
" so vulgar peril " is pure James, and James indeed
might have written it all in utter seriousness, saving the
Pas si bête, which purposefully betrays " Max " and his
little joke without reference to the context.

But the relationship between the two men is by no
means mere mannerism. " Max," announcing himself
" a dilettante, a *petit maître*," dubbed a " popinjay " in
Punch, regarded by all and sundry as the complete
butterfly of the arts, was, and is, an artist with a purpose,
and his purpose was Henry James's purpose. In both
was the idea that in the *beau monde*, as each knew it, lay
the stronghold of civilisation. Each saw the arts linked
inevitably with the amenities of polite society. Only
" Max " knew far better than James that the stronghold
was not strong, was indeed most ridiculously weak,
and, what is more, quite possibly indefensible on any
moral grounds, or on any other grounds whatsoever.
Hence the difference in their methods. With appalling
irreverence a fellow-novelist once described James as
an elephant engaged in picking up peas with his trunk.
In fact, he does seem to be concerned perpetually about
trifles, though it is only fair to remember that the sum
of trifles may be enormous, and, while the *conte* rather
than the full-length novel was his usual vehicle of
expression, his normal manner was pontifical, not to

say ponderous. " Max," it may be, exceeded even James in the amount of " scrutiny and titivation " to which he subjected his published work, but the effort, though patent to any practised critic, escapes the simple. An adept at hoaxing, his most cunning hoax of all was to persuade the world to consider him as first and last a graceful lounger.

In one of his cleverest cartoons he shows Sir Edmund Gosse, introducing the ghost of Stevenson to a company of modern novelists, all standing upon tubs, and Stevenson suggests that, having now met the pamphleteers and preachers, he would like to meet some writers. " Max," as usual, is hoaxing. He means you to think how different he is from any of those earnest persons. When he writes of the " sterling affectations " and " frivolous convictions " of Mr. Bernard Shaw he is hoaxing again, and hoaxing far better than when he wrote of one Luntic Kolniyatsch, whose masterpiece he, almost alone in England, could read in the original Gibrisch. For nobody worth deceiving was ever deceived about Luntic, whereas he most likely did mislead you regarding himself and Shaw. He made you fancy that he was laughing at Shaw because he did not care the toss of a counterfeit coin for any of those battles in which the dramatist fought.

Really, he was laughing because he believed in laughter as a weapon, and because he had at least a notion that it was the sole reliable weapon his side possessed. " Max " was the genius as trifler, and exquisite polish in trifling was a joy no less than a religion with him. But he had some settled ideas, for the most part curiously conventional for a man of his type; and when he was moved, he was moved not to solemnity but to his most precious persiflage. A relatively rough satire sufficed for the demolition of a more literary lunacy or *bêtise*. The most delicate and deadly weapon was reserved for a serious opponent like Shaw. Assuredly he and Shaw were nine times out of ten upon opposite sides. The Irishman was Puritan, stark and stern, whilst " Max " was of those who wore frills, and not just because frills may be accounted pretty, but because frills are an advance on nature and to doff them is to take a step backward into barbarism. Shaw, again, was Socialist. " Max's " temperament made him the natural enemy of Socialism. He had, no doubt, few politics and fewer economics, but Socialism does, presumably, imply one of two things. Either it means rule by a small body of intellectuals, or else " dictatorship of the proletariat," and it is safe to say that " Max " must always have objected to either regimen. He was a child of the 'nineties; and, as even his most recent caricatures of the Labour leaders show, the masses and all sprung from them are to him the " great unwashed," dull, ugly, brutish. As to the intellectuals, anyhow the intellectuals who might conceivably govern a Socialist England, they would be yet more distasteful to him. The mob, after all, can produce a thrill, and there may be pleasure in a thrill even when the thrill is an apprehensive shudder. Mr. Wells, to cite one who is not at all obviously dull, offers no such excitement. Given a choice of evils, " Max " would rather ride to death in the tumbril than be sentenced to imprisonment for life in any of the many worlds which Mr. Wells has at various times constructed upon paper. " Max " has confessed in middle age that we may yet return to simpler ways of life, and, perhaps, not unwillingly. Again, as a choice of evils, he would prefer the existence of a peasant to the existence of a machine-minder. There is at least one justification for his choice. The arts can and do flourish side by side with a sort of primitive rudeness. Experience is proving that they wilt in a mechanised age and country.

All we now see in " Max " had not developed in him before the end of the decade with which this book deals. He was always shrewd as well as witty, but there is a wisdom sprung from human sympathies to be discerned in his later essays that would have astounded and even shocked his admirers of the epoch when he was writing his weekly articles for the *Saturday Review*. The " Max " of the early and middle period had not discovered the superiority of the mountain spring to the hot-water tap. He would not and could not have written at the end of *The Golden Drugget* : " I pause to bathe in the light that is as the span of our human life, granted between one great darkness and another."

In the Edwardian period he was a typical Edwardian, and because one great mark of the period was not seeing, or pretending not to see, the obvious, he was a pretender. The statesmen of the time can be divided into two classes : those who never saw the German menace and those who made others fancy they had never seen it. Yet more general and certainly more genuine was the blindness to the rise of Labour as a political power. " Max " conformed to the convention. Perhaps he lacked the ability of Henry James to banish a displeasing idea by sheer effort of will, but he was as elaborately careful as any of them to avoid beholding a disagreeable prospect. Everybody knows the tale of " Max " going by train to Brighton, and suddenly surprising his fellow-passengers by pulling down the carriage blinds. " Hush ! " he whispered in answer to inquiries. " We shall soon be passing the Crystal Palace." I might ask, in passing, what in the most exquisite human soul that could be tortured by the Crystal Palace would not also suffer laceration in

HENRY JAMES AND MAX BEERBOHM   271

the neighbourhood of the West Pier.   But, to return
to the point, most contemporaries would have shut their
eyes, or, open-eyed, would have noticed nothing.   The
eyes of "Max" bulged, as is demonstrated by his
caricatures, and could not be closed.   If it were not
notorious that prophets are always stoned, "Max"
might have been a prophet.   As it was, he spent the
ten years joyously stoning everything, or, at least,
pelting with paper pellets furnished with something
sharp and metallic enough to prick everybody and
everything.

There was another way, too, in which he was essentially Edwardian.   Critics allege that his best work
was done in the 'nineties and in the teens of the twentieth
century, and that in the intervening years, though his
fame reached its highest, he was stopped from producing
anything memorable by his task of regularly producing
Saturday articles.   Now it is undeniable that most men
produce their best under the spur of necessity.   In an
art, as at a game, it is odds on the professional being
better than the amateur.   But the Edwardian period
seems to have been exceptional.   Regular duties were
performed under protest, and branded on all sides as
irksome.   Everywhere the amateur was encouraged to
think himself the better man : the cobbler was urged
to desert his last, everybody recommended to be all
things by turn and nothing for very long.   "Max"
himself had been advised by his brother not to adopt
the regular profession of the Bar, but to be "a sort of a
writer, and then, perhaps, drift into diplomacy."   It
was all part of the general plot for not taking anything
quite seriously, that is seen at its plainest in the
politics of those days if one compares the airy fashion
in which serious matters were handled under Balfour and
Asquith with the earnest manner of handling affairs of
no particular moment under Gladstone and Salisbury.

" Max " conformed.   One cannot picture " Max "
a Nonconformist.   The humour of the decade was to
fritter talents and energies, and to kick against every
restraint, even the slight restraint of two columns
weekly.   The critics are right.   " Max " when he had
his weekly pulpit and his largest audience did least
justice to himself.   As has been said, he was influential,
yet he never used a tithe of his potential influence.
" My gifts are small," he said, and most people imagined
he had no more to give.   Still, from one and another
comes the familiar phrase :   " Max had no axe to
grind."   In truth, he ground it so fine that the edge
was very often imperceptible to most.

CERTAIN IRISHMEN

DURING the 'nineties the political fortunes of the Irish Nationalists had, largely owing to their own dissensions, reached nadir. The party which Parnell had made was divided into two factions, not to mention Mr. T. M. Healy and sundry sub-sections. But as the old century was wearing to a close, and whilst the Parnellite remnant and the whilom " Carties " were still raging against one another at Westminster, the people of Ireland grew tired of this intestine strife, and in the country itself, under the tutelage of Mr. William O'Brien, there came into existence a body known as the United Irish League.

At first the faction-leaders sniffed, sneered, or snorted, according to their several temperaments, but the League, founded in the wilds of County Mayo, grew, spread and flourished. Mr. O'Brien had a rare talent for organisation. What is more, he had set his mind definitely on peace, and just because he waved his olive-branch as other men wave a blackthorn, he drew to himself the hearts of his many compatriots, who love nothing better than a fight. One fine day the M.P.'s woke to find their constituents reunited, interested once more in the question of Home Rule and the land, and no longer caring about Kitty O'Shea's petticoat. Thereupon they did one thing that was left for them to do ; they decided themselves to reunite. All that remained was to decide who should be the leader.

At the opening of the session of 1900, in a committee-room of the House of Commons, Mr. John Redmond was chosen to take command. Partly, if not mainly, the choice was dictated by the same reason which had decided the selection of Parnell as a Parliamentary candidate many years earlier. Redmond, like his old chief, was " a bit of a country gentleman." A Redmond, or, anyhow, a reputed ancestor, called Raymond le Gros had " come over " with Strongbow, Earl of Pembroke. In the seventeenth century a Redmond had held his castle against the Cromwellians. In " 'ninety-eight " an amazon of the family had ridden at the head of " the boys of Wexford," and on the distaff side, too, there was a creditable record, including several hangings, which to the patriotic mind meant even more than quarterings. John Redmond himself might be no more than a squireen owning shockingly encumbered acres, and in England, of course, nobody would have thought the name of this unmoneyed aristocrat worth putting on the prospectus of a bogus company. In Ireland, however, where the raising of live stock is a national industry, blood by itself is an asset. It would be, as one said to another, a fine thing to have a Redmond speaking for the poor old country.

Moreover, John Redmond had already proved himself a man. A devout Catholic, he had stood by Parnell when a bishop had intimated that the Parnellite who escaped cruel torment would have had an uncommonly close shave. As chief of the little band of those who were faithful to the memory of the uncrowned king he had led them, and comported himself, with a dignity made the more impressive by the wranglings and the antics and the subserviences of the faithless majority. Except in numbers his group had never been despicable, although at elections they had had to depend on the votes of a heterogeneous crowd of hill-side men and Tories, whereas the " Carties," though they had on their side the great Liberal party and the hierarchy, if not heaven itself, had always been " the gutter sparrows."

John Redmond was certainly a fine figure of a man, and probably has been written down in the Judgment Book as a good man, but, unfortunately, he was not the great man who could command the unquestioning support of a nation or a national party. On the other hand he was by no means the small man who could be elected leader one day and jockeyed out of his seat the next. Some there were who foresaw that the choice was bound to lead to trouble, and yet it was almost impossible to dispute that it had been inevitable. It would have been all but unthinkable to reject Redmond in favour of any of the other Irish chiefs. To look at him and at Mr. Dillon as they sat on the Irish benches was to understand why Shakespeare's Cæsar said : " Let me have men about me that are fat." Any French or Italian stranger in the gallery would have remarked that Mr. Dillon had the face of a sacristan, and, though that might convey nothing to an Englishman and nothing necessarily unfavourable to an Irishman, there could be no denying that he had " a lean and hungry look." Fitly enough, prototypes for the three most prominent of the anti-Parnellites could be found among the conspirators against Cæsar as we know them in the play. If Mr. Dillon recalled Cassius, there was in Mr. Healy a frequent suggestion of " the envious Casca," whilst in the Irish press of the day Mr. William O'Brien had been aptly stigmatised as Brutus—" dead Cæsar's Brutus." Mr. O'Brien was, before all else, " an honourable man "; in his own opinion, at all events, he had been Parnell's "angel," and yet he had struck with the rest, whilst his subsequent apologies and explanations in speech and writing all went to prove that he was the very incarnation of the stage Roman.

For a country weary of intrigue and plot John Redmond was the obvious choice. Judged by his career or his appearance he was absolutely solid and inspired confidence. And for a while all went well. Ireland, neglected since the failure of Gladstone's last Home Rule Bill, quickly attracted British attention when the factions united under Redmond's lead. At first, indeed, the attention was hostile. The Irish were pro-Boers to a man, gloried in it, and did not hesitate to find a seat for Colonel Lynch, who, in the words of Synge's farmer, had been " fighting bloody wars for Kruger." But even those who could only think of such a one as rebel and traitor, and who lifted up their hands in horror when cattle-driving became again the popular recreation of the west, could not quite dismiss the leader with an abusive epithet. " All I am," he said once, " I owe to the Jesuit Fathers," and at Clongowes he had been trained carefully in elocution. On Academy Days he could declaim passages from a Ciceronian speech with considerable effect. One of his masters has left it on record that at school he wrote excellent essays, especially notable for the " elevated and dignified way he had of looking at any given subject." In later life these things remained with him. He who had worn a convict's broad arrows and existed in a cell on bread and water was one of the two last members of the House of Commons to practise the " *ore rotundo* " style of oratory. When it is added that the only other holding to the old fashion was Henry Chaplin, an idea is given of the irony always to be found in the relations of Ireland and England.

After a little while English statesmen began to think that it might be not only advantageous but safe to treat with this Irishman, so utterly antithetical was he to all preconceived notions of the Nationalist politician as half Fenian and half pantaloon. On the other hand he never took the pose of the mere pleader for a little country. There was no going cap in hand to the conqueror. In the early days of Redmond's leadership Ireland became again a thorn in the English side. Irish M.P.'s began to annoy the Chief Secretary by getting themselves once more into gaol. Agrarian troubles began again. The editor and manager of a London newspaper were compelled to apologise at the Bar of the House for aspersions on the Nationalist party. An Irish revival was obvious, and, as a consequence, Campbell-Bannerman began to talk again of Home Rule, whilst the Government introduced a Land Bill which, not being favourable enough to the tenants, was promptly rejected by the representatives of Ireland and thereafter dropped.

Concurrently there was a change in the attitude of many Irish landlords towards the popular side, and it can scarcely be questioned that this was largely due to confidence in Redmond. Whatever his opinions were, whatever the language he used on American platforms, he was one of their own order, and, very plainly, without even a touch of that ruthlessness which had made Parnell so terrible. Hence the land conference, of which he was a member, and hence Wyndham's Land Act of 1903, in which the main recommendations of the conference were embodied. The Land Act, by which nearly a quarter of a million occupying tenants became with the aid of the British Treasury their own landlords, some £77,000,000 worth of property changing hands, was a great triumph for Redmond's statesmanship, and its results are a memorial to him more enduring than brass. Yet in the very hour of triumph a certain weakness in him was revealed. Much as the Act did for Ireland, it might have done a great deal more had its administration not been hampered by certain disgruntled personages over whom the leader failed to exercise his authority. It might, too, have paved the way to Home Rule. With their chief problem settled the landlords of the south soon formed an idea that a Parliament in Dublin would not be at all a bad thing, and accordingly formed the Reform Association, of which the object was to obtain for their country, by devolution, " a large measure of self-government."

Mr. Redmond was in America when the Association's policy was announced, but when news of it reached him he cabled home that it was " of the utmost importance."

> " It is," he said, " simply a declaration for Home Rule and is quite a wonderful thing. With these men with us, Home Rule may come at any moment."

However, the same men who had hampered a full and friendly settlement of the agrarian problem again intervened, and once more Mr Redmond surrendered to them. " A politician first, a politician second, a politician third," Stead once wrote of him, and with some truth. Mr. O'Brien has written of John Redmond that he " never acquired any first-hand power of judging popular feeling." On the morrow of the Wyndham Act the Irish people were in the mood for reconciliation, and so was their leader himself, but he was turned from the path of peace and victory because, instead of putting himself at their head, he allowed himself to be scared by a handful of political bosses. Touch with the people was never afterwards established, and when in the next decade the testing-time came it was found that the Parliamentary party had neither knowledge of nor hold over the public it had been so long falsely supposed to represent.

The four principal wreckers of the conciliation policy were Mr. Davitt, Mr. Dillon, Mr. Sexton and Mr. T. P. O'Connor. Mr. Davitt's opposition was comprehensible. The single Socialist of any repute in his country, he naturally hated a land settlement which was once and for all to make Socialism an impossibility in Ireland. Mr. Dillon may have been less singleminded. It has been hinted that he might have thought better of the land conference and its results if he had been invited to sit as one of its members. At all events he told Mr. Scawen Blunt that the land trouble was a weapon in Nationalist hands, and that to settle it finally would be to risk Home Rule. Having conceived this notion he did his best to keep the sore open. Mr. Sexton probably agreed with him. Mr. Sexton had been a great figure in Ireland, was a bitterly disappointed man, and now used all his immense influence as manager of the *Freeman's Journal* to mar the new promises of harmony. As to Mr. O'Connor, his position was clear enough. Hand and glove with the English Liberals, he was naturally anxious to prevent an alliance between his compatriots and the Tories.

The one really influential member of the party who was ready to go to all lengths for conciliation, and to support Mr. Redmond against all the wire-pullers and cavemen, was Mr. William O'Brien. Had these two stood together the subsequent history of Ireland might have been written differently. There were, however, temperamental differences between them. Mr. O'Brien could not restrain a tendency to gush. John Redmond was a man of impenetrable reserves. " As an individual entity," Stead wrote, " he is almost unknown to any except his intimates." Blarney was to him the eighth deadly sin, and, anxious as he was to see closed the

long feud between his party and his class, he may well
have been revolted by all the handshakings and em-
braces with which some others would have inaugurated
the new era. At certain critical moments he was,
perhaps, too much inclined to stand on that wonderful
dignity which so often was his greatest asset as a leader.
Could a composite Redmond have been made of John
and his brother William, the perfect Irishman would
have resulted. When William Redmond died a
soldier's death in France, men who had met him
casually in the army could scarcely speak of him with
a dry eye. His heart was always on his sleeve, but the
heart was so obviously of gold without alloy that his
way of wearing it was forgiven him.

Mr. O'Brien and John Redmond were too differently
constituted to march far together with ease or comfort,
yet for the sake of the country they might have kept
step had not the latter committed a blunder which
delivered him bound into the hands of the foes of settlement. John Redmond, as has been said, was a country
gentleman, and after the Wyndham Act he sold his
lands in Wexford to his tenants. What is more, he
arranged to sell them at a price above the average
fixed as equitable by the meeting of the National
Directory over which he himself had presided. The
thing was, indeed, done in such innocence that Mr.
Redmond actually communicated the terms of sale to
the *Freeman's Journal*. Moreover, the land was worth
every penny promised for it, and was so encumbered
that he could have derived no personal advantage from
the price obtained. None the less a deplorable situation was created. Other landlords naturally began to
demand " Redmond prices," and little good was done
when the Irish leader, waking suddenly to the brewing
storm, concluded the sale by letting his tenants have
their acres at a figure well below what they had willingly

agreed to give. Nobody heeded the alteration ; every-body remembered the originally published bargain. Had John Redmond thereafter joined hands with the other southern landlords in an effort to secure agrarian peace and political agreement he would have been de-nounced on every anti-conciliation platform as entering into a conspiracy of greed and grab. Nothing was left to him but to surrender to Messrs Dillon, Davitt, Sexton and O'Connor, to abandon the idea of working with Mr. Wyndham, and to consider what could be got out of the Liberals when they came back to power.

Everybody knows the sequel. When the Liberals came back to power they had an overwhelming majority from the British constituencies and offered the Irish nothing that the Irish wanted. Only at the very end of the decade, when Mr. George's Budget had con-vulsed politics, did the Nationalist party even seem to occupy a strong position. And even thereafter, when Mr. Redmond was telling the Liberals to " toe the line," and Unionists were calling him " dollar dic-tator " and using him as bogey-man, the strength was merely Parliamentary. Mr. Asquith and Mr. Birrell may have dreaded him in the division lobby, but their qualms were quickly forgotten in the greater dread that overcame them when the stick-at-nothing Orange-men of the north began to import rifles from Germany.

It is doubtful whether other ministers would have viewed the situation differently. Carson, after all, had a people behind him, whereas Redmond had at most a party. At Westminster " the old eagle " may have been the despotic leader of the Nationalist M.P.'s, just as British fancy painted him. His words had the ring of authority, and he looked the part to perfection. Unquestionably the rank and file members rendered him implicit obedience, but there is reason to believe that some at least of the orders he issued were in fact

Mr. Dillon's. Once, certainly, in August 1914 he spoke his own mind, but that is another story, and does not belong to the period with which we are dealing. Hidden from the British, hidden from the Irish, too, there must have been struggles for supremacy within the party, and more often than not, perhaps, John Redmond gave way. According to a priest who had been his master at school he had the one defect of laziness. At a supreme moment he could exert himself and take his own course, but in his life the moment came too late. When he emerged as absolute commander of his party, his party had long ceased to command more than lip-service from the people whom he and his lieutenants had half, or more than half, forgotten in the preoccupation of Parliamentary and political intrigue.

And yet, strange to say, John Redmond was not one of those who love politics for their own sake. His biographer, Mr. Redmond Howard, remarks that when he could take a day or a week away from the party and the House, he could and did banish all thought of them. He had the traditional squire's love of sport, and he loved books as well. For the outward pomps of leadership he cared nothing. In the midst of the House of Lords crisis I saw him with his daughter in two back seats of the upper circle at the Haymarket Theatre. Recognition was instant. The features were those of the face of the " Dictator " which glared at one from Unionist placards on every hoarding, only the face did not glare. On the contrary it was very calm, very tired. It was, as his admirers said, Roman. And so far as it revealed the soul, it carried a suggestion, " the long quiet reigns of the Antonines."

But if Mr. Redmond in those days held the centre of the Irish stage, there were others at work in Ireland whose mark on the country seems likely to prove more durable. Mr. O'Brien, although his " All for Ireland " movement never gained ground beyond County Cork, did, in spite of gush and ravings, put before the people an ideal of unity among creeds and classes which the founders of the Irish Free State are, at all events, still preaching. Mr. Healy, the " extremist in a party of one," at the beginning of the century regarded as the most unreasonable being that ever came from an unreasonable island, has, of course, survived all storms to become a governor-general and the respected mentor of all the young men who are trying to govern Ireland. Nobody ever predicted such a metamorphosis, yet it may be recalled that he had long ago styled himself the " political jackdaw of Rheims," the object of all curses, but with his feathers never a whit the worse. Also, when Mr. Healy is compared with his coevals, it can be seen that in more respects than one he had abilities that they all lacked. He was more vigorous than John Redmond. Unlike Mr. O'Brien, he could and always did draw a firm line between the sublime and the ridiculous. As a pleader for his country or for his religion he was more effective than Mr. Dillon, because, though there was often an appeal to the emotions in his words, there was never a whine in them. What is more, as an incorrigible independent, whilst the others were absorbed by party questions, he had the leisure to keep his eyes on Ireland, and in the wilderness to which he was condemned he studied statesmanship. Whilst the generation which had known Parnell formed the majority of the Irish race, the only choice for Mr. Healy was between standing alone or being a subordinate, and for the latter rôle he had no inclination. He had said things which put him outside the pale, as most thought, for the duration of his natural life. However, the new generation has taken him to its heart. The sign is not without promise.

If Mr. Healy's sins are forgiven, the curse of Cromwell may be passing.

Outside the Nationalist party others, too, were in the early years of the century working for ideals which, in the broad sense of the word, were national. Most prominent among them was Sir Horace Plunkett. Once Conservative member for South Dublin, he had to leave Parliament when the Orange drum was beaten against him on account of his sympathy with what Mr. Justice Moore once described as " the cowardly, rotten and sickening policy of conciliation." To him, as patron and promoter of agricultural co-operation, particularly in the years following the Wyndham Act, Ireland owes a great debt ; yet, admirable as were his intentions, it may be doubted whether any success would have crowned them had he not enjoyed the services of an inspired lieutenant. Mr. George Moore has written a description of Sir Horace Plunkett that cannot be bettered :—

> " Plunkett . . . a timid man . . . fears to meet any one with a sense of humour . . . dreads laughter as a cat dreads cold water . . . courteous and dignified, clearly of the Protestant ascendancy. . . . There is something pathetic in him which strikes one at first in the brow, in the grey eyes under it, and all over the flat face marked with a prominent nose, and in the hesitancy of his speech, which straggles with his beard, and his exclamation, ' Er-er-er,' without which he cannot speak half-a-dozen words."

The picture of the well-meaning, ineffective man is complete, but it chanced that Sir Horace (the " doctrinaire dairyman," as a lady in a novel by Mr. Wells called him) was one day introduced to a curious person who sometimes kept the books in a Dublin draper's shop and sometimes expounded the Upaiushads at the street corners. This person, called " Æ " by poets, but known among drapers and book-keepers as Mr. George Russell, was promptly enlisted in the co-operation cause, and with little more delay mounted his bicycle, to ride over Ireland thereon, spreading the new gospel. Where he succeeded, the more practical individual would have failed. The merely practical individual never gets away from the superstition that two and two make four, whereas the herald of co-operation must always insist that two and two will at least make five. "Æ," being a mystic, preached this sort of arithmetic with the fervour of conviction, and persuaded the peasant farmers to put it to the test. That they did so with the best possible results is now matter of history. Thereafter "Æ," having seen the material regeneration of his country, began to preach a spiritual crusade also, and for his special target he took the segregation of the sexes as practised in the " Pope's green isle." For the subsequent appearance of women in the political drama of Ireland he must be held largely responsible, though whether he can be congratulated on this success is a different question. In the opinion of the average Irishman, at all events, whilst the creameries and piggeries have been grand, the women have been more bother than they are worth. If the practical individual never knows where to begin, the mystic and idealist never knows where to stop.

Whether mention should be made of Arthur Griffith in a book dealing with the first ten years of the century is a moot point. It may be doubted whether in England one in a million had ever heard of the little dark man, but in Dublin, at all events, he was quite notorious, and everybody could have told an English visitor that he was a celebrated crank. As far back as 1902 he had outlined for his compatriots what was called the " Hungarian policy," by the terms of which Ireland was to occupy the same position in regard to

Britain that Hungary held to Austria, that is to say, they were to be two nations independent of one another save that their crowns should be worn by one monarch. To complete the parallel, the Irish M.P.'s were to stay away from Westminster even as the Magyars under Deák had stayed away from the Imperial Parliament of Austria. Three years later " Sinn Fein " as a political organisation came into existence with Griffith as its guiding spirit. In 1908 it ran a candidate at a Parliamentary by-election and was heavily defeated. The Irish public did not give it much more serious attention than a London crowd bestows on the little band of neo-Jacobites who annually decorate the statue of King Charles in Trafalgar Square. But whereas the Jacobites are dull the Sinn Feiners were lively, and contrived to obtain such notice as is vouchsafed to naughty boys. Their pin-pricks goaded John Redmond into solemn denunciation. Their disrespectful references to the Royal Family won them quotation in the English press. Not that Griffith was himself lively. He was, on the contrary, rather dull, with no gift of speech, and with a mind stuffed full of economics. He talked Friedrich List to everybody who would listen to him, and his listeners went away with a very vague idea of what the German protagonist of high protection might be meaning, but with his creed boiled down to a war-cry of " Burn everything English except the coal."

But by 1910, with Home Rule said to be in sight, with John Redmond triumphant in the House of Commons and in America, Sinn Fein seemed as near death and damnation as made no matter. It was only Arthur Griffith who did not give up the ghost. Among other things he was the most obstinate man that ever lived in Ireland. He was called " the man who never changed." He virtually went out of politics (he had never been very far into them), read more history, and waited for the day when the English would drive the people to him. And because, unlike John Redmond, he had never mixed much with the English he knew them. They did just what he always had expected. They discredited Redmond and the Parliamentary party. They ignored O'Brien and " All for Ireland." They shook their heads over Plunkett. And then they sat down at a table with Griffith and gave him the " Hungarian status " that nearly twenty years earlier he had been mad enough to demand.

MINISTERS FOR WAR

THE English people, though no more insensible than any other to the lure of military pageantry and martial music, seldom pretend to any intelligent interest in their army. Until recently, the average Englishman was ignorant how fours were formed or bayonets were fixed, and he had a shrewd notion that his ignorance was bliss. The few who adopted the profession of arms did so of their own free will, and for their subsequent fortunes the mass of citizens felt no special responsibility. The amateur soldier was, of course, a stock joke. Generally speaking, the army had proved equal to its tasks. There had certainly been scandals in connection with the Crimean War, but the heroism of Balaclava, thanks to Lord Tennyson, was remembered long after the blunders and failures, recorded in official publications, had been forgotten. Also, there had been Majuba, but, as that mishap had befallen under a Liberal administration, it could be regarded as in the course of nature. During almost the whole of the nineteenth century the public was profoundly unconcerned about military matters.

That, it seems, is the normal English frame of mind, but in the beginning of the twentieth century England was in some ways abnormal. The second Boer War had at once roused interest in the army and shaken the dull confidence hitherto reposed in it, and when peace returned the old apathy was not, strange to say, quickly and easily restored. Throughout King Edward's reign the country remained more or less upon the *qui vive*. It was a period of foreboding. If a great war was not actually expected, the idea of a great war no longer seemed, as to the happy Victorians, quite absurd. Assuredly the Edwardians did not want conscription or anything like it, nor would they willingly have had a penny added to the income-tax for anything except the navy, but, though they neither wished to serve in the army nor to pay for it, they had come to the conclusion, illogically it may be, that they not only needed an army, but an army fit for something beyond ceremonial parades and beating niggers.

Hence the positions taken in the public eye by Mr. Brodrick, Mr. Arnold-Forster and Mr. Haldane, who followed one another in the office of Secretary of State for War. Past occupants of that post had lived obscurely but not unhappily, despite occasional brushes with the Duke of Cambridge. Since Mr. Cardwell had abolished the numbering of the infantry regiments, they had acquiesced in the masterly inactivity expected of them. One after the other Gathorne-Hardy, Childers, W. H. Smith, Stanhope and Campbell-Bannerman had had their reigns, long or short but always quiet, in Pall Mall. True, there was some superficial pretence that the last-named had been responsible for the downfall of Lord Rosebery's Government, but nobody was deceived. Lord Lansdowne had gone to the War Office with the comfortable knowledge that nothing was required of him beyond *vis inertiæ*. Then, unfortunately, the South African hostilities supervened. Long before their conclusion Lord Lansdowne had sagaciously removed himself to another sphere. Mr. Brodrick, promoted to his place, had to bear the blame for all that his predecessors during a quarter of a century had left undone, until he in his turn handed the " poisoned chalice " to another.

T

In the circumstances it would have been wise for
him to set about his new duties with some show of
modesty and with an appeal for sympathy. For a while,
of course, unjust attacks would have been made upon
him, for in an unsuccessful war there must always be a
scapegoat, and the temporarily responsible minister will
invariably be selected. But in time there would have
been a revulsion of feeling. In time it would have
been realised that the mess and muddle had not been
of his making, that his acceptance of the disastrous
heritage had been an act of patriotism, that any effort
he was making to reform a department which a distinguished general had called a " terrible congeries of
confused opinion and congested clerkship " was praise-
worthy.

However, William St. John Fremantle Brodrick
went to work in another fashion. Humility was a
virtue he did not possess and could not assume.
Twenty years earlier, when he had first entered politics,
it had been observed of him by Sir Richard Temple
that " in a party sense " he could claim " many social
advantages." He had " a fulcrum and leverage not
pertaining to ordinary persons." He had " local
influence in the County of Surrey." The reward of all
this had been a minor front bench post after half-a-dozen
years in Parliament, and from the age of thirty he, a
largish minnow, had consorted with the tritons. The
tritons perhaps treated him somewhat casually, whilst
he, to redress the balance, developed a tendency to
retaliate upon the minnows who were merely minnows.
Men who had been his contemporaries at Eton used to
differ widely in their recollections of him. Some
recalled him with amused tolerance ; he had been their
butt. More remembered him less kindly; he had
been a bully. Premature arrival at ministerial rank had,
no doubt, accentuated certain points in his character.

Mr. Brodrick took over the War Office with a flourish of trumpets that might have announced the advent of a second Carnot. There was to be no more favouritism, no more red tape. Mr. Brodrick, having served at the War Office as an underling, knew all that was to be known about its dark and devious ways, and, therefore, was the very man to carry out the reforms required. Yet there were those who shook their heads. Some thought that one who had lived so long in the Pall Mall tradition must have been infected with its virus. Others opined that no strong man ever looked quite as aggressively strong as the new Secretary of State.

As to the war itself, Mr. Brodrick seemed to take some gloomy pleasure in informing the House of Commons that it was going very badly. After all he had not been conducting it. The first brief session of the Khaki Parliament was saddened by the speech in which he asked for a supplementary vote of £16,000,000 to pay for our defeats, and not everybody was convinced that everything was going to change for the better under the new dispensation. More than a year later it was his painful duty to read to the House of Commons, amid frantic Irish cheers, the despatch announcing the disaster to General Methuen. But Mr. Brodrick could neither learn nor forget. He could not learn that " influence in the County of Surrey " did not spell omnipotence. He could not forget his " many social advantages."

Long before the war was over Mr. Brodrick was unfolding to an awed though puzzled House his great scheme for reorganisation of the army. Like General Trochu, during the siege of Paris, he had a plan, but how the plan could be put into effect when practically every effective military unit was on active service six thousand miles away few ever understood.

Mr. Brodrick, however, would listen to no counsels of delay. We must, he proclaimed, have army corps at once, and it could not be denied that all the chief military nations actually possessed army corps. We were to have one army corp in Ireland, another in Scotland, a third on Salisbury Plain, and three more for service beyond the seas, each complete with staff. The militia and yeomanry were to be increased. A new style of headgear was introduced for officers and men, and alone among Mr. Brodrick's reforms it has survived to immortalise his name. It tends, it is said, to produce baldness in the wearer, but it is otherwise unobjectionable.

Patiently or impatiently, the public waited for the army corps to materialise, but Mr. Brodrick had no luck. In small matters as in large the fates, who love to disturb arrogance, worried him with pin-pricks. First there was the Colville case, when the Opposition suddenly united to champion an officer deprived of his command. Afterwards there was the Guards' "ragring " case. Mr. Brodrick knew happier moments when, having acquired a khaki uniform, he departed in company with Lord Roberts to study army corps in Germany, where they existed in the flesh as well as upon paper. As spectator of the German manœuvres he was duly photographed, booted and spurred, complete with sword. Before his return home he had received the Order of the Red Eagle.

But at Westminster Mr. Brodrick had no respite from worry. There was a hint of troubles to come when attention was called to the fantastic prices which had been paid for remounts in Hungary, and when a committee had investigated the matter, honest Tories described its report as " whitewashing " and " tame and bleating." Most of the South African scandals were only revealed when Mr. Brodrick, following Lord

Lansdowne's example, had left the War Office, but they were scented long before they were actually brought to light. Young Conservatives, anxious to pester their elders and betters, concentrated with one accord on army questions. Mr. Churchill described how Mr. Brodrick made army corps " by a mental process and a scratch of the pen." Mr. Beckett denounced Mr. Brodrick's management of the War Office as " mess, muddle and make-believe." Lord Hugh Cecil, Major Seeley, Sir John Dickson-Poynder, Mr. Ivor Guest all joined in the sport.

Mr. Brodrick, of course, was not responsible for a tithe of the sins for which he had to answer, but then the British system of government is so designed that nobody ever is to blame. And for the rest he was given a longer run with the taxpayers' money than results warranted. His scheme of army reorganisation was largely, as Sir Henry Campbell-Bannerman said, a concession to panic. Lord Rosebery had talked darkly of conscription, and Mr. Balfour had said the Brodrick plan was the sole alternative to conscription. Therefore the scales were at first weighted in his favour. But he could never give the soft answer which turns away wrath. He seldom had the air of understanding the facts and figures in his own proposals, and certainly did not contrive to make them clear to others. Only, he grew to look stronger and stronger : more and more the autocrat, as though to live up to his Red Eagle. " German Measles " was Mr. Churchill's diagnosis.

The six army corps, save as an expense to the nation, remained a phantom army to the end. They never existed except upon paper. In the autumn of 1903 Mr. Brodrick was shifted to the India Office, and Mr. Arnold-Foster succeeded him at the War Office. Mr. Arnold-Foster was the schoolmaster in politics. He

was the grandson of Dr. Arnold of Rugby. He was
the adopted son of Mr. W. E. Forster, the pioneer of
elementary education. From such antecedents no man
could escape. Mr. Arnold-Forster, as a director of a
publishing company, had justified the promise of his
double-barrelled name by writing and publishing the
Citizens' Reader, a work which is believed to have gone
through more editions than any other school-book ever
produced in England. Also, he had always been a
serious student of military and naval matters. As a
politician he had inclined to independence, and had,
indeed, first come to note as a critic of the South
African Chartered Company and of Mr. Rhodes.
Minor office, it may be, had been given him with an
idea that he was a person who thought, wrote and
talked too much, and should be kept quiet.

In minor office, however, he had continued thinking,
and, though he had been employed at the Admiralty, it
would seem his thoughts had run largely on the other
Service. He arrived at the War Office with many
notions on what needed to be done, and with the one
dominating notion that Mr. Brodrick's work must, at
all costs, be undone. Very soon he was abolishing
everything Mr. Brodrick had established : army corps,
reserve regiments, militia reserve, short service, all were
to go. So far nobody objected in the least. In a
Government that was growing more and more unpopular, Mr. Arnold-Forster was, for a moment, the
most popular member. Where Mr. Brodrick had been
stiff, domineering and official, he was affable, polite
and human. His industry was amazing. After a
sitting that lasted all night and well into the next afternoon, instead of going to bed he attended a meeting of
militia officers to learn their opinion on some affairs
of detail. Also, despite his willingness to listen to
persons of ordinary calibre, he enjoyed a reputation for

encyclopædic knowledge. In addition to the *Citizens' Reader*, he had written a history of England and a geography of the world (both for use in schools), whilst his sketch, entitled *In a Conning Tower*, had been mistaken by more than one sailor for the work of a naval officer. If his plan for army reform seemed at least as elaborate as Mr. Brodrick's had been, there was a prevalent belief that he himself understood it. That was a change for the better. Mr. Brodrick's plan, apparently, mystified nobody more than Mr. Brodrick. The only mystery about Mr. Arnold-Forster's plan was that, being quite shapeless, it did not look like a plan at all ; it had to be considered rather as a mixed grill.

However, Mr. Arnold-Forster won admiration by his candour. His exposure of all that had been amiss before he took command was notably courageous. Mr. Brodrick in possession of an ugly secret had always relegated it to a file, and the file to the dust which, in Government offices, saves so many reputations. There was, for instance, the affair of the jam. There had been 1,350,816 tins of it, all bought for the consumption of our troops as holding one pound each. But the pound, by some mistake, had been apothecary's weight : a pound of twelve and not sixteen ounces. Pall Mall had been aware of the error before Mr. Brodrick's departure, yet it was left to Mr. Arnold-Forster to institute the searching inquiry. No thought for the reputations of his predecessors or his colleagues ever deterred the author of the *Citizens' Reader* from following the path of civic virtue.

But in a Government doomed to destruction even the most conscientious, industrious and omniscient minister will sooner or later find himself personally in trouble. Mr. Arnold-Forster made the mistake, common among educationists, of imagining that the passion for self-improvement is universal. He looked upon the volunteers and beheld a numerous and singularly inefficient body. He decided that, without loss to the country, the number might be reduced and that the remainder should be trained into a really effective force. Against such an edict nothing much could be said in public, but in the privacy of the polling-station quite a lot could be expressed with the sign of the cross. Mr. Balfour's Government had against it the labour vote, the chapel vote, the free trade vote, the Irish vote. Owing to Mr. Arnold-Forster the volunteer vote was also lost.

When the Liberal administration was formed, the War Office was awarded to Mr. Haldane. His selection was generally approved. During the Boer War he had distinguished himself as a champion of the army against the pacifists in his own party. Furthermore, his intimate acquaintance with Germany seemed a double qualification for his post. His appointment to the War Office could be interpreted as a gesture of amity to Germany, but it could also be regarded as an insurance against risk, for he, if anyone, could surely read the German mind. And then, to everybody's amazement and relief, he did not pull out of his red despatch case a scheme for military reform immediately on reaching the Treasury Bench. Mr. Brodrick and Mr. Arnold-Forster had had their plans cut and dried. Mr. Haldane, on the contrary, told the country with agreeable modesty that anything he did in a hurry would most likely turn out wrong. Meanwhile he made a few preliminary economies, and delivered a lecture on the virtues of " Clear Thinking," which reads to-day much better than it sounded in the House of Commons. Mr. Haldane in his time has said many things well, but nature did not intend him to be an orator. Mr. Wells once wrote of his voice as reminiscent of a beast in pain.

Indeed, the time had been when the Speaker had only to call on Mr. Haldane to cause a stampede of members from the chamber. Had his tone been the most dulcet, Richard Burdon Haldane, a Scottish philosopher trained in Germany, would yet have alarmed any audience of average Englishmen. Tories who questioned the patriotism of C.-B. might have been pardoned for suspecting the new War Minister had been appointed in the hope that he might kill all public interest in the army. However, events were to show that it was an interest which could be killed by nothing save a victorious war. Whenever Mr. Haldane had a pronouncement to make upon military affairs he had a full house and a good press, and there is no doubt that his speeches, in an abbreviated form, were read by thousands of young men whose normal concern was not with politics. Lord Morley once wrote of Mr. Haldane's "trumpet call." Assuredly he was a strange performer on the trumpet, but the two words used in reference to the creator of the Territorial Army have more of earnest in them than of jest.

And there is this to be said : if Mr. Haldane started with the disadvantage, from the English point of view, of being a sort of professor, he had at least the advantage of being a different sort of professor from Mr. Arnold-Forster. The latter, as has been observed, was encyclopædic. It might almost be added that he was Cassell's *Cyclopædia* made flesh. Even those who disliked the flavour of Weimar, Gottingen and Jena had to admit that Mr. Haldane was on another intellectual plane. Judged as the Minister for War, Mr. Haldane deserved well of his country. He found an army of regulars, militia and volunteers, maintained at a great expense and serving nobody exactly knew what purpose. He began by effecting certain economies, though their extent was a bitter disappointment to a big section of his party which remained blind to the German danger.   He went on to produce order out of chaos, always acting on the elementary though often neglected principle that utility for war is the sole criterion of value in soldiers and things military.   When he found battalions of line infantry which could not be put into the field, because they were chronically below strength or because there was insufficient artillery to support them, he terminated their existence.   He took the militia, which had long ceased to have any definite function, and converted it into a first of reserve for the regular army.   He took the volunteers and, without doing hurt to their feelings, turned that much derided body into the territorial army which, when the War came, provided some of the best divisions for the Front. Out of the very unpromising material of the university bug-shooters he produced officers' training corps.

All told, it was a wonderful performance for one man, and that one man under the constant fire of Tories who were sure that under a Liberal Government the army must be going to the dogs, and of Liberals, not to mention Socialists, who could see nothing but criminal folly in a Government of the Left mending instead of ending our military system.   In all he did, Mr. Haldane had, of course, the support of the military experts, but as that support had been bestowed before on the wholly contradictory plans of Mr. Brodrick and Mr. Arnold-Forster its weight must not be exaggerated.   Of more importance was the support he received from the general public, particularly in regard to the territorials. Mr. Haldane was terribly voluble.   One of his army speeches took three hours to deliver, but, despite dabblings in metaphysics, he could be lucid.   When he said what he wanted, ordinary citizens understood and responded.

The pity of it is that to the end, although he said so

much, he never told more than half of what he wanted
and less of what he feared.   For, from the time he took
office under Sir Henry Campbell-Bannerman, Mr. Haldane was of that innermost circle of the Cabinet wherein
it was known that war with Germany, though it might
be avoided, was not improbable.   Under Mr. Haldane's
direction preparations for that eventuality were made
even down to the " *dix minutes d'arrêt*," in which the
British Expeditionary Force were to have tea after
disembarkation in France.   But the preparations,
though perfect in their way, were necessarily on a tiny
scale, for the country was kept in ignorance of what
was toward.   Now and then, in something said by
Mr. Haldane, one can detect, rather faintly, the " trumpet note."   His mere use of the words " expeditionary
force " had a significance which, after the event, cannot
be missed.   But against every guarded warning he
may have given can be set an expression of unguarded
optimism from the ministers who were not " in the
know " ; from Mr. George, from Mr. Churchill, from
Sir John Simon, from Mr. Harcourt.

Truly the story of Mr. Haldane at the War Office is
a strange one, full of irony.   In all England no man
was more truly a " pro-German " than he.   With others
the thing was usually a political affectation, a result of
ignorance, a perversity, or a snobbery.   With him the
thing was deep, genuine, and the result of close knowledge.   But for half-a-dozen years he was engaged
laying the foundations of an army for which he knew
there could be but one likely object—a life-or-death
conflict with the German Empire.

MEN OF THE LAW

IT is partly, I suppose, a diminished zest that makes me feel that the Bench and Bar of to-day are not so rich in character as when Edward was king. But, I think, after all allowances have been made for the personal equation, the fact remains of a lessened piquancy. We have much learning and eloquence, but they are less allied with amusing (or irritating) idiosyncrasy. Of course, all professions tend nowadays to lose their distinctive character : a doctor may look like a stockbroker ; a stockbroker may give the impression of a bishop ; a bishop may have something of the style of a book-maker. The law does still stamp its mark on most of its followers. There is a peculiar expression still about lawyers of a fatigued vigilance, an air of rather hostile toleration of everything and everybody not legal, that gesture which Dickens called " the jury droop," that curiously leathery kind of complexion which goes with all colours, from pasty " law-calf " to the full purple of morocco. " All lawyers," said Disraeli, " lead loose lives in their youth," and though they may have long outlived that aspersion there is still in the relative asceticism of their busy years something that suggests wild nights of long ago. The Bar is the only profession which maintains in adult life the communal relations of student days ; the Bar mess brings young and old together, and marks the separation of both from ordinary humanity. Thus there is still opportunity for a certain development of individuality. But, on the other hand, the law mixes much more than it used to do in society, and there is a marked falling-off in that singular kind of Bohemianism which distinguished so many learned counsel and judges of a bygone time.

Perhaps this is largely due to the fact that the criminal courts are so much less the nursery of great advocates. In no place has there been more change than in the Old Bailey. The real Old Bailey still stood in the first years of the century, a shabby next-door neighbour to the grim and massive Newgate prison, which, dark and minatory, festooned with gigantic fetters, frowned, a savage anachronism, on the busy modern street. The Old Bailey was an evil place in every sense of the word, commonly designed, commonly furnished, dark, poky and inconvenient, exhaling in its most concentrated form that atmosphere of stale breath, heated clothing and damp umbrellas which is characteristic of all places where British justice is administered.

To-day all of that is changed that can be changed. The new Old Bailey is spick and span almost to jauntiness. But to a sensitive mind it is, perhaps, even more inhuman than its shabby predecessor : it suggests the widening gulf between man and man, between those who sin and those who judge. Old Bailey lawyers in the old days were often coarse and brutal, but they were not aloof. They took a certain personal interest in the people they defended ; congratulated in human fashion those whom they saved from hanging, and sometimes wore mourning rings for the unfortunate. To-day the Old Bailey is less intimate all round. Among the lawyers composing the Bar there is little of the sense of being a close corporation, little of the rough jollity and "snugness " of the old days. A good many men go eastward after their call because they can generally reckon on some kind of brief at some kind of fee, and there is always the chance of getting into

the public eye.   But few take to the Old Bailey with
the idea of sticking to it.   The way of the judge in
Trial by Jury is not the approved modern path to legal
eminence.   The day of the great specialised criminal
lawyer is gone.   At one time the High Courts Bench
was largely recruited from the ranks of famous advocates
at the Central Criminal Court.   Without taking note
of Jeffreys, who rose from the Old Bailey to the Woolsack, we have only to go back a few years to another
distinguished Lord Chancellor, Lord Halsbury, who
was one of a group of brilliant barristers long living on
criminal briefs.   Lord Brampton, as Mr. Henry
Hawkins, was chiefly known as a criminal lawyer ; and
there were others who almost looked on the neighbour-
ing Newgate as a mediæval baron might have done on
his deer-park.   They were a mighty race, given to
florid eloquence and ingenious cavil, terrors to witnesses
and even sometimes to judges, and many of them
cultivated to the utmost the powers of their leathern
lungs.

The late Sir Charles Mathews, one of the most deadly
of great Old Bailey counsel, and conspicuous for the
prosecution in the first decade, was a delicate little man
with a curiously tired voice tending to drop at every
tenth word, and it was he who, to a large extent, inaugurated the quieter modern fashion.   But some of
his predecessors, to a great extent, relied for their
verdicts on terrifying loudness of tone ; they roared
like all the bulls of Bashan.   A newly appointed judge
was once startled during his first Old Bailey sitting
by a dreadful noise.   " What's that ? " he exclaimed.
" Is it thunder ? "   " No, m'lud ; only Mr. Sleigh
making an application in the next court," was the reply.

The departure of the prestige of the Old Bailey Bar
is easily explained.   The business of defending crim-
inals is no longer lucrative, according to modern

standards. A burglar of to-day may be able to afford something more than a burglar of the 'sixties, but not very much ; crime, after all, does not permit of syndication beyond a certain extent, Sir Arthur Conan Doyle's Professor Moriarty belongs to pure fiction, and the best-managed thieves' kitchen does not accumulate much in the way of a reserve fund. On the other hand, with the growth of big business, there is hardly a limit to be placed on the money that great firms are willing to pay for the best that can be had in the way of legal aid. Thus the whole outlook of lawyers has changed. Thirty years ago it was possible to pick up a very good living at the Old Bailey, and it was not easy to accumulate a vast fortune in a few years elsewhere. To-day the prospects of the first career remain much what they were, while famous K.C.'s can get enormous fees from big commercial and society suitors. Sir John Simon was offered as much as seven thousand pounds to appear in a single case.

It is therefore natural enough that criminal practice has come to be regarded mainly as a stepping-stone to better and to higher things ; a reputation made at the Old Bailey is valuable chiefly for what it leads to. Two results follow. The Central Criminal Court has now few particular stars of its own, and the style adopted by beginners is far quieter and more ordinary than was once the case ; it is a general purposes style, and not specially designed to mesmerise the common juryman. When the magic of words is badly wanted, and can be paid for at fancy rates, a fashionable K.C. is apt to be imported from outside.

Thus Sir John Simon, whose first beginnings were at the criminal Bar, early left burglars for company directors, who could pay very much better. But the Old Bailey has called him back from time to time, both as prosecutor and as counsel for the defence. Sir John

Simon has not often been heard in a criminal court since his youth, and the constant jingle of the guinea—or rather thousand guineas—has so softened his manner that it is often forgotten that he can be, when he likes, a very terrible cross-examiner ; on one occasion he reduced a prisoner to inarticulate sobs. But ordinarily his chief weapon is a deadly suavity, like that of the boa-constrictor hypnotising the rabbit.

Quite different in method was the other great King's Counsel who dominated the Law Courts during the first few years of the century, and was occasionally tempted by large fees, or impelled by the demands of his official position, to the Old Bailey. Sir Edward Carson was a terrible prosecutor ; he learned his business in Ireland, where legal manners are sterner than here, and, as he long went about in fear of his life from desperadoes, it was natural that he should be bitter when he got one in the dock before him. But his fame as counsel for the defence was hardly less high in the legal profession. " I would rather be defended by Ted Carson when I was wrong than by any other man when I was right," was the opinion of a high authority. At a Bar mess some famous legal men were discussing Sir Edward and his great rival of the moment. The debate was concluded by an admirer thus : " I should be ready to hunt tigers with Carson ; I wouldn't hunt cats with the other."

Sir Edward always carefully preserved his rich brogue, but it was never heard to such advantage as in a Court of Justice, and was especially luscious when he leant forward, with his hungry, hatchet face drawn in every muscle with the kind of excitement one sees in a greyhound straining at the leash, to demolish a hostile witness. The thing had a most curious effect. Here were the very tones of the music-hall Irishman, and the purport was so grim. It was as if you heard Sir

Harry Lauder declaiming the Athanasian Creed. Sir Edward had a trick of repeating the word " any "—which he pronounced " Annie "—with such emphasis that the most good-natured juryman felt that he must convict, or recommend that the chief witness for the prosecution should be proceeded against for perjury, as the case might be. It was a liberal education for any young barrister who wanted the elements of his business to listen to the great counsel laying down the law as to what should happen to Annie man, or for that matter Annie woman, who in Annie circumstances, without Annie justification, or being in Annie fear of Annie serious injury to himself, or Annie one belonging to him, commits Annie violence against, or inflicts Annie injury on, Annie other person. Apart from the constancy of his accent, Sir Edward had the most flexible voice imaginable, and could pass at will from thunder-tones to a not less menacing calm, or from a cynical drawl to a deadly hiss. Once he even burst into tears as the result of his own eloquence.

Coming to smaller men, a considerable reputation was founded early in the first decade of the century by the advocate who now sits on the Bench as Sir Ernest Wild. He made himself by his brilliant defence of the man Gardiner, twice tried for what was called the Peasenhall mystery. He was then opposed to Mr. Dickens, K.C., and there could have been no greater contrast between the gravely responsible style of the prosecutor and the fiery energy of the counsel for the defence. Sir Ernest Wild was not a profound lawyer, but he had many of the qualities of a very great advocate. For a forlorn hope, that might be realised by sheer audacity and pertinacious worrying of witness, judge and jury, he had few fellows.

Turning to the eminent lawyer who is now Marquess of Reading, but who as Rufus Isaacs pervaded the

U

Law Courts in the first ten years of the century, I do not recall any appearance of his at the Old Bailey, though he had a great part in one of the most sensational causes of the period, that of Whittaker Wright. He was, in his earlier years, often junior to Sir Lawson Walton, whose early death prevented the realisation of high political ambitions. Rufus Isaacs, as everyone knows, started life as a sailor. Then he went into business. Then, after a short experience as a stock-broker's clerk, he set up for himself in the enchanted land of bulls and bears, but the bulls tossed him and the bears hugged him so unkindly that at twenty-seven he was once more in search of a career. Then, in no great spirit of optimism, he turned to the Bar, where his success was almost instantaneous. "He is the only man I know," said Walton, " who has not had to go through the grind of quarter sessions and county court like the rest of us." He had become a K.C. some two years before the old century ended, largely because the demands on him as a junior were such that his health must have broken down had he continued indefinitely to cope with them. But though he may be said to have taken silk for his health, it brought him only a very relative repose.

It was quickly discovered that he was the one man to brief in commercial cases. His early experiences had not been wasted. His familiarity with the sea, his knowledge of business, his grasp of all the mysteries of finance made him an advocate of peculiar value in such suits. Barristers are not as a class versed in the arcana of the world of buyers and sellers, and, accustomed though they are to get a rapid grip of any kind of facts, they are perhaps at their worst in groping their way through mazes of figures and trade technicalities. To Rufus Isaacs, on the other hand, what with his inborn Jewish aptitude for calculation and his close acquaintance with the business world, figures spoke as poetry does to some men. Just as there are some people who can repeat *The Ancient Mariner* after reading it twice, so Rufus Isaacs could carry in his mind all the details of a balance-sheet after little more than a glance. When it fell to him to prosecute the unfortunate Whittaker Wright, experienced business men were amazed at the superb mastery he exhibited of every feature of a case of appalling complexity.

His energy while at the crest of his forensic success was marvellous. He would often work till the small hours while habitually rising not later than five. For a long time he was regularly astir at four, doing four hours' full reading before sitting down to breakfast. Most men, even of strong physique, would be wrecks after a few months of such unremitting toil. But nobody ever found Rufus Isaacs during all those years other than alert, energetic and good-tempered. Nothing seemed to be able to affect his superb nervous organisation or to diminish by a trifle the taut erectness of his spare figure.

Rufus Isaacs was a prince of cross-examiners. His forensic speeches were in every way excellent, lucid, vigorous, closely argued, exquisitely tactful, occasionally rising to considerable heights of sober eloquence. But it was in the handling of evidence that his supreme gifts were shown. If anything damaging were to be got out of an adverse witness Rufus Isaacs would get it, and that without resort to any of the traditional brow-beating tactics. There was never a more affable or a more deadly cross-examiner, while no man knew better how to bring out his own case without offering points of attack to the enemy.

In some ways, indeed, he was surpassed. He never attained the almost elemental force of Sir Charles Russell at his best. He lacked the mordant power of

Sir Edward Carson.   Sir John Simon, perhaps, afterwards brought methods very like his own to a greater
pitch of perfection.   Very many barristers long forgotten have surpassed him in knowledge of law and
subtlety of intellect.   His strong point mentally was a
sublimated common sense which told him precisely
what to accentuate and what to omit or slur over.
The rest was explained partly by an amazing skill and
tact, and partly by the sheer force of a pleasant but
masterful personality.   The man who was always the
same, never ruffled, never at a loss, equable in reverse,
moderate in triumph, deferential without servility, firm
without arrogance, determined and pertinacious always,
could not but impress himself on judges, who are but
human, as well as on juries, which are very human
indeed.

The money value of these qualities was, of course,
enormous.   In one great case, which lasted twenty
days, Mr. Isaac's retaining fee was three thousand
guineas, with a " refresher " of two hundred guineas
a day.   The year before he accepted the post of
Solicitor-General he made over thirty thousand pounds.

Sir Edward Carson's energy was of quite a different
character.   He was never a strong man physically, and
only extraordinary courage and determination could
have enabled him to overcome the handicap of an
inadequate vitality.   He was often ill, and always lazy.
That may seem a bold statement to make of a man
whose life for so many years was one of hard work and
frequent nervous strain of exceptional intensity.   But
though he had the power, like so many indolent and
rather delicate men, of forcing himself to strenuous
exertion his natural tendency was always to inertia.
There was a time when his distaste for any kind of
trouble went to extraordinary lengths.   Habits of
business ultimately conquered the procrastinating dis-

position which would make him rise from his desk
because his pen was scratchy or the light annoyed him.
But the disposition itself always remained, and the
occasional exorbitance of Sir Edward's fees at the Bar
was dictated far less by a desire for money—money
never held more than a moderate place in his philosophy
—than by a disinclination for overwork. His enormous success at the Bar, the unique position he occupied
for so many years, was the more remarkable when we
consider that his exertions, instead of flowing naturally
from an excess of mental energy, were all against the
grain of his disposition.

To turn to the judges, we have admittedly no
present-day figure so picturesque as Lord Halsbury,
who was delivering brisk judgments from the Woolsack
during the period, and still preserving, in his 'eighties,
enough energy to become later what one of his less
judicious political admirers called " an antique bantam
of the fighting breed." I remember the curt common
sense with which he pricked the bubble of an organ-
grinder's pretensions to a peerage. He had a way of
summarily sweeping aside sophistries of counsel which
must have been immensely disconcerting to those
gentlemen. And when it was all over he would go to a
chemist's over against Westminster Bridge and drink
an ice-cream concoction from the soda fountain with all
the innocence and physical hardihood of a boy of ten.

Nor is there such an eccentric as Vaughan Williams,
the learned and untidy, who wore the same tall hat for
years, and astonished people in assize towns with his
pipe and his bull-dog. We have no such perfect Tory
as Grantham, and no such suave unmaker of marriages
as Jeune. But happily with us, though not on the
Bench, is Lord Darling, whose quips enlivened the
whole period under review. He owed his promotion
to the discriminating notice of Lord Halsbury. It has

been said that in office Liberals forget their principles, and Conservatives remember their friends. Nobody, at any rate, could suspect Lord Halsbury of not seeing the best side of a good party man. He saw the best side of Mr. Darling, and, as things turned out, that best side was very good. "It was managed by a job," sings (*pianissimo*) the learned lawyer who presides in *Trial by Jury*. "Job" is sometimes the crude description of a most beneficial departure from routine. It is natural that when a Lord Chancellor elevates to the Bench a comparatively unpractised barrister the cry should go up that the public interest has been sacrificed to private partiality; and no doubt that view is sometimes justified. "People talk of a scandal," said one Lord Chancellor, with reference to his appointments. "Which is the worst scandal? That three men who perhaps don't know quite as much law as they might should be put in a position where they can learn it, or that three men of excellent family should go through the Bankruptcy Court?" That is an extreme case, but it is a fact that many Chancellors go, as Mr. J. A. Strahan points out in his interesting book on Bench and Bar, looking first for a gentleman, and " if he knows a little law, so much the better." But, curious as it may seem, such appointments often turn out extremely well, while there are many failures among the judges appointed on what Lord Melbourne called " damned merit."

It was so with Sir Charles Darling. He was appointed in 1897. Mr. Justice Darling existed for over a quarter of a century, and Lord Darling is still a valued and valuable public servant. The length and distinction of this wonderful career are surely sufficient vindication of Lord Halsbury's partiality.

The fact is that there are two kinds of judges who justify themselves. One is the profound lawyer who ends naturally in the House of Lords as one of the final arbiters on the most knotty problems of law and equity. The other is the common-sense judge, with a considerable knowledge of human nature, and a faculty of getting to the heart of any matter not too abstruse. Mr. Justice Darling belonged to the second class. He was emphatically the " human " judge ; he liked " human " cases ; and he generally managed to get them. Hence his habitual association with " laughter in court."

" As there is a Crown law," says Halifax, " there is a Crown wit also. To use it with reserve is very good and very rare. There is a dignity in doing things seldom, even without any other circumstance. Where wit will run continually, the spring is apt to fail ; so that it groweth vulgar and the more it is practised the more it is debased." Some of Mr. Justice Darling's *obiter dicta* were undeniably more than witticisms ; they were wit itself. But possibly he was too prone to miss the dignity of doing things seldom. Still, there is a real use for " laughter in court." It makes the whole little world of Bench Bar and jurymen kin. It may, like a good dinner, " lubricate business." It is sometimes, moreover, a useful means of reducing a pretender or pricking a fallacy ; and Sir Charles Darling often brought his verbal felicities to bear with effect on serious issues. More than once he tumbled over a great fabric of sophistry by an apt whimsicality. For example : counsel was once arguing that a farm was really a non-textile factory. " Ought Bloomfield," asked the judge, " when he wrote *The Farmer's Boy*, to have put it ' The Non-Textile Factory Boy ' ? " Common sense could not have been expressed with more point.

It was this native shrewdness which was his main strength. He brought to the Bench not only an alert and compact intelligence, but the point of view of an experienced man of the world who knows, on the whole, exactly how many beans make five by the law of nature and arithmetic, and is rather impatient with any attempt to prove them four or six by any other law. The Law, though generally far more common sense than is generally admitted, may be often strained to absurdity, and a jest is often the most effective way of exhibiting the naked unreason of what is being most rationally argued. Sir Charles Darling could crush a scamp as well as prick a bubble with a joke. Once, in the early years of the century, he spoke of a cause which had been withdrawn as an " impudent action." Next morning counsel in the case applied that it should be re-instated, in order to show that the plaintiff, however ill-advised, had acted in good faith. The judge beamed on the barrister. " Mr. Blank," he said, " like David, I spoke yesterday in my haste. I should not have used the word ' impudent.' " Counsel interrupted with purring self-satisfaction. " Of course —ludship's explanation—wholly satisfactory—my client —only wished, m'lud—make it clear——" " Mr. Blank," said the judge, " I was about to observe that I spoke in my haste when I described this as an *impudent* action. I now say at leisure that it was a *blackmailing* action. The application is refused."

The most cutting and eloquent denunciation could hardly have had such an effect.

LABOUR LEADERS

WHEN the Parliament of 1900 assembled for the first time, all but one of the members of the House of Commons attended on the Whip of a party leader.

The solitary exception was James Keir Hardie. He was what the Japanese used to call a *ronin*, a " wave man," or man without master. In 1892, when a majority of voters were more tired of the Conservatives than enthusiastic for the Liberals, he had made his first appearance at Westminster. It was a remarkable business. Whitehall heard a trumpet and saw a two-horse brake, from which descended a man of grave face and already grizzled hair, whose general intensity of expression contrasted curiously with the tawdriness of all this advertisement. Those were the days when nearly everybody about St. Stephen's wore customary suits of solemn black ; even John Burns, preferring blue, contrived that, if aggressive, his reefer should not be indecorous. Hardie insisted on tweeds of the tweediest, and crowned himself with a cloth cap to match. He inspired the policemen with a momentary doubt. He shocked the attendants. The fame of him, spread abroad by the newspapers, variously affected the public. Some found him merely ridiculous. Some regarded him as a portent of wrath to come, a sinister star forecasting permanent discord of the spheres. Others, again, imagined him a wandering comet that would presently pass and leave no trace. The wisest men of the time had taken the last view.

" A little splotch of red " was the commentary of Sir William Harcourt, waving him aside, Podsnap-like, as something unpleasant, but not disquieting. For a while the wisest people seemed justified. The " damned spot " disappeared. From 1895 to 1900 decorum was disturbed only by Radicals who could be understood even when not approved, people who at the worst wore bowlers and serge. The cloth cap was forgotten. But suddenly Keir Hardie returned when he was least expected, at the height of the khaki fever, the cloth cap more aggressive and significant than ever, opposing not only the top-hat but the " Brodrick." What was more, he was evidently in for life.

There were, of course, other Labour members even in those days. There was Burt, already highly considered, and later to be honoured as father of the House. There was John Burns, still with a touch of the subversive about him, but rapidly acquiring merit in middle-class eyes. There was " Mabon " Abrahams. There was Bell, the railway man. But these and others were all part of the retinue of the Liberal leader. Some of them were very unruly followers, occasionally abusive on the floor and unreliable in the Lobby. But, in the jargon of the hour, they could all be classed as " Lib-Labs." Their aims and views were certainly not the aims and views of the sleek Nonconformist tradesman or the peerage-hunting manufacturer, but they could have importance only through the Liberal party, and on all issues that mattered they might be depended on to follow the Liberal whip. Hardie, on the other hand, was a Labour man and Socialist pure and simple. He carried independence to the logical extreme. He had just contested two constituencies. At Preston he fought a Tory. At Merthyr, to show there was no ill-feeling—or rather no good-feeling—he opposed a Liberal ; and it was through

Merthyr that he won his way back to the House. The election there may be justly regarded as one of the great elections of history.

For Hardie was a man of considerable importance. Even now, when Labour has ousted Liberalism from its position as one of the two great parties, it is hard, for an Englishman at any rate, to realise of how much importance. That touch of showmanship that was in him misled many as to the basic character of one of whom it was possible to admire and easy to hate, but very hard for a Southerner to understand. Mr. Chesterton once threw a ray of light on him when he said that Hardie was " very like a poor man in Sir Walter Scott." There is, again, a passage in Lord Morley's *Recollections* which, though it does not allude to the Waverley novels, coincides with this verdict. " A hard-headed honest fellow," wrote Morley, " but rather vain and crammed full of vehement preoccupations, especially on all the most delicate and dubious parts of politics." Few Englishmen can recall an acquaintance possessing this particular assortment of incongruous qualities. But let him open *Old Mortality*, and he will find them incarnate in the person of Balfour of Burley. Let him read a speech or article by Hardie, and the odds are that he will catch ever and anon an echo of the Covenanting hero's very tone and words. Hardie was not so simple a thing as an ordinary Scot, though, in truth, Scots, however ordinary, are far from simple. He was a Scot of a type that the Act of Union and the broadening of the southward road have made rare. Neither in essentials nor in inessentials did he ever Anglicise himself ; and in England friends, enemies and neutrals were all equally at a loss to make anything of the alien in their midst.

Thus he was honest, almost glaringly honest. Probably the House of Commons contained no man

whose word more closely corresponded with his thought.
Yet his honesty was often questioned because of his
yet more glaring vanity. A dash of conceit in one
who has risen from the ranks must be expected. Its
absence would be contrary to nature. It is found in all
the early Labour members, and it is familiar enough on
the Socialist benches and platforms of to-day. The
Right Honourable John Burns was always a standing
miracle to the Right Honourable John Burns, and
quite comprehensibly so. Crooks patted himself on
the back from morn to midnight. But they and others
like them found time to approve people who might be
outside their circle. Their good conceit of themselves
was not exclusive. A well-meaning Prime Minister
was not beyond the range of their charity. They could
even extend tolerance to a deserving peer. With
Hardie it was quite otherwise. Surveying the House
of Commons, Mr. Bernard Shaw acutely denominated
him " the damnedest aristocrat of the lot." There was
a Calvinistic exclusiveness in Hardie, and a Calvinistic
want of charity. He was proud of himself in fact. He
was proud of his class in theory. Outside of himself,
and outside of his class, he saw little or nothing to love
or to tolerate. Others conceived of the Proletarian as
an economic phenomenon. He conceived of the
Proletarian as the member of a sect—Carlyle's sect
of " Poorslaves." Between him and the enemy there
was the war of Israelite and Philistine. If he was
as sincere as a Joshua he was also as merciless.
Once he was interrupted in a debate on unemployment.
" Well-fed beasts," he ejaculated. Doubtless he spoke
in heat, as he said in formal apology to the Speaker, but
he spoke only what he would have thought in cool
blood. He did actually see mankind in terms of well-fed
beasts and ill-fed drudges. On one occasion he declared
that he would not belong to a club that admitted Lord

Salisbury. That was no insolent gasconade. Un-doubtedly he did feel just like that. St. Just felt like that too ; Fifeshire is much nearer to France than Kent.

It was Keir Hardie, such as he was, that did more than any man to make Socialism a political force. The narrowness of his charity, no less than the intransig-ence of his logic, served where English geniality and vagueness could hardly have effected the purpose. When he entered the House of Commons for the second time, Socialism was little more than a middle-class fad. It had no existence outside debating societies, trade unions and obscure borough councils. It had next to no organic connection with the world outside. Socialism, in brief, was Fabianism, and Fabianism was mainly talk. For Hardie, Britain was a cramped stage. He aspired to greater things. His faith, to say nothing of his vanity, sent him globe-trotting—to America, Africa, India, the Antipodes ; and in all his wandering he was sustained by his conviction that capitalist and militarist Jerichos were crumbling at his voice. His self-confidence was amazing. Sir Henry Lucy, meaning to be complimentary to the Labour men of his time, noted that " they confine their interposition in debate to topics with which they are personally familiar." Not so Hardie. His topics were as various as the colours of his ties. There was nothing on which he felt a compulsion to silence, nothing on which he did not speak with the full assurance that what he had to say was of value from his own and his party's point of view. His fancy for the " delicate and dubious parts of politics " was, of course, a heritage from the Cameron-ians. To Burley and his kind, Heaven and Hell were as plainly mapped as Lanarkshire. Why should Hardie be diffident over India ? The furthest steppe of Asia held no mystery for him.

Therefore to Lucy, and to many more, he was only
" sounding brass and tinkling cymbal." He was just
a rather tiresome self-advertiser. But bombast is not
solely the product of insincerity. Sincere people are
given to it also ; and the greater the sincerity the more
preposterous often the bombast. Scott's Covenanters
were full of it, yet they died for their cause. Hardie
was full of it, yet he lived for his, and lived for it in
poverty. I remember him well, after a meeting which
he had addressed in terms of almost lunatic class-hatred,
going to take a cup of muddy coffee at a place which
most corporation dustmen would have jibbed at ; and
there he talked as modestly, naturally and good-
naturedly as if he had been a dustman himself. His
scorn of the material things which he valued, and even
overvalued, in his political scheme was, indeed, nothing
short of majestic. By a trifling compromise, legitimate
and honourable, he could have assured himself a
competence, and delivered his family from all financial
embarrassment. Such compromise was invariably
refused. It is not only saints who are careless about
riches. But Hardie seemed not so much careless as
afraid. Mr Gardiner told the truth when he said that
it was " the quality of gilt as well as of pitch to defile,"
and that Hardie would " not be defiled by the gilt of
the prosperous." The attitude was majestic, as I have
said, in its stoicism ; we can but honour disinterested-
ness when we find it, even though we see no compulsion
to admire the occasion of its display. But men as
honest as Hardie, yet without his fanaticism, do not
feel like him. Crooks, for example, might have dined
off gold plate for a month without deeming himself
defiled. He would have made a great joke of it.
Hardie's strength was not in temperance, but in
abstinence, and was to that extent a weakness. The
like weakness may be discerned in Burley's fury over

" a painted chamber and a prince's table." Such scorn
of the perfect ascetic pays an inverted compliment to
the world, the flesh and the devil. The ascetic forgets
that it is really much more contemptuous to use than to
avoid.

But with all this went the hardness of head which
Lord Morley perceived in the leader of the Independent
Labour Party. The fanatic was also a statesman. In
the inner circle this turbulent person was always the
conciliator; the venom he distilled was for outside
application only. He was famous for his formulas.
One delegate might shout for the omnipotent State.
Another might propound doctrines of pure anarchism.
Hardie, as though born to the Front Bench, would
point out that the differences between the two were
merely verbal, and could be bridged by a little goodwill.
While he raved in public, he could be judicial, as well
as judicious, in dealing with his own people. A revolution ? Certainly, nothing better, but no revolution
could succeed without the support of public opinion ;
was public opinion sufficiently advanced ? A republic ?
By all means, but that must come of itself, and the time
was not yet. The class war ? It could be a reality
only when the people were class-conscious, and they
were not.

Hardie's own people often laughed at him, and even
railed ; and in truth they had, on the surface, some
reason. In some ways he offended the working-man's
fine sense of decorum ; in other ways he stimulated
dangerously the working-man's equally well-developed
sense of humour. The cloth-cap ritual, for example,
stamped him as unrepresentative of the real working-
man ; the real working-man does not wear a cloth cap
on occasions of ceremony. Neither does the real
working-man affect, as Hardie did later, the style of a
minor poet. " White-livered poltroons " is very much

in the Burley style, but is not the sort of expression that springs naturally to the lips of a Battersea artisan ; and an amendment to the Address in reply to the Gracious Speech from the Throne, deploring that the Monarchy was not abolished, could hardly strike the average trade-unionist as either good sense or good humour.

But it is now pretty plain that Hardie had method in his madness, or at least that, like the famous dog, he went mad to serve an end. Behind the scenes he was sane enough, and a good deal more realistic than that sturdy squire of Socialism, H. M. Hyndman, who used to predict the imminence of the Social Revolution, much as Old Moore foretold fogs for London in November and trouble in the Balkans in spring. Moreover, his rants advertised Labour, just as Parnell's obstruction advertised Home Rule. Burt, in frock-coated respectability, might have the ear of the House at odd times, just as Butt was allowed his annual Irish motion, but the country thought as little of him as it had done of Butt. Nobody was allowed to avoid thinking of Keir Hardie, and, consequently, had to give a thought to Keir Hardie's cause and class. His party was in the position of having nothing to lose and everything to win. Hardie, if he were anything, could only be an asset.

This was seen when by degrees the Hardie following grew. In the 1906 Parliament he was no longer alone. For colleagues he had Ramsay Macdonald, with his gifts for Parliamentary manipulation ; Barnes, a solid Scotsman ; Henderson, the ideal Methodist ; Pete Curran, the Irish play-boy, who, despite Socialist professions, was always ready to hoist the green above the red ; Ward, the " handsome navvy," who had been a soldier once and was to be a soldier again ; Jowett, the mildest pirate who ever essayed to scuttle the capitalist ship ; Victor Grayson, blazing and finally vanishing like a complicated piece of fire-work; Hodge, the brawny Yorkshireman; Walsh, the Lancashire comedian; and Philip Snowden.

Mr. Snowden, at the beginning of the century, had a certain reputation. I remember once comparing him and another Labour leader to the two executioners in *Quentin Durward*. Mr. Snowden was " Jean qui pleure," the, other was " Jean qui rit." I remarked that both were equally bent on the hanging. That was the impression of Mr. Snowden in his early days. He was regarded as distinctly dangerous. " A slender, twisted figure," Mr. Wells wrote of him in a novel, " supporting itself on a stick and speaking with a fire that was altogether revolutionary." Nobody can think of Mr. Snowden in those terms since he produced a Gladstonian Budget, and I will not waste time in appraising the revolutionary that might have been " altogether " and who was never even " somewhat." There was another sitting in Hardie's group, the perfect foil to Hardie, who better repays attention here.

Will Crooks, who sat in Parliament for Woolwich, was, irrespective of politics, representative of the English worker everywhere. Crooks managed, by some magic, to be both typical and highly individual. There would be no end to a catalogue of the points in which he differed from Hardie. But in no respect were they more unlike than in their reactions to bitter early experience. Both had an unhappy childhood; but the more painful memories were, if anything, those of Crooks. He was brought up in a workhouse; whereas the Hardies, despite grinding poverty, had never lost a sort of independence. Hardie's upbringing was not happy, and may sometimes have been horrible; but his boyish woes did not include the supreme punishment of separation from his kin and virtual imprisonment in a dreary poor-law bastille. Again,

x

each had known what it was in early manhood to get the
" sack " for agitation—an experience making for much
psychological complication. But the consequences to
Crooks had been the harsher. Hardie had contrived
to start a tiny shop and had earned a few shillings in
the field of journalism. Crooks had been driven on
tramp, had put up at the hotel of the *Belle Etoile*, had
gone long on a tragically empty belly. He might
even, without undue exaggeration, have charged his
persecution with being the indirect cause of a child's
death.

Hardie, looking back on his past, on the childhood
he had missed and the wrongs he had suffered, was the
more bitter, because he thought he did well to be angry.
He not only wanted the goods of the " well-fed beasts,"
to divide them among still ill-fed victims. He desired
punitive justice no less. Somebody ought to smart for
it all. If he could not forget, he could even less forgive.
Crooks's memory was not less vivid. But he was
chiefly concerned that, so far as in him lay, his sufferings
should not be repeated in another generation. That
was his motive in entering public life, and it was the
object that led him into a course of policy which,
travestied by others, exposed him to criticisms which
hurt him to the quick. But though he was emphatically
and specially the champion of the under-dog, he
was affable to top-dogs of good breed and intent. He
might not rejoice in the existence of kings and millionaires. If he had such a thing as a genuine political
philosophy, which is entirely doubtful, it may have
been as anti-capitalist and as anti-monarchical as that
of Hardie. But if a king or a millionaire could be got
to do something for the poor of Poplar, Crooks was
there to give his benison and encouragement. It was
their money he wanted chiefly, but apart from money
he had no disposition to churlishness. Hardie felt one

of the greatest moments of his life when he discovered that he had not been invited to the Buckingham Palace garden-party because of his denunciation of the Czar. Crooks was near the height of human happiness when in scarlet robe and gold-laced hat he received the Prince and Princess of Wales at a Poplar party in King Edward's coronation year.

But all this geniality was destitute of any suspicion of class treason. Nobody could have been more innocent than Crooks of desiring to " better " himself in a social sense. He never dreamed of quitting the class in which he had been born. He never left the East End. There, he realised, he was wanted. Indeed, he could not help realising it, for a hundred times every day his door-bell advertised the fact that somebody needed his advice or help. Sometimes the appeal was to the Guardian or the Member of Parliament. But as often as not it was made simply to the man of open heart and generous mind, stored with that homely wisdom that springs from a good disposition rather than from a capacious intelligence. As a peacemaker between husbands and wives Crooks deserves beatification. A stopped sink was generally regarded as one of the problems he could most hopefully be called on to solve.

Like more than one Labour leader of his time, Crooks's politics were mixed. He was half a Radical of the old type, with immense belief in thrift, sobriety, self-help and the Smiles virtues generally, excepting avarice. From his platform by the docks he talked to the workers quite as much about the wrongs they did themselves as about those they suffered from others. By example and precept he essayed to prove that total abstinence and good-fellowship were not, after all, mutually exclusive, and he had nothing but loathing for the drunkard. But Crooks was without the callousness which disfigured the manly self-reliance of so many old Radicals. He believed in self-help for the strong, but he also believed that it was part of the duty of the strong to help the weak. He felt the dint of pity. He did not think, with some one in a Galsworthy novel, that if we could not do much for the poor, we should at least have the utmost sympathy with them. He regarded half-a-crown in the right place as much more important than tears of sensibility. And this feeling inclined him to something which he, no doubt, thought of as Socialism, though its better name is Christian charity. First he wanted the poor to help themselves. If they failed he insisted that they must be helped.

His chief work was, of course, not done in Parliament, but in local government. In Poor Law administration he fought and defeated Bumble, and if the rout was afterwards carried too far, the fact must not blind us to the rational humanitarianism of most of his reforms. At the Poplar Workhouse he abolished " skilly " from the dietary, and the pauper dress from the old people's wardrobes. He improved the quality of the inmates' bread while reducing its cost. He fought for un-skimmed milk and unadulterated groceries. He obtained a concession of tobacco for aged men, and won ancient women sugar for their tea. He saw that the children had a brighter life than had been his own as a " workhouse brat." His colleagues bitterly resented all this, as well as his war on their own conviviality. But Crooks, backed by Henry Chaplin at the Local Government Board, won his fight. His ideas were recommended elsewhere. Mr. Long, later in the seats of the mighty at Whitehall, took the same line as Chaplin. " Am I to understand," he asked a protesting deputation, " that you do not want to feed your poor people properly ? "

Despite the softness of his heart, his head was reasonably hard. Kindness and decency were in his administration, but while he himself had control there was nothing that could be called, except by Scrooge and Gradgrind standards, extravagance. Only when he went to Parliament did trouble of that kind begin. He had then been chairman of the Poplar Board for half-a-dozen years. When he was urged to retain office he consented with some reluctance. The pressure of his new duties was considerable. The House took up much of his time. Speaking and lecturing up and down England occupied more. He was a temperance man, a Labour man, a Pleasant Sunday Afternoon man, a Free Trade man, and in the multiplicity of his engagements he inevitably lost grip on Poplar. Mr. Lansbury, his lieutenant there, had not his common sense. Expenditure mounted. The relief Crooks gave to the unfortunate, the very old, and the very young began to flow into the pockets of the merely lazy. Then, as must always happen when purse-strings are unduly relaxed, corruption crept in. Guardians and officials, among them Crooks's political adversaries, were suspected of benefiting at the ratepayers' expense. Soon the storm broke.

Mr. Burns was then at the Local Government Board, a vigilant watchdog of finance, and naturally vigilant in a special degree where carelessness might be misinterpreted as political or class favouritism. During the first year of his presidency he boasted that under him twenty members of local authorities had been gaoled and two had killed themselves. He ordered an inquisition into the affairs of Poplar, and Poplar emerged badly. Crooks, indeed, came out scatheless in all that concerned his honour, but was censured for follies and extravagances committed behind his back. He might have got away with apology or disavowal. Instead he was ill-advised enough to defy the lightning of Jupiter. Jupiter was, to all appearances, unconcerned ; but Crooks, one of the best-humoured men in the world, could never afterwards refer to the matter in perfect calm.

But, whatever the precise rights or wrongs of the Poplar inquiry, he survived it, better loved than ever by the people among whom he lived. He believed in them, and they in him. His belief in them made him unique among Labour leaders, and won him a popularity which other champions have never quite attained. He had none of the ordinary Socialist's idea that proletarians must be better regimented as well as better housed and fed. " I'm proud of the poor," he once said, and in those words told the secret of his hold on them. It is worth noting that he had been a good workman. An old cooper who had employed him, said in later years, " Yes, Crooks was always spouting about the rights of labour, but his work used to show that he never forgot the rights of an employer." "They've made that common fellow our mayor, and he's no better than a workman," was the comment of the wife of an East End shopkeeper. " Quite right, ma'am," said Crooks, raising his hat as he passed her in the street, " no better than a workman." It was good enough for him.

Crooks did not merely take the side of the workers ; he was on their side. If they trusted Hardie to be their deputy, it was in the same way that they had trusted a Disraeli or a Gladstone, a being utterly unlike themselves, who seemed to be sent from heaven for their service. But they had confidence in Crooks as their mate. On nine subjects out of ten his ideas and theirs were the same, and when he and they did not see eye to eye they could at least understand what he meant. They did not agree on the drink question, but they

could see that Crooks the teetotaller had in his nature
already the best thing about beer, the atmosphere of
geniality it can sometimes induce in decent people who
would be tongue-tied without it.   Again, on woman's
suffrage he might appear a crank, but his arguments
went home.   Women were the best managers in the
house ; why not have their help in managing that big
house, the State ?   The logical fallacy was unnoticed
by the husband of a good and capable wife.

Once Cobbett spoke with the authentic voice of the
old English peasantry.   Crooks was the first man in
public life to express truly the heart and mind of the
new English proletariat.   It must be added that we
still await his successor.

INDEX

Admirals, Obstructive talents of, 243

" Admiral of the Atlantic," 14

" Æ." (Mr. George Russell), 284–5

Afrikanders, Milner and, 78–9

Akers-Douglas, Rt. Hon. A., 73

Alexander, George, matinée idol, 147 ; social and municipal preoccupations, 148 ; personal characteristics, 149

Amery, Rt. Hon. L. S., 83

Arnold, Matthew, 258

Arnold-Forster, Rt. Hon. H. O., antecedents and character, 293–4 ; reputation for candour, 295 ; attitude to volunteers, 296

Asquith, Rt. Hon. H. H., afterwards Earl of Oxford, King Edward's relations with, 22 ; services in Tariff Reform controversy, 194–5 ; limitations, 196–7 ; airy manner of handling serious matters, 271 ; mentioned, 32, 96, 281

Asquith, Mrs. (Countess of Oxford), view of Milner, 20 ; of " C.-B.," 29

Atbara, battle of, 167, 172

" BACKWOODSMAN " peers, impoverishment of, 24–5

Bancroft, Sir Squire, 149

Balfour, Rt. Hon. A. J., afterwards Earl of, King Edward's relations with, 22 ; Irish Land Bill, 67 ; abandonment of Wyndham, 71 ; attitude to Entente cordiale, 72 ; as Etonian, 151 ; attitude to Tariff Reform, 193

Baring, family of Lord Cromer, 92–3

Barker, Granville, 145, 147

Barrie, Sir James, O.M., Peter Pan, 59 ; view of Rosebery, 59 ; criticism of, 60 et seq. ; mentioned, 147

Beardsley, Aubrey, 265

Beerbohm, Max, on Bernard Shaw, 50 ; on Tree's theatre, 143 ; influence on period, 266 ; shrewd judgment, 267 ; laughter as weapon, 268 ; typical Edwardian, 270 ; no axe to grind, 272

Belloc, Hilaire, 38 et seq., 43, 49, 133

Bengal, division of, 86

Bennett, Arnold, early employment, 55 ; journalistic work, 56 ; characteristics, 57 ; mentioned, 147

Benson, Mgr., passage to Rome, 110 ; purpose in novels, 111 ; services to religion, 112

Beresford, Lord Charles, afterwards Lord, reputation for zeal, 245 ; Condor feat, 246 ; in Parliament, 247 ; hostility to Fisher, 252 ; showing the flag, 254 ; farewell to Navy, 255–6

Birrell, Rt. Hon. Augustine, importance in " C.-B.'s " Cabinet, 202 ; nature of Irish policy, 203 ; mentioned, 281

Blunt, Scawen, quoted, 66, 76, 279

Boyd, Charles, on Wyndham, 73

Brampton, Lord (Sir H. Hawkins), 302

Brodrick, Rt. Hon. William St. John F., Secretary for War, 289 ; social advantages, 290 ; scheme of Army reorganisation, 291 et seq.; made scapegoat for " mess, muddle and make-believe," 293 ; goes to India Office, 293

329

Bryce, Rt. Hon. James, afterwards Lord, Irish Secretary and Ambassador to Washington, 203 ; vast information, 204 ; position in letters, 205–6

Budget of 1909, 82, 90, 91, 96, 173

Burns, Rt. Hon. John, 197, 313, 314, 316, 325

Buxton, Rt. Hon. Sidney, afterwards Lord, 197

CAMBRIDGE, Duke of, impression of " C.-B.," 29

Campbell, Rev. R. J., new theology, 107 ; quotable character of preaching, 108 ; joins Anglican Church, 109 ; on conflict of science and religion, 109

Campbell-Bannerman, Rt. Hon. Sir Henry, Prime Minister, King Edward's resentment of his Army criticisms, 22 ; taste for French novels, 26 ; distrust of Kaiser, 27 ; inclination to *Entente cordiale*, 26–8 ; attitude to Boer War and Dogger Bank incident, 29 ; " methods of barbarism," 30 ; hostility to Dilke, 32 ; compared with Walpole and Melbourne, 33 ; wife as confidante, 29, 33 ; humour and knowledge of world, 34 ; concedes self-government to South Africa, 36 ; mentioned, 202, 249, 289, 293, 299

Canadian Pacific Railway, Lord Strathcona's policy regarding, 212–17

Carson, Rt. Hon. Sir Edward, afterwards Lord, forensic style of, 304–5 ; delicacy of constitution, 318 ; mentioned, 281

Cassel, Sir Ernest, 17, 18, 24

Cecil, Lord Hugh, 194, 226, 293

Cecil, Lord Robert, 194

Chamberlain, Rt. Hon. Joseph, Tariff Reform scheme, 190–3 ; mentioned, 29, 30, 67, 80, 82, 200, 218, 235

Chaplin, Rt. Hon. Henry, 324

Chesterton, Gilbert Keith, inspired to hostility by Kipling, 39 ; association with Belloc, 40 ;

literary weapons, 41 ; influence on Wells, 45 ; mentioned, 43, 49, 133, 226, 231

Chirol, Sir Valentine, quoted on Cromer, 95

Church in Wales, Lyttelton and Disestablishment Bill, 158

Church of England, decline of Victorian feuds, 98 ; Archbishop Davidson's influence on, 99 *et seq.* ; position of Bishop Gore in, 101 *et seq.*

Churchill, Rt. Hon. Winston, part in Tariff Reform controversy, 198–201 ; criticism of Brodrick's Army administration, 293 ; mentioned, 166, 299

Clifford, Dr. John, boyhood, 104 ; defective education, 105 ; leads Passive Resistance movement, 106

Conrad, Joseph, 58

Cromer, Earl of, character, 78 ; descent, 92 ; Puritan tendencies, 93 ; views on Egyptians, 95 ; part in British politics, 95 *et seq.*

Crooks, William, 321 *et seq.*

Curzon, Rt. Hon. Nathaniel George, afterwards Marquess, Dulac's cartoon of, 77 ; industry at Eton, 84 ; Indian policy and attitude to native princes, 87 ; occasional imprudence in speech, 90 ; lost chance of Premiership ; 91 ; mentioned, 151, 152, 160

Daily Express, 121, 123

Daily Mail, 28, 116, 121, 128, 133–7

Daily Mirror, 123, 130, 131

Daily News, 133

Darling, Sir Charles, afterwards Lord, appointment as High Court judge by Halsbury, 309–10 ; common-sense judgments, 311 ; wit, 311–12

Davidson, Dr. Randall, Archbishop of Canterbury, Scottish origin of, 99 ; tranquillising policy of, 99–100 ; relations with Nonconformists, 100–1 ; views on " Chinese slavery," 157

Davitt, Michael, 279
Decadents and Anti-Decadents, 38–9
Delane, Thaddeus, editor of *The Times*, 219
"Devolution," Wyndham's scheme of, 68 *et seq.*
Devonshire, Duke of, 194
Dickens, Sir H. F., 305
Dickson-Poynder, Sir John, afterwards Lord Islington, 293
Dillon, John, 275
Disraeli, Benjamin, name for King Edward, 16
Dogger Bank incident, " C.-B.'s " attitude, 29
" Dollar dictator," Redmond called, 232, 281
Douglas, George, on Kailyard school, 59
Dudley, Earl of, 68
Dulac, Edmond, cartoon of Curzon, 77
Dunraven, Lord, 68
Durbar, criticisms of Curzon in reference to, 88–9

EDWARD VII, King, influence on period, 9 ; character and personality, 10 *et seq.* ; interest in ceremonial, 13–14 ; engrossment in foreign policy, 15 *et seq.* ; worldly knowledge, 17 ; Max Harden on friendships, 18 ; dislike of Kaiser, 18 *et seq.* ; services to *Entente*, 21 ; belief in solidarity of crowned heads, 21 *et seq.* ; views on domestic issues, 22; helps to impoverish aristocracy, 24 ; sense of humour, 25 ; friendly relations with " C.-B.," 34 ; supports Kitchener for Indian Viceroyalty, 173 ; Gardiner's view of, 226
Editorship, qualities for, 219–20
Egypt, Milner's work in, 78 ; prosperity of, under Cromer, 92 ; Cromer's low opinion of natives, 94–5
Entente cordiale, 15, 20, 21, 26, 27, 37, 72
Esher, Viscount, on Kitchener, 169

Evening News, Harmsworth's acquisition of, 123 ; Kennedy Jones and, 135

FISHER, Sir John, afterwards Lord, compared with Beresford, 245 *et seq.* ; early years at sea, 246 ; relations with civilians, 247 ; talking powers, 248 ; views of fighting values, 252 ; press attacks on, 252 ; friction with Beresford, 252 *et seq.* ; ultimate triumph, 255
Fitzgerald, Lord Edward, 66
Fowler, Sir Henry, afterwards Viscount Wolverhampton, 202
France, King Edward's liking for, 20 *et seq.* ; " C.-B.'s " attitude to, 26 *et seq.* ; Wyndham's sacrifices for *Entente* with, 72
Freeman's Journal, publishes terms of sale of J. Redmond's lands to tenants, 280

GALSWORTHY, John, " bland violence " of, 38 ; perfection of style, 46 ; effect of legal training on, 47 ; refinement, 49 ; affection for dogs, 49 ; quoted, 63 ; mentioned, 147
Gardiner, A. J., on King Edward, 11–13 ; on Bryce, 227 ; qualities as editor and writer, 225–8 ; mentioned, 133, 201, 204, 318
Garvin, J. L., journalistic beginnings, 229 ; qualities as writer and political thinker, 230–5 ; influence on Unionist thought, 239
Germany, the book that would not sell, 118 ; Fisher's preparations against, 251 *et seq.*
Gilbert, W. S., on National Anthem, 11 ; quoted, 46, 90
Gladstone, Rt. Hon. W. E., 34, 139, 160
Gladstone, Rt. Hon. Herbert, afterwards Lord, 197
Gordon, General, Kitchener's interest in, 178
Gore, Dr., character, 101–3 ; classed as modernist, 102 ; loss of influence, 103

Gosse, Sir Edmund, 269
Grantham, Sir William, 309
Grey, Rt. Hon. Sir Edward, after-
wards Viscount, 32, 40, 240
Griffith, Arthur, 285–7
Guest, Ivor, 293

HALDANE, Rt. Hon. R. B., after-
wards Viscount, called " Schop-
enhauer " by " C.-B.," 32 ;
Secretary for War, 296 ; Ger-
man influences in his mind, 296 ;
services to Army, 297 ; volu-
bility, 298 ; paradox of his
career, 299
Halibut, King Edward and " C.-
B." discuss, 34
Halifax, Earl of, quoted, 311
Halsbury, Lord, 302, 309
Halsbury Club, 91
Hamilton, Lord George, 194
Harcourt, Rt. Hon. Sir William,
202
Harcourt, Rt. Hon. L. V. Q., afterwards Viscount, 299, 314
Harden, Max, 18–20
Hardie, Keir, 313 et seq.
Harmsworth, Alfred Charles, Lord
Northcliffe, newspaper genius,
115 ; early shyness, 116 ; lack
of political mind, 117 ; business
perception, 118 et seq. ; solidity
of his enterprises, 123 ; nature
of his friendships, 124 et seq. ;
Daily Mirror failure, 130, and
final success, 131 ; distrust of
brilliance, 133 ; concentration
of interests, 134–5 ; debt to
Kennedy Jones and Lord
Rothermere, 135 et seq. ; litiga-
tion with Leverhulme, 185
Healy, Rt. Hon. Timothy, 283–4
Henderson, Rt. Hon. Arthur, 320
Hewlett, Maurice, 58, 59
Hicks-Beach, Rt. Hon. Michael,
64, 202
Hirsch, Baron, friend of King
Edward, 17, 18
Holidays, danger of political, 69–
70
Howard, Redmond, biographer of
John Redmond, 282
Hulton, Sir Edward, 137–8

Huxley, Aldous, 241
Hyndman, H. M., 320

IBSEN, Tree's rendering of, 141 ;
Shaw's admiration for, 54 ;
James's denunciation of, 263
India, Curzon's administration, 84
et seq. ; Milner considered as
Secretary for, 84
Inge, Dean, 57, 162
Ireland, King Edward and, 22 ;
Wyndham's policy, 67 et seq. ;
course of Irish politics during
decade, 273 et seq.
Irving, Sir Henry, compared with
Tree, 139 et seq. ; Shaw's want
of reverence for, 54
Isaacs, Rufus, K.C., afterwards
Marquess of Reading, early
experiences, 305–6 ; industry,
107 ; characteristics as advocate,
307–8

JACKSON, Holbrooke, 266
James, Henry, special position in
letters, 257 ; things he under-
stood, 259 ; character of educa-
tion, 260 ; his " ivory tower,"
263 ; Order of Merit, 365
Japan, Kitchener's view of national
spirit, 175
Jesuits, Redmond's debt to, 276
Jeune, Sir Francis, 309
Jeyes, S. H., 132
Jones, Kennedy, 135–6

KENSIT, John, 98
Kipling, Rudyard, revulsion from
" art for art's sake," 38 ; G. K.
Chesterton a hostile follower of,
39 ; South African poems, 49 ;
writings for the young, 50 ;
quoted, 14 ; mentioned, 218,
261
Kitchener, Sir Herbert, afterwards
Earl, contrasted with Roberts,
164 ; transgresses Army regulations, 165 ; participates in
Egyptian operations, 166 ; Atbara and Omdurman, 167 ;
talent for statesmanship, 170 ;
masterly conduct of negotiations
at Fashoda and Vereeniging,

170 ; tendency to loquacity, 173 ;
Indian administration, 171–2 ;
artistic strain in, 173 ; attitude
to Ulster trouble, 173–4 ; complexities of character, 178–9

LABOUCHERE, H., 64
Land purchase, Irish, 67, 280
Landsowne, Marquess of, 72, 240,
289
Law, Rt. Hon. A. Bonar, 203
Lawson, Sir Wilfrid, 35
Lee, Sir Sidney, on King Edward
VII, 16, 18
Leopold II, King of the Belgians,
22
Leslie, Shane, quoted, 113
Lever, Hesketh William, after-
wards Lord Leverhulme, origins
and character, 180 ; foundation
of Port Sunlight, 183–4 ; colli-
sion with Northcliffe, 185 ;
political views and business
policy, 187–9 ; mentioned,
226
Lloyd George, Rt. Hon. David,
32, 34, 37, 40, 91, 92, 96, 197–8,
226, 240–1, 299
London County Council, George
Alexander's membership, 148
Long, Rt. Hon. Walter, 324
Low, Sir Sidney, 132
Lucy, Sir H., 317
" Lux Mundi," 102
Lynch, Bohun, 266–7
Lynch, Colonel, 276
Lyttelton, Rt. Hon. Alfred, suc-
ceeds Chamberlain as Colonial
Secretary, 151 ; the perfect
Etonian, 151–2 ; legal standing,
153 ; cricket, 151, 152, 156,
158 ; understanding and educa-
tion, 153–4 ; affection for Bal-
four, 156 ; Chinese labour, 156
et seq. ; model of the English
gentleman, 162

MACDONALD, Sir John, Canadian
Prime Minister, 211–3, 215
MacDonald, Rt. Hon. Ramsay, 320
Macdonnell, Sir A., afterwards
Lord, 68

Mackintosh, Sir James, compared
with James Bryce, 203–6
M'Kenna, Rt. Hon. Reginald, at
Admiralty, 254
Maine, Sir Henry, quoted, 88
Marchand, General, 170
Marconi debate, Lyttelton's con-
tribution to, 158
Martindale, Father, quoted, 112
Massingham, W. M., position and
influence as editor, 239–42
Mathews, Sir Charles, 302
Melbourne, Lord, compared with
" C.-B.," 33 ; mentioned, 35
Methuen, General Lord, 291
Milner, Sir Alfred, afterwards
Viscount, miscalled " prancing,"
77 ; influence of Germany and
Balliol, 78 ; misjudges South
African situation, 79 ; " vio-
lence " of his mind, 80 et seq. ;
part in home politics, 82 et seq. ;
Rosebery's estimate of, 83 ;
mentioned, 30, 156
Minoru, King Edward's Derby
winner, 17
Minto, Lord, on Kitchener, 173
Moore, George, 266, 284
Morley, Rt. Hon. John, afterwards
Viscount, 33, 173, 176, 315, 319
Morning Post, expresses Milner's
views, 82 ; championship of
Beresford, 252

Nation newspaper, 242
Naval policy, dispute between
Beresford and Fisher and re-
organisation under latter, 243
et seq.
Nelson, Lord, his interpretation of
discipline, 244
Nevill, Lady Dorothy, quoted, 113
" New Theology," Rev. R. J.
Campbell and, 107–9
Northbrook, Lord, appoints Fisher
captain of Inflexible, 248
Northcliffe, Viscount, see Harms-
worth, Alfred.

O'BRIEN, William, 68, 273
O'Connor, Rt. Hon. T. P., 279
Old Bailey, change in character of
Bar, 301

Oppenheim, Phillips, 56
Omdurman, battle of, 167
" Organ-grinding viscount," Halsbury and, 309
O'Shea, Mrs, 273

PARNELL, Charles Stewart, 274, 275
Passive Resistance, Dr. Clifford and, 106
Pearson, Cyril Arthur, afterwards Sir Arthur, early career compared with Northcliffe's, 115; obtains control of *Standard* newspaper, 117; interest in politics, 121; causes of relative non-success, 123-4; friendships and interests, 125-33
Peel, Sir Robert, compared with Asquith, 195-6
Pensions, Old Age, Cromer's objection to, 96
Philæ, submersion of, 95
Phillips, Stephen, ranked with Sophocles, Dante and younger Dumas, 58; Tree's patronage of, 146
Plunkett, Sir H., 284, 287
" Pop," Lyttelton as leader of, 153, 160
Private Secretary, Tree as Rev. Robert Spalding, 141

QUEUX, William le, 56, 252

" RADICAL JACK," soubriquet for Fisher, 247
Reading, Marquess of, *see* Isaacs, Rufus
Redmond, John, 68, 203, 232; position in Irish party during trouble over Parnell, 274-5; chosen leader of party, 276; relations with O'Brien, 280
Redmond, William, 280
Rhodes, Rt. Hon. Cecil, 64, 65, 79, 80, 209, 218, 294
Ripon, Marquis of, friend of " C.-B.," 33
Riel rebellion, Lord Strathcona's part in, 211
Ritchie, Rt. Hon. C. T., 67, 202

Roberts, Earl, compared with Kitchener, 164; affection he inspired, 169; part in South African War, 171; scheme of military training, 175; Morley on his "curious belatedness," 176; simple character, 178-9; goes to Germany with Brodrick, 292
Rosebery, Earl of, tribute to Milner, 83; nickname of " Barnbougle," 32
Rossa, O'Donovan, J. L. Garvin and, 229
Rothermere, Viscount, 136-7
Royalism, revival of, 15
Russell, Sir Charles, afterwards Lord Russell of Killowen, 307
Russia, King Edward's influence on *Entente* with, 20; Dogger Bank incident, 29; " C.-B." on the Duma, 31

SALISBURY, Marquess of, 64
Saunderson, Colonel, 70
Schreiner, Olive, quoted, 81
Scott, Sir Percy, 253
Selborne, Earl of, 249
Serbia, King Edward's resentment of royal assassination, 22
Sexton, W., 279
Shakespeare, Tree's performances in, 142-5
Shaw, George Bernard, regarded as " subversive," 50; tipster, but not a major prophet, 51; character of Shavian philosophy, 52 *et seq.*; mentioned, 147, 264, 268, 316
Simon, Rt. Hon. Sir John, occasional appearances at the Old Bailey, 303; position and earnings at the Bar, 304; style compared with Rufus Isaacs, 308; mentioned, 299
Sinn Fein, 286-7
Smith, Rt. Hon. F. E., afterwards Earl of Birkenhead, 74
Smuts, General, 170
Snowden, Rt. Hon. Philip, 321
Soap, litigation concerning, between Leverhulme and Northcliffe, 183

Socialism, Milner's inclinations to Germanic ideas, 82 ; bugbear of Leverhulme, 186

Society, sins of, sermons by Father Vaughan, 112 *et seq.*

South Africa, " C.-B." and, 29 *et seq.* ; Milner's High Commissionership, 78 *et seq.* ; Lyttelton and Chinese labour, 155 *et seq.*

Spectator, under Strachey, 235 *et seq.* ; attacks Fisher, 252

Spender, J. A., qualities as editor and writer, 219–25

Spender, Harold, 223

Standard, 117, 123, 132 252

Stead, W. T., on Milner, 80–1 ; on Redmond, 279

Steevens, G. W., 133

Strachey, Lytton, quoted, 10, 78, 93

Strachey, St. Loe, identified with *Spectator*, 235–6 ; qualities as journalist, 237 ; embarrassments, 238–9

Strathcona, Lord, laments shortness of life, 207 ; early experiences, 209 ; Riel rebellion, 211 ; part in Canadian politics, 211–16 ; High Commissioner, 217 ; stately entertaining at Knebworth, 217 ; popularising the Empire, 218

TARIFF REFORM, King Edward's criticism of, 22 ; Milner's attitude to, 82 ; Curzon's conversion to, 90 ; contrast in Northcliffe's and Pearson's attitude to, 122–3 ; general discussion of question and personalities, 190 *et seq.*

Theatre, change of tradition in, 139 *et seq.* ; productions at His Majesty's, 142 *et seq.* ; policy of St. James's under Alexander, 147 *et seq.*

Traill, H. D., biographer of Cromer, 93, 97

Tranby Croft scandal, 17, 19

Tree, Sir Herbert Beerbohm, social advantages and connections, 140 ; idiosyncrasies, 141 ; taste for costly pageantry, 142, 144–6 ; neglect of rising talent in drama, 147

Tree, Lady, 140

Tweedmouth, Lord, 252

UITLANDERS, 80, 155

Ulster, dissatisfaction with Wyndham, 68 *et seq.* ; R. J. Campbell's native place, 109 ; Kitchener's attitude to, 173–4 ; J. L. Garvin and, 231

" University tip," retained by Milner, 78

VAUGHAN, Father Bernard, " Sins of Society " sermons, 113 ; new pattern Jesuit, 114

Vereeniging, Peace of, 170–1

Victoria, Queen, 10, 15, 23

Walpole, Sir Robert, compared with " C.-B.," 33

WALTON, Sir Lawson, 306

War Office, " C.-B.'s " defence of, 30 ; Haldane sent to it as " unhealthy," 33 ; Wyndham's brilliant defence of, 65 ; under Brodrick, Arnold-Forster and Haldane, 288 *et seq.*

Webb, Sidney, 35

Wells, H. G., passing interest in theology, 40–1 ; literary method, 41 ; novels noticed, 42 *et seq.* ; views on spiritualism, etiquette, private property and nationalism, peasantries and the Romans, 43–52 ; mentioned, 230, 264, 269, 296, 321

Whibley, Charles, on Wyndham, 75

Wild, Sir Ernest, 305

Wilde, Oscar, 147, 148, 265

Wilhelm II, German Emperor, 14, 18–21, 27

Williams, Lord Justice Vaughan, 309

Wright, Whittaker, 307

Wyndham, Rt. Hon. George, fineness of character and handsome appearance, 63–4 ; approved by Cecil Rhodes, 64 ; brilliant success as Under-Secretary for War, 64–5 ; Irish policy, 66–7 ; attitude to Tariff Reform, 67 ; land purchase triumph, 67–8 ; incautiously takes a holiday, and is thrown over by Balfour on agitation of Ulster, 69–72 ; death, 75 ; qualities and deficiencies, 63–4, 75 ; mentioned, 151, 281